PEASANTS, CLASS, AND CAPITALISM

PEASANTS, CLASS, AND CAPITALISM

The Rural Research of L. N. Kritsman and his School

TERRY COX

CLARENDON PRESS · OXFORD
1986

Oxford University Press, Walton Street, Oxford OX2 6DP

Oxford New York Toronto
Delhi Bombay Calcutta Madras Karachi
Kuala Lumpur Singapore Hong Kong Tokyo
Nairobi Dar es Salaam Cape Town
Melbourne Auckland
and associates in
Beirut Berlin Ibadan Nicosia

Oxford is a trade mark of Oxford University Press

Published in the United States
by Oxford University Press, New York

© T. M. Cox 1986

British Library Cataloguing in Publication Data
Cox, Terry
Peasants, class, and capitalism: the
rural research of L. N. Kritsman and his
school.
1. Communism—Soviet Union—History
2. Soviet Union—Economic conditions
—1918–1945   3. Soviet Union—
Rural conditions
I. Title
330.947'084   HC335.2
ISBN 0–19–878014–1

Library of Congress Cataloging in Publication Data
Cox, Terry.
Peasants, class, and capitalism.
Bibliography: p.
Includes index.
1. Peasantry—Soviet Union—Historiography.
2. Social classes—Soviet Union—Historiography.
3. Agriculture and state—Soviet Union—Historiography.
4. Soviet Union—Rural conditions—Historiography.
5. Kristman, L. (Lev), 1890–1938.   I. Title.
HD1536.S65C69 1986   305.5'63   86–2362
ISBN 0–19–878014–1

Set by Cambrian Typesetters, Frimley
Printed in Great Britain
at the University Printing House, Oxford
by David Stanford
Printer to the University

For Sylvia

Acknowledgements

I am grateful to a great many people for their help and support in writing this book. In particular, my thanks are due to Hillel Ticktin who supervised the thesis on which the book is based, and to Terry Byres, Neil Charlesworth, John Harriss, Susie Jacobs, Judith Pallot, and Gavin Williams who also read all or parts of my thesis. They all provided me with useful comments or criticisms which improved my work, though none is responsible for remaining errors, or for the views expressed here. I am especially grateful to Gavin Williams for his constant encouragement and support over a number of years.

I would also like to thank Tanya Ticktin for her efforts to teach me Russian which allowed me to carry out my research. Alison Aitchison and Janice Stewart bore the brunt of deciphering my handwriting and turning it into typescript, and to them I also give my thanks. Above all I would like to thank Sylvia Cox for her understanding, advice, and support.

Contents

Glossary and Abbreviations

artel'	An association or collective of producers, made up craftsmen or peasants
barshchina	A system of feudal forced labour required from peasants by landowners
batrak	Agricultural wage labourer
bednyak	Poor peasant
CPSU	Communist Party of the Soviet Union
CW	*Collected Works*
desyatin	A measurement of area: 1 desyatin = 1.09 hectares = 2.7 acres
dvor	Peasant household
Gosplan	State Planning Commission
guberniya	Province
khozyain	Head of the household
khutor	A farmstead, physically separate from a village, and not subject to communal repartition
kolkhoz	Collective farm
kombedy	Committees of poor peasants
kulak	Rich peasant, usually hiring labour
mir	Peasant community; government of the community
Narkomtrud	Peoples' Commissariat of Labour
NEP	New Economic Policy
oblast	Largest administrative unit of local government after 1929 when it replaced the *guberniya*
obshchina	Commune
okrug	Subdivision of the *oblast*
otrub	Consolidated farm land, outside the village, and not subject to communal repartition, but without the farm-house which remained inside the village
promysly	Crafts, trades or outside work producing an income
Rabkrin	Peoples' Commissariat of Workers' and Peasants' Inspection
raion	Subdivision of *okrug* and *oblast*

RSDLP	Russian Social Democratic Labour Party
RSFSR	Russian Soviet Federal Socialist Republic
serednyak	Middle peasant
smychka	Alliance between the working class and peasants
SRs	Socialist Revolutionary Party
TsSU	Central Statistical Administration
tyaglo	Team of draught animals and ploughman
uezd	Subdivision of the *guberniya*
volost'	Subdivision of the *uezd*
Vserabotzemles	All Russian Union of Agricultural and Forestry Workers
VSNKh	Supreme Council of the National Economy
zazhitochnye	Well-off peasant
zemstvo	Institution of local government in the pre-Revolutionary Russian countryside at *guberniya* or *uezd* levels

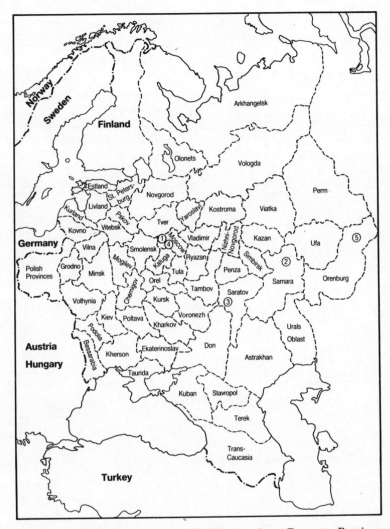

Sketch map of European Russia, 1900. The map shows European Russia at
its largest before the revolution, when the various *zemstvo* studies were
carried out. After the revolution, Finland, the Polish territory, and part of
Bessarabia were lost; otherwise the provincial (*guberniya*) names and
boundaries remained largely the same in the 1920s. Numbers on the map
represent the approximate locations of the various research projects carried
out by the Agrarian Marxists:

(1) Anisimov *et al.* (1927)
(2) Vermenichev *et al.* (1928)
(3) Sulkovskii (1930)
(4) Naumov and Shardin (1928)
(5) Nemchinov (1926b)

Introduction

The main concern of this book is with the question of capitalist development in Russian peasant society and the attempts of Russian social researchers to understand the nature of the relationship between capitalism and the peasantry. In the years between the emancipation of the serfs in 1861 and the collectivization of the peasantry in 1930, as Russia became increasingly affected by world capitalism, and commodity production became increasingly pervasive among the Russian peasantry, various changes occurred in Russian rural society. The nature and significance of these changes was the subject of intense debate in Russia at the time, focusing in particular on the question of whether capitalism was actually developing as the predominant form of organization in Russian peasant farming. While some writers argued that capitalism would have a negligible effect on the peasantry, others argued that it was bringing about significant changes. Within the latter camp, further differences emerged between those who thought that capitalist development would allow an independent peasantry to continue in existence, adapting itself to the growth of a commodity economy, and those who thought that capitalism was progressively undermining peasant society and bringing about a differentiation of the peasantry into the separate social classes of capitalism, namely, an agrarian bourgeoisie and a proletariat.

To begin with, the debate was conducted mainly at the level of theory with little systematic provision of evidence. Gradually, however, a movement grew among the Russian intelligentsia to gather information about Russian peasant society, and in turn some of this information began to be incorporated into debates on the peasant question. The result was a body of research literature on peasant society which is probably richer and more extensive than has been developed in relation to any other peasant society in the world.

The debate on the nature of peasant society in Russia attracted a great deal of interest at the time; furthermore, interest in it has remained high among students of agrarian problems in modern societies with large peasant populations. For example, reference is often made to the Russian research in modern works on agrarian problems in Asia, Africa, or Latin America; and to some extent, the concepts and research methods developed in Russia have influenced the way in which modern debates and research have been conducted.[1] The lasting interest in the Russian research can no doubt be explained partly by its high level of sophistication and its extensiveness, but it also reflects the continuing political significance of the question of whether capitalist development does or does not undermine peasant agriculture and promote the differentiation of the peasantry.[2]

Both in discussions of rural development strategies (whether involving technological innovations or land reforms) and in political debates on questions of the political outlook, interests, and involvement of peasants in various parts of the world, judgements about the differentiation of the peasantry have been central. Moreover, in many cases, the desire to establish the facts about the extent of differentiation in a given country has led to references back to the Russian literature.

However, in view of such continuing interest, it is perhaps surprising that only a partial view of the Russian research as a whole is available to modern readers. While on the one hand the case for the differentiation of the peasantry is available in the works of Lenin, and on the other hand arguments for the continuation of a relatively homogeneous independent peasantry have been provided by the translation of some of Chayanov's work (Thorner *et al.* 1966), as well as the more recent reworking of some of the Russian research by Shanin, few other contributions to the Russian debates are available to modern readers. This book is intended to help fill some of the gaps by offering an outline history of developments in Russian research on the differentiation of the peasantry and its relation to capitalist development.

The following chapters attempt to trace the development of the Russian social research tradition to its culmination in the work of Kritsman and his group, the so-called 'Agrarian Marxists', in the second half of the 1920s. Chapter 1 introduces the main issues as they were first raised in Marxist theory and examines the social context in which the debate was developed in Russia. Chapter 2 then offers a parallel treatment of developments in the concepts and techniques of empirical social research on the Russian peasantry, from the work of the *zemstvo* statisticians towards the end of the nineteenth century through to the approaches in use in the 1920s. These two chapters provide details of the two main traditions on which the research of the Kritsman group was to draw.

Chapter 3 describes the initial development of the ideas of Kritsman and his colleagues, concentrating on Kritsman's development of Lenin's ideas on the nature of Soviet society in the 1920s and the critiques by Kritsman and others of existing approaches to the study of the peasantry in the Soviet Union. Chapters 4 and 5 examine the various research projects on the question of the differentiation of the peasantry carried out in the Soviet countryside by members of the Kritsman group, focusing on questions of methodology and research methods and the organizing concepts through which the data were analysed. Chapter 6 then describes some of the main findings of these research projects, assessing the extent to which they allow us to build up a picture of the key processes in Soviet rural society at the time. Although the differentiation issue formed the main focus for the work of the Kritsman school, towards the end of the 1920s they were also beginning to branch into other topics concerning peasant society and the economics of peasant agriculture. These are discussed in Chapter 7.

Finally, Chapter 8 outlines the various criticisms that have been levelled against the work of Kritsman and his school, both by contemporary Soviet writers and by more recent Western writers. The validity of these criticisms is questioned before going on to offer an alternative appraisal of the strengths and limitations of the research of the Kritsman school. It is argued that, despite a number of problems with their research which had not been resolved by the end of the 1920s, the Kritsman group offered an original approach which could potentially make a valuable contribution to modern research on the relation between the peasantry and capitalist development in various parts of the world. In this context comparisons are made between the approaches used by the Kritsman group and those made in more recent research in Third World countries today.

A major critical theme that is developed concerns the argument that history has proven the early Marxists to be wrong in their expectation that class differentiation and capitalist development in peasant agriculture would normally follow from the wider development of capitalism and the incorporation of peasant societies into the world capitalist system. In this context, Kritsman and his colleagues were clearly part of the tradition of classical Marxism. However, although they saw their main contribution as providing an improved method of identifying the emergence of classes within the peasantry, it is argued here that the actual value of their work was in developing ways of studying the relations of exploitation between households, irrespective of whether any clear process of class differentiation was taking place or not.

Notes

1. See for example for India, Harriss (1982a); for Tanzania, Shivji (1976); and for Latin America, Goodman and Redclift (1981).
2. For a useful selection of readings, reflecting much of the range of discussions of this issue in recent years, see Harriss (1982b).

Marxist Theory and Russian Peasant Society

1 Marx on Capitalism and the Peasantry

To a large extent, the terms of the debate on the Russian peasantry were set by Marxist theory. In developing an analysis of their own society, Russian Marxists drew on Marx's writings on the development of capitalist agriculture in western Europe, and, as a result, took on a set of assumptions concerning the Russian peasantry—in particular, that they would undergo a similar process of change of their counterparts in the West.

For Marx, drawing on the case of England, the main feature of capitalist agriculture was that capitalist farmers had to extract surplus value through the employment of 'free labour' which had been created by 'the expropriation of the rural labourers from the land and their subordination to a capitalist' (Marx 1865, 614–15). As part of this process, agricultural production had been reorganized so that it became less and less like peasant production, geared to simple reproduction and subsistence, and increasingly came to resemble capitalist production in general, oriented to expanded reproduction, with the reinvestment of profits into further accumulation.

On the basis of this view of capitalist agriculture, Marx then sought to explain its historical development, and thus to discuss the relation between peasant farming and capitalism. He did this mainly through a discussion of changes in rent relations in the transition from feudalism, tracing them through the growth of commodity exchange and money rent in agriculture, and thus to the possibility of capitalist farming. The establishment of a requirement to engage in commodity production led increasingly to a situation where the landowner would rent out land for the highest price, and where land would be rented by those who could produce the biggest profit from it. Peasant subjects would therefore tend to be replaced by capitalist tenants, who would be either outsiders, seeking to invest in capitalist agricultural production using hired labour, or well-off peasants, turning themselves into capitalists, expanding their operations, and hiring the labour of their weaker neighbours. In this way money rent would give rise to fully capitalist relations in agriculture, involving a differentiation of the peasantry into two main classes, an agrarian bourgeoisie and a proletariat, some of whom would remain in agriculture (Marx 1865, 797–9).

In this way, Marx attempted to explain the historical development of the form of agriculture which he took to be representative of developed capitalism.[1] His approach seemed to imply that, with the growth of commodity production, the growth of capitalist agriculture would inevitably follow, involving the differentiation of the peasantry and the employment of wage labour by capitalist owners or tenants.[2] However, although this is the way in which Marx has often been understood, a number of qualifications and complicating factors in Marx's discussion should be noted.

First, Marx thought that there were ways in which capitalism could allow the persistence of peasant agriculture, with peasants retaining control over at least some of their main means of production. These took the form of share-cropping (Marx 1865, 803) and independent peasant farming, which in certain conditions, Marx recognized, could actually compete with capitalism, especially since, in the absence of a profit motive, peasants might be prepared to pay more for land than capitalist farmers, and charge less for their produce (Marx 1865, 804–7).

However, despite such considerations, it was Marx's expectation that small peasant agriculture was nevertheless unstable and would not be able to resist capitalist penetration. In his view, it was a 'necessary transitional stage for the development of agriculture itself' (Marx 1865, 807). The factors that would contribute to its downfall, apart from the direct state repression of small peasant farming discussed in *Capital*, Vol. 1 (Marx 1867, Chs. 26–8), included the removal of the main subsidiary and supporting economic activities that went along with peasant farming (i.e., rural domestic industry and common grazing), and competition from larger-scale and technically more advanced forms of agriculture.

In the long term, for Marx, independent peasant agriculture must be unstable and, under conditions of a growing commodity economy, would dissolve into the relations of the capitalist mode of production. To begin with,

It is possible that these producers, working with their own means of production, not only reproduce their labour-power but create surplus value, while their position enables them to appropriate for themselves their own surplus labour or a part of it. . . . And here we come up against a peculiarity that is characteristic of a society in which one definitive mode of production predominates, even though not all productive relations have been subordinated to it. . . . . The independent peasant or handicraftsman is cut up into two persons. As owner of the means of production he is capitalist: as labourer he is his own wage-labourer. . . . in fact, this way of presenting it, however irrational it may be on first view, is nevertheless so far correct, that in this case the producer in fact creates his own surplus-value, in other words, only his own labour is materialised in the whole product. But that he is able to appropriate *for himself* the whole product of his own labour, and that the excess of the value of his produce over the average price for instance of his day's labour is not appropriated by a third person, *a master*, he owes not to his labour—which does not distinguish him from other labourers— but to his ownership of the means of production. It is therefore only through his ownership of these that he takes possession of his own surplus labour, and thus bears to himself as wage-labourer the relation of being his own capitalist. . . . Separation is maintained as the relation even when one person unites the separate functions. Here emerges in a very striking way the fact that the capitalist as such is only a function of capital, the labourer a function of labour power. For it is also a law that economic development distributes functions among different persons, and the handicraftsman or peasant who produces with his own means of production will either gradually be transformed into a small capitalist who also exploits the labour of others, or he will suffer the loss of his means of production (in the first instance the latter may happen although he remains their nominal owner, as in the case of mortgages) and be transformed into a wage-labourer. This is the tendency in the form of society in which the capitalist mode of production predominates.

(Marx 1873, part 1, 395–6)

In the above passage Marx was suggesting that, in a society whose relations were dominated by the capitalist mode, even though developed capitalist class relations were not prevalent, it made sense to identify and analyse the roles and functions of capital and labour although they may not have been embodied in the separate roles of different people. Behind this idea is the basic assumption that the whole logic of capitalist development promotes the development of the separate functions of capital and labour, and that, although in specific conditions these may be united within the roles of the same person for a considerable period of time, in general, capitalism leads to the separation of the different functions in the roles of different people, capitalists and proletarians. Thus, although independent peasant production is a clearly recognizable, and relatively lasting, system of production in the context of a wider capitalist development, the logic of capitalism in the long run must tend towards the class differentiation of the independent peasantry.

Second, however, there was at least the possibility that not all societies in which simple commodity production evolved would necessarily develop money rent and the leasing of land to capitalists as the predominant form in agriculture. Such a development was generally possible, Marx thought, only 'when the world market, commerce, and manufacture have reached a relatively high level', and 'only in those countries which dominate the world market in the period of transition from the feudal to the capitalist mode of production' (Marx 1865, 799).

Thus, while Marx clearly saw the classic pattern of capitalist development as involving a necessary transition to capitalist production once simple commodity production had come to predominate in a society, involving a necessary differentiation of the peasantry,[3] there are at least grounds for doubting whether this necessarily applied to Russia. Unfortunately, Marx did not expand on this point, and although he later considered the Russian peasant commune and the possibilities of Russia avoiding capitalist development (to be discussed below in Section 3), his conclusions there did not connect with the more general questions of the place of Russia in the world market and its implications for internal developments in Russian peasant agriculture.

The main impression given by Marx's writings, and the main way he was interpreted by Russian Marxists, was that, first, with the growth of commodity production in peasant agriculture, and in the wider context of world capitalist development, peasant production was determined basically by capitalism, however modified the specific form of production; and second, although there might be alternative patterns to the classical path of the transition to capitalism in agriculture, in the long run the growth of commodity relations in peasant agriculture would result in the development of agrarian capitalism and the separation of the labourer from the land, that is, in the class differentiation of the peasantry, in some form.

Although many writers since have accepted the first point, the second has attracted more criticism. Among the earliest critics were the Russian Populists, who, for all their approval of Marx's analysis of industrial capitalism, held that there were specific features of Russian peasant society which could resist and prevent capitalist development and class differentiation. Their ideas, and those of the early Russian Marxists, with whom they debated, will be discussed in Section 3, following an outline description of some of the main characteristics of contemporary Russian peasant society.

2 Social Change in the Russian Peasantry

A major problem for any analysis of the Russian peasantry within the framework of the ideas outlined above is that capitalist development in Russia deviated significantly from the 'classical' pattern described by Marx. The context in which the Russian peasantry came to be confronted by capitalism was therefore different from the way it had been anticipated by Russian Marxists.

In the mid-nineteenth century, practically all Russian peasants lived in communes. There, each household cultivated its own strips of land which had been allocated to it by the commune and which were spread out in different fields around the village. Decision-making was through a meeting of male heads of household which elected an elder as leader and spokesman. Some communes were based on hereditary tenure, wherein each household held its strips of land more or less in perpetuity, but the majority of communes were based on repartitional tenure, where the strips were period-ically reallocated according to some criteria of the household's needs or capacities. Usually households were given land either according to the number of working males or the number of mouths to feed. Methods of cultivation were primitive, often with a simple wooden plough as the main implement available. The usual system of cultivation of the strips in European Russia was a three-field rotation, whereby all strips belonging to different households in the same field went through a cycle of winter crop, spring crop, and fallow.[4] It was a wasteful system, which required land to go out of cultivation a total of one year in every three, and also required relatively large amounts of land to act as boundary lanes between the strips of different households. It was also a system that required communal decision-making concerning basic questions such as when to plough or when to harvest.

In such a system there was little room for extensive commerce or commodity production. The consequences of low productivity, primitive production methods, and the heavy burdens of dues and taxes, as well as restrictions on the mobility of peasants, all meant that there was very little surplus from peasant agriculture. Furthermore, and partly as a result of the lack of available surplus, there was little significant urban development in Russia, and no strong merchant sector was able to emerge with the kind of corporate identity achieved by merchants in western European cities. The existing commerce took the form of local trade and peasant craft production for exchange. In a society made up of socially and geographically isolated communities, the links established by small-scale traders became very important, but the form of their development was not conducive to capitalist development.[5]

Equally, there was little room for any significant differentiation of the peasantry. There were some inequalities between households and between communes, in terms of both living standards and status, but the general poverty and low levels of production, along with periodic redistribution of land in the majority of communes, made any significant degree of differentiation the exception rather than the rule (Robinson 1932, 40; Volin 1970, 16–19).[6]

During the nineteenth century, however, changes began to occur, and the peasants increasingly felt the effects of a growing commodity economy. Perhaps the main change affecting them was the emancipation of the serfs in 1861. This, and later associated legislation, was the contradictory outcome of various conflicting interests, especially between many landowners, who wanted to retain their hold on servile labour on their estates, and the state, which sought to promote commerce and industrial development to strengthen the economic basis of Russia's international power position.

The legislation of 1861 granted land to the peasants but retained communal tenure, along with the legal role of the commune, which, with the removal of the lord's authority over the peasants, now became the main institution of regulation of peasant life. The amount of land to be received by the peasants through their membership of the commune was to be less than the amount they had previously cultivated on their own account as serfs. In return for their allotments of land, moreover, the peasants had to pay redemption payments to their former lords. These were in fact paid by the state at the time of the emancipation as a compulsory loan to the peasants, who were then required to repay them through the commune over a period of forty-nine years.[7]

The resulting situation in Russian peasant agriculture in the last decades of the nineteenth century was a highly contradictory one. On the one hand, the retention of the household and the commune as the main institutions of peasant society, and the requirement imposed on the commune of the payment of taxes and redemption fees, meant that a growing peasant population was constrained to stay in their home villages, farming smaller and smaller areas of land. Many peasants suffered increasing poverty and indebtedness, suffering from a lack of land or resources to reorganize and expand their production.

On the other hand, the new obligation created by the emancipation legislation to pay taxes and dues in money acted as a stimulus to petty commerce and commodity production among the peasantry. Land became a significant commodity, with a rapid growth in both the purchase and rent of land by peasants; there was a growth in peasant production of cash crops, and increasing regional specialization in peasant agriculture. As a result, despite general poverty and low productivity, there was a growth in inequality between peasant households (Robinson 1932, 81–2, 112–15; Atkinson 1983, 132).

After the 1905 revolution, when peasant militancy led the autocracy to lose faith in the commune as a basis for a conservative regime, a number of measures were introduced which had the effect of further promoting both the growth of a commodity economy and differentiation among the peasantry. The Stolypin reforms, beginning in 1906, contributed both to a further commoditization of land, as it became easier to transfer allotments from communal to private ownership, and to a reorganization of farming among a small proportion of households. The reforms supported the rights of individual households to consolidate their lands, either in an *otrub*, where all the land of a households was brought together but the family's house and farm buildings remained in the village, or in a *khutor*, where land was consolidated and a new house and farm buildings were established on the household's land. Consolidation provided the opportunity for reorganization in order to use land more intensively, to produce more commodities for the market, and perhaps to employ wage labour.

Furthermore, there were other signs of inequalities emerging in peasant farming as a result of the growth of a commodity economy.

Some studies, for example, showed significant differences between households in the ownership of horses (Shanin 1972, 48), while other studies showed a differentiation in the market activity of peasant farms depending on their size of land holding (Kerblay 1968, 90–1).[8]

In summary, it can be stated that, in the years between 1861 and 1917, Russian peasant society clearly experienced a number of changes involving the growth of commodity production and an increase in differentiation between peasant households. However, what is far from clear is how the evidence of such changes related to the classical Marxist view of the class differentiation of the peasantry as part of a transition from petty commodity production to capitalism. On the one hand, the growth of markets, including that in land, and the legislation enabling the consolidation of individually owned farms created possibilities for some peasants to expand their farms and even take up capitalist farming, while the same trends helped undermine other peasant households and contributed to their impoverishment, or even their proletarianization. On the other hand, the majority of peasants stayed within the commune, farming on a small scale, primarily for their own subsistence, with little recourse either to buying or selling wage labour. Despite economic trends, and government policies after 1905, the commune remained a central institution of Russian peasant society, competing as a major purchaser of land with the emerging peasant 'private sector', and generally retaining the allegiance of many peasants. The problem, both for contemporary researchers and for historians since, has been how to interpret the contradictory evidence, and, indeed, how to decide what should count as evidence of the social character of Russian peasant farming. These were the issues to be debated by scholars in Russia, beginning with those involved in the debates at the end of the nineteenth century between Populists and Marxists.

3 Early Marxism and the Debate on the Russian Peasantry

Although Marx's thoughts on the relation of capitalism to the peasantry had been marginal to the main focus of his work, such issues were of central significance to Russian writers of the time. It was among Populist[9] writers that Marx's work first received a favourable reception in Russia, because, despite the direction of Marx's thoughts, they saw in his work a very clear warning of the dangers of capitalism. However, the Populists could not accept his arguments about the progressive role of capitalism in socializing production, breaking up communal and small-scale private property, and thereby laying the basis for an advanced form of communism. Above all, they could not accept the implications of his analysis that communism had to be achieved as a result, in the long term, of the breakup and class differentiation of the peasantry.

Although many of the Populist writers, and particularly Flerovskii, had provided evidence of ways in which capitalism was already beginning to disrupt traditional forms of production and promote a certain amount of differentiation of the peasantry, they all believed it would still be possible to arrest such developments, and, armed with a theoretical understanding, largely drawn from Marx, to build new advanced forms of socialism based on the development of existing communal institutions. Such ideas were often expressed in opposition to what was taken as a proposal by Marxists that there were 'iron laws' of history which events were predetermined to follow. As an alternative to this, Populists put forward the greater significance of subjective and voluntaristic factors in history (Walicki 1969, 140–6).

Perhaps the 'iron law' most vehemently rejected by Populist writers was that concerning the necessary dissolution and expropriation of the peasantry as a result of capitalist development. Marxism was interpreted as predicting the imminent and inevitable breakup of the commune and the differentiation of the peasantry. At the same time, however, it was noted that Marx appeared to recognize a degree of continued vitality on the part of the peasantry. In order to clear up what they took to be a confusion, some Populists wrote to Marx seeking clarification. In a series of letters with various Russian Populists, Marx and Engels gave their reply.

First, in his reply to the editorial board of *Otechestvennie Zapiski*, Marx refuted Populist criticisms that he was proposing absolute laws of history (Marx and Engels 1955, 379). Then, in a letter to Vera Zasulich in 1881, he argued that, while his analysis in *Capital* had neither accepted nor rejected the possibility of peasant communalism as a basis for developed socialism, nevertheless, for the Russian commune to serve as such a basis, it would have to overcome certain 'deleterious influences' which were already undermining it (Marx and Engels 1955, 412). For Marx, Russian society had already been affected by world capitalist development and the commune had, as a result, already been partly undermined.

However, as he suggested a year later in the Preface to the Russian edition of the *Communist Manifesto*, 'If the Russian revolution becomes the signal for a proletarian revolution in the West, so that both complement each other, the present Russian common owner-ship of land may serve as the starting point for a communist development' (Marx and Engels 1882, 56).

Where capitalism developed with a weak native bourgeoisie, as in Russia of the 1880's, the peasantry took on an independent role as a united class and could even provide the basis for a direct development to communism. However, as is clear from the quotation above, such a development would not be a result of the peasantry's own spontaneous development, as the Populists thought, but would occur only if a proletarian revolution in the advanced capitalist countries could provide material and political support. What is clearly implied is that, without the support of advanced socialist states, even a communal peasantry is doomed to dissolution and differentiation as a result of capitalist development.

However, while in his own writings on Russia, Marx thus made some moves towards the Populists, in the political debates within Russia all the leading Russian Marxists tended to take up positions more dramatically opposed to Populism.[10] The first major Russian Marxist thinker was G. V. Plekhanov. Following Marx, Plekhanov rejected any idea of universal historical laws, and indeed saw Russia as having taken a different pre-capitalist path from western European feudalism, describing Russia as a type of 'oriental society' dominated by a despotic state which assumed control over land and other means of production, reduced all classes to dependence on it, and squeezed a surplus out of a primitive peasant agriculture organized into small, self-sufficient, and widely scattered communal villages. However, although Russia's particular historical develop-ment gave rise to certain 'peculiarities' in its transition to capitalism, nevertheless, for Plekhanov, once capitalist development was under way, it then conformed to a law-bound process (Plekhanov 1895, 760). As far as Plekhanov was concerned, capitalism already occupied a determinant position over Russian social development, and he attempted to demonstrate this by using figures from his Populist adversary, 'Nikolai-on',[11] on the extent of capital accumu-lation, money circulation, and credit in Russia (Plekhanov 1885, 266).

In practice, for Plekhanov, capitalist accumulation would have similar effects in Russia as in Marx's 'classic case' of Britain. Drawing on data from census and *zemstvo* surveys, and especially from the work of V. I. Orlov, he attempted to show evidence of the dissolution of peasant communal agriculture and of the differentiation of the peasantry into the major classes of capitalism. For Plekhanov, the development of a commodity economy removed the support offered by a natural economy for the village community, thus setting in train its dissolution and differentiation. The beginnings of this process were to be found in the emancipation of the serfs. This obliged peasants for the first time to make redemption payments for their land in money form, thus forcing them into commodity production. Involvement in the market promoted individual competition between peasant households, with the weaker households failing to meet their redemption payments and becoming indebted to richer peasants or *kulaks* (Plekhanov 1885, 274).

The new relations of exploitation and dependence set up a combination of interests in favour of the breakup of the commune. The richer peasants required perpetual individual rights to their land in order to consolidate their investment in them and their position of strength in the village. For the poorer peasants and especially, according to Plekhanov, the quarter of the peasant population with no horse, their allotments were 'unnecessary' encumbrances that they could not afford to farm or to make the payments on (Plekhanov 1885, 281). Thus, the preconditions were created for a class differentiation into, on the one hand, proto-capitalist peasants, providing credit, hiring labour, and expanding their farming by renting extra land, and, on the other hand, semi-proletarian peasants, unable to provide sufficient capital to farm their land or meet the redemption payments on it, who fell into debt to the richer peasants and were forced to rent out their land, and sell their labour in order to survive.

In this way, Plekhanov lay the basis for the Marxist analysis of the differentiation of the Russian peasantry. However, his analysis remained highly abstract and did not take account of the complexities of the effects of capitalist development on the peasantry. The considerable task of developing a Marxist analysis of the available empirical evidence, and a detailed critique of Populist analysis, was to be taken up by V. I. Lenin.

4   Lenin and the Development of Capitalism in Russia

The main task undertaken by Lenin in his early works of the 1890s was a critique of Populist arguments that capitalism could not develop in Russia. The predominant Populist view of the time was that Russian capitalism was not developing, either because of the low level of technological development of the Russian economy in general, or because the predominance of an impoverished peasant subsistence sector in the Russian economy prevented the growth of a home market for Russian capitalist industry.[12] Lenin's reply was based, on the one hand, on a questioning of Populist definitions of the problem, and in particular of their definition of capitalism, and, on the other hand, on the collection of detailed information to show how the differentiation of the peasantry was making dependence on commodity exchange more prevalent among the peasantry, thus helping to create a home market.

For Lenin, the 'essential features of capitalism' were, first, that commodity production was 'the *general* form of production', and, second, that 'human labour had assumed a commodity form'. This meant that proof of whether capitalism was developing would depend on evidence of these basic features rather than the more circumstantial evidence sought by the Populists. In this way Lenin's approach offered the possibility of more accurate empirical determination of the existence of capitalist relations. However, Lenin then complicated the issue by introducing a further argument that 'the degree to which the commodity form of labour power is developed is an indication of the degree to which capitalism is developed' (Lenin 1894b, 437).

In other words, instead of specifying a certain degree of the development of 'the commodity form of labour' as the minimum necessary for the clear emergence of capitalism within a given sector, Lenin saw a low degree of commoditization of labour power not as a possible subordinate form within a pre-capitalist mode of production, but as a low degree of *capitalist* development. Thus, following the dominant theme in Marx's discussion of the question, Lenin too seemed to see a necessary development of capitalism following from the growth of general commodity production. Following Marx, Lenin traced the transition to capitalism in stages from a predominance of merchant capital, to usury capital, to industrial capital. General commodity production and the increasing commoditization of labour power developed through these stages, but only in the final stage would the independent production of the peasants be fully subordinated to capitalism (Lenin 1894b, 438). Thus, on the basis of such an approach, Lenin's aim in the presentation of evidence against Populist arguments was not to prove that labour had already generally taken the commodity form, but to suggest that it would increasingly do so as a result of the growth of commodity production and the gradual effects of capitalist development. Lenin sought evidence, therefore, of both an increasing specialization of production into different sectors, and a greater differentiation of the population into different social classes. Both these processes served to undermine the self-sufficiency of a natural economy and create demands which could only be met through the purchase of commodities, either for rich peasants, on capital goods markets, or for poor peasants, on consumer goods markets.

Lenin marshalled evidence to support his argument in his various works of the 1890s, culminating in his detailed study, *The Development of Capitalism in Russia*, in 1899. In that book he produced evidence of the specialization of agriculture into different commercial crops, of the separation of former handicrafts and their development into specialized capitalist industries, and of the growth of capitalism in agriculture. The latter trend was developing, Lenin argued, both on the estates of the landowners and within peasant farming.[13]

Within the peasantry, Lenin thought, there was already a noticeable process of class differentiation. Clear inequalities between households were emerging in the distribution of land, horses, and other means of production. As a result, households with insufficient means to produce their own subsistence were being proletarianized, while those with surplus means were increasingly employing wage labour. This trend affected in turn the situation of the large estates. Increasingly, the estates were unable to find peasants able to enter into labour service arrangements, and thereby to provide labour and means of production for the cultivation of the landowners' lands. On the one hand, poor peasants were now less likely to own sufficient means of production, while on the other hand, peasants with sufficient means of production would prefer to use them in their own farming, expanding their operations by renting or buying extra land. As a result, the estates themselves had to turn to capitalist farming, i.e., owning all the necessary means of production and employing wage labour, or they would go into decline.

Thus, by the turn of the century Lenin had set out in his work the possibility of two different paths of agrarian capitalist development in Russia: through the differentiation of the peasants, and as a result of changes on the big estates. In the 1890s Lenin's main concern was simply to set out these possibilities, since evidence of both paths counted equally as support for his arguments that the future of Russia lay in capitalism rather than in a direct transition to peasant socialism; his chief purpose had been to develop a critique of Populism and establish the reality of capitalist development in Russia. However, by the early years of the twentieth century he became more concerned with practical considerations of political strategy. As a result, the demands put on his empirical analysis of Russian society changed, including his analysis of the relation between the peasantry and capitalism. The question of the class differentiation of the peasantry now became part of political discussions concerning the relative strengths of different class forces and interests in Russian society.

Lenin's general position was that, since the peasantry were becoming increasingly differentiated, they should not be treated as a homogeneous class for the purposes of the revolutionary movement, but rather as an unstable agglomeration of different class forces. Over some issues all peasants would share common interests, but over others there would be differences of interest between different emerging class groups. In general, Lenin's approach was that the support of all peasants should be secured for measures to abolish the last remnants of serfdom, and to achieve a democratic bourgeois revolution, but where a difference of interest occurred, the workers' movement should support poor peasant and rural proletarian interests, since these groups would crystallize as firm allies in the future struggle for a socialist revolution.

Such was the thinking behind Lenin's argument that the labour movement in Russia should only campaign for the reinstatement of the 'cut-off lands' which the peasants had formerly had rights to but had lost as a result of the emancipation settlement. Such a policy, Lenin argued, was to be preferred to one favouring the confiscation of all landowners' land by the peasants. For Lenin, the former issue would unite all the peasants against the remnants of serfdom, but the latter issue would confuse matters by encouraging the myth of a homogeneous peasant class which could engage in independent farming if only it had enough land (Lenin 1902, 134).

However, the events of 1905 in the countryside were to reveal that the vast majority of peasants still did support peasant class interests, with peasants acting as a whole in many areas against the estates, and in many cases seizing estate lands as well as 'cut-off lands'. In various writings on agriculture after 1905, Lenin accepted that he had previously overestimated the extent to which capitalist differentiation had already taken place and that large estates in general should be seen as part of the remnants of a system based on serfdom (Lenin 1908, 57–8).

In general, though, Lenin argued for the overall correctness of his analysis. Capitalism was developing in Russian agriculture and differentiation was taking place among the peasantry, albeit more slowly than he had anticipated. The aim of the workers' movement should still be to campaign with the peasantry for the removal of all remnants of serfdom (now seen as all landlord estates), as part of the achievement of the democratic revolution, after which capitalism would develop apace and the proletarianized section of the peasantry would ally themselves with the workers. In order to support his arguments that class differentiation was continuing, Lenin produced new figures to update his analysis of ten years before, again using data on inequality between peasant households to indicate the emergence of class differences with the peasantry. (Lenin 1908, 225–7).[14]

Such, in outline, was Lenin's analysis of the development of capitalism within Russian agriculture. It was based on the argument that capitalist development had already begun, but that a bourgeois revolution was now required to provide the political context for the full development of capitalism. Since the Russian bourgeoisie itself was very weak, however, the leadership of such a revolution would fall to the proletariat, and, in their struggle, they needed to know what sectors of the peasantry could be relied on as allies. In this context, therefore, the question of the differentiation of the peasantry was politically of great importance.

However, by the time the revolution came in 1917, Lenin's understanding of the nature of Russian social development had undergone a significant change, which, ironically, resulted in his according less importance to the question of the differentiation of the peasantry. By then, Lenin had come to see the Russian revolution as part of an international proletarian revolution which would provide the conditions for the establishment of a 'commune state', based on the control of the direct producers, whether they were workers or peasants. Given such an understanding, the question of political alliances with different sections of the peasantry, and therefore the question of peasant differentiation itself, became less important. Such questions were to receive serious attention again from leading Russian Marxists only after the first few months of Soviet power, when it became clear that the Russian revolution was not necessarily to be part of an international revolution, and that therefore its problems would have to be solved mainly on the basis of social forces in Russia itself.

5 Marxism and the Russian Peasantry in the Early Years of Soviet Power

The revolution in the countryside during 1917 and 1918 seemed, on the surface, to confirm the experience of 1905 that any tendencies towards peasant differentiation had not developed to the point where the political actions and interests of different groups of peasants had diverged significantly. Peasants seized estate lands and stock, and redistributed them among themselves through the agency of the commune. The ensuing general redistribution of the land included the reclamation of *khutor* and *otrub* lands by communes and a general equalization of landholdings. The commune seemed to become the dominant political institution in the countryside, negating at a stroke the attempts of policy-makers since 1906 to undermine it (Atkinson 1983, 160–1, 181–3). Moreover, for the first few months of Soviet power, this impression of a homogeneous peasantry seemed consistent with the new view of the nature of the revolution outlined above.

However, both practical and theoretical issues were soon to revive the question of the class differentiation of the peasantry. Increasing realization that the revolution in Russia had not prompted revolutions in the advanced capitalist West were to undermine the prospects of immediately carrying the Russian revolution through into the building of socialism without further basic class conflicts. More immediately, the disruption of production and communications by war and revolution led to food shortages in early 1918, and attention became focused on the political relations between those holding grain surpluses and those in need of food. The immediate assumption was that rich peasants were hoarding grain (Lenin 1918b, 391–2).

Such problems led to a shift in theoretical concerns. Lenin began to argue that, if the new Soviet government was to preserve itself and the future possibility of socialism, then it would have to rule as a 'dictatorship of the proletariat' over other hostile classes.[15] This involved examining the nature of Soviet society to decide who would be the class allies of the proletariat during its dictatorship, and thus led to a renewed interest in the question of the differentiation of the peasants. The nature of post-revolutionary society was, Lenin argued, that of a transitional society involving not only a struggle between capitalism and socialism but, in fact, the complex coexistence of five elements or 'socio-economic structures', each penetrating and affecting the workings of the others. For Lenin (1918a, 335–6), the five structures were:

1. patriarchal economy (i.e. self-sufficient peasant 'natural' economy);

2. small commodity production (i.e. independent peasant and handicraft production for the market);

3. private capitalism (i.e. expanded reproduction for profit based on the employment of wage labour);

4. state capitalism (i.e. capitalist enterprises under the general direction and control of the proletarian state);

5. socialism (i.e. socialized production planned by the proletarian state).

According to Lenin, the progressive elements which were favourable to socialist construction were state capitalism and socialism. State capitalism involved the Soviet government allowing certain capitalist firms to operate and make profits, but under strict controls and regulations set down by the government. As such, he thought, it could be of use to socialism in helping rebuild the economy while, because of the restrictions on it, it could pose no serious threat of a revival of capitalism.

On the other hand, the main threat to the Soviet government came from the small commodity production of the petty bourgeoisie in alliance with private capitalism. In the interests of their own profit-making, thought Lenin, these groups would be opposed to any kind of state interference in economic matters. While the revolution of 1917 had been based on an alliance of workers and the peasantry as a whole, and had successfully overcome the old landowning interests, from now on Lenin thought that the peasantry would be increasingly split between its petty bourgeois members, aspiring to become capitalists, and those whose interests lay on the side of socialist development. As such, the revolution in the countryside was now entering its socialist phase, involving a struggle between bourgeois and proletarian interest (Lenin 1918a, 336–7).

Accompanying such theoretical shifts, policy also changed in the direction of more class conflict. During 1918 there were attempts at the forcible requisitioning of grain from 'rich peasants' by detachments of workers, and the establishment of *kombedy* (committees of poor peasants) to extract surpluses from rich peasants, to organize access to scarce grain and means of production for poor peasants in need, and generally to politicize poor peasants as the main potential supporters of socialist construction in the countryside.[16] By the end of 1918, however, it had become clear that such measures were generally not very successful. Indiscriminate requisitioning of grain resulted in the widespread hoarding of their produce not only by rich peasants, but also by many of their less wealthy neighbours. Suport for the *kombedy* also had been less than hoped for by the government. As a result, there were further revisions in the government's view of relations in the countryside. While the peasantry was still seen as differentiated into different strata, stress shifted from class struggle led by poor peasants to the aim of winning middle peasants, as well as the poor, to support for the Soviet government (*V. K. P. (B) . . .* 1936, 301).

The cast of official thinking about the peasantry was now beginning to set in the form it would take for most of the 1920s. While the idea of the danger of capitalist development within peasant agriculture remained in the background, the immediate concern was increasingly with the problem of winning over the middle peasants to the regime. The idea was accepted that the majority middle group was made up of independent peasants who, for the most part, neither exploited others nor were exploited by them.

Once again, it seemed, Lenin had overestimated the degree to which the peasantry had differentiated on class lines. Just as the events of 1905 had led him to revise his time scale for the dissolution of a peasant class with common interests, so now the failure of policies of class struggle in the countryside again forced him to change course. Along with the majority of his fellow Bolsheviks,

Lenin argued for coexistence with the middle peasantry and policies to win them over to socialism.

In the spring of 1921, the government finally abandoned its policy of direct extraction of grain and went over to a system of exchange with the peasantry through the market. This became part of the New Economic Policy (NEP). The first steps were the introduction of a tax in kind on agricultural produce, which was to be levied on a progressive scale to ease the burden on poor and middle peasants; the introduction of individual rather than communal responsibility for payment of the tax; and, in general, the removal of obstacles to free commodity exchange in the countryside. At first, the leasing of land and the hire and sale of labour were still prohibited, but then these were allowed in 'exceptional circumstances' in 1922, and restrictions were eased more substantially in 1925. The policies of the NEP were thus able progressively to encourage small commodity production with the explicit aim of helping improve productivity in peasant agriculture and build up surpluses of agricultural produce. The tax in kind would encourage this process by leaving a substantial surplus for trade after the tax had been paid.[17]

The adoption of the NEP could not, of course, be seen purely as a neutral device to improve productivity. Following on from the earlier analyses of Marx and Lenin himself, encouraging the development of a commodity economy would implicitly encourage capitalism and class differentiation. As Lenin noted in *The Tax in Kind*, 'once you have exchange, the small economy is bound to develop the petty bourgeois capitalist way' (Lenin 1921a, 344). He even went so far as to repeat his views of 1918 that one must see 'the petty bourgeois economic conditions and the petty bourgeois element as the *principal enemy* of socialism in our country'[18] (Lenin 1921a, 330). On the other hand, Lenin now argued that this petty bourgeois capitalist threat was not something to be fought head on: instead, it had to be controlled and directed by state policies in the same way as he had already argued for state capitalist industry. As far as the peasantry were concerned, this meant the encouragement of agricultural co-operatives (Lenin 1921a: 344–8).

Through the co-operatives, peasants could become accustomed to working together towards wider goals than when engaged in private family farming. Moreover, co-operatives were a very practical way of achieving such an education of the peasants because they could begin from an appeal to the peasants' self-interest. If the government gave sufficient material support to co-operatives, such as a favourable bank rate or state loans, then peasants would be prepared to give up individual farming to join them. The co-operatives would grow up in a petty commodity economy, but by helping to socialize production they could help transcend such conditions and contribute to the building of socialism. Essentially, the process would be a cultural revolution to change peasants' attitudes to property and production (Lenin 1923, 468–9, 474–5).

In setting out this approach, Lenin prescribed both the basis for analysis of the Soviet social structure, and the outlines of policy on peasant agriculture to be followed for most of the 1920s. His policy of accommodation with independent commodity production, combined with an attempt to transform it into more socialized production through co-operatives, was an attempt to construct a policy for a complex and contradictory set of conditions. As a result, Lenin made various remarks which could, in isolation, be read as mutually contradictory. It is perhaps not surprising, therefore, that as time went on, and as the debate grew about how long the NEP compromise should be allowed to continue, different participants in the debate would be able to stress different sides of Lenin's ideas.

Until the later part of the 1920s, the predominant view was that the NEP was working well and should be continued for a considerable time. The first few years saw steady increases both in the area of land under cultivation and in yields of crops, until prewar levels were reached again by 1926. Credit was increasingly made available to peasants, the co-operative movement was re-established, and work on the rationalization of land holdings began again. After the disruption of market relations during the war and revolution, and the attempt to curtail commodity exchange during war communism, peasant life quickly became dominated by a commodity economy once again (Atkinson 1983, 257–60; Davies 1980a, 4–5, 11–15).

There were a number of problems, however. The technological level of agriculture remained very low, with the land redistribution of the revolution having made the inefficient system of farming small scattered strips of land even more pervasive than before the revolution. There were also severe shortages of draught animals and machinery, and despite lip-service to encouragement of collective agriculture, very little was achieved in practice. Finally, in spite of improvements in levels of production, the proportions of produce that were marketed were lower than before the revolution (Davies 1980a, 6–10; TsSU 1927, 120).

Despite the problems, however, in the early and mid-1920s the predominant view within the Party was that the NEP was working well, in that production was increasing and the re-emergence of class differentiation was not proceeding rapidly enough to pose any problems in the foreseeable future.[19] The leading figure putting forward such views was Bukharin, who went so far as to argue for further removal of restrictions on well-off peasants to enable them to accumulate capital and expand production (Bukharin 1925a). According to this view, capitalist and socialist elements in the economy could co-exist, trading with each other on the market. This did not involve any threat of the re-emergence of a dominant capitalism because the socialist sector would become bigger and more efficient, and therefore more successful on the market than the small peasant enterprises. In this view, it would seem, commodity production and market relations did not involve significant conflicts of interest.[20] For Bukharin, the main concern was with the balance between 'agriculture' and 'industry' as sectors rather than with class relations. Industry, he argued, should develop slowly, producing for the peasant market and gradually expanding on the basis of its income from this trade.[21]

Such views as these were strongly opposed, however, by a minority section on the left of Party, and especially by Preobrazhenskii and Trotsky. The earliest statement of such views was by Preobrazhenskii in the set of theses he presented to the Party Central Committee in March 1922. There he argued, first, that, with the reintroduction of a commodity economy under the NEP, stronger farms would have new opportunities to expand commercial activities, either by developing capital-intensive production of cash crops or, in Siberia and some of the border lands, by expanding large-scale farming and employing permanent wage labour. Second, he argued, weaker households were suffering a decline in their productive capacity, with shortages of various means of production, which would force them into the labour market to be exploited by richer peasants.

As yet, in 1922, Preobrazhenskii thought, the main result had not been the emergence of clearly capitalist or proletarian households to any significant extent, but nevertheless the differentiation process had started again (Preobrazhenskii 1922a, 440–1). The main point of his theses was to offer a warning that it had begun, and to argue that support, or even neutral tolerance, of the newly emerging stratum of strong peasants was a mistake, and that the Party should adopt non-coercive means to restrict their expansion, while giving greater support to agricultural extension and co-operative ventures biased towards middle and weaker peasant farms (Preobrazhenskii 1922a, 441–3).

While Lenin's reaction to Preobrazhenskii's theses was dismissive,[22] and the points he raised did not receive serious attention within the Party, the general issue of differentiation continued to receive attention in Party discussions. Preobrazhenskii himself went on to broaden his analysis into a critical study of the whole range of social relations of Soviet society in the 1920s. His key theme was one of a growing contradiction between a law of socialist planning and a law of the market which would support the re-emergence of capitalist tendencies (Preobrazhenskii 1922b, 1926). In *The New Economics*, Preobrazhenskii (1926) also developed the concept of 'primitive socialist accumulation'. This involved the use of such methods as taxation, income from the external trade monopoly, and non-equivalent exchanges with the peasantry to 'pump out' a surplus from the peasantry for investment in an expanded socialist industrial sector. Without this, Preobrazhenskii thought, the development of capitalism in the petty commodity sector would increasingly undermine the chances of socialist construction.[23]

Trotsky, meanwhile, had also provided an early reminder of the continuing possibility of a re-emergence of capitalism in Russia. In his second speech to the 12th Party Congress in 1923 he discussed the issue in a broader framework than was common in the Soviet debates of the 1920s. For Trotsky, the question was one of the political and economic influence of capital not only in agricultural production, but also in trade. Developing a theme from his analysis of pre-revolutionary Russian society, he pointed out that a long-standing feature of the Russian countryside had been the isolation of villages and their dependence on small trading capital as virtually the only economic link between them and the wider society. In this context, it followed that *kulaks* and small rural traders could exert a strong influence over peasant society as a whole out of all proportion to their size, and that the conditions of NEP, permitting private retail trade as well as peasant commodity production, would support the further growth of such influence (Trotsky 1923, 365–83).

While Preobrazhenskii and Trotsky had been among the earliest Bolshevik leaders to raise the problem of class differentiation, they shared such concerns with others on what was to become the left of the party, and an increasing number of those closer to the centre. In 1925, following the publication by the TsSU of figures showing the existence of a stratum of rich peasants which produced 61 per cent of the total grain surplus, a significant group within the party, with Kamenev as its chief spokesman, concluded that there was a danger of such differentiation producing a *kulak* class which could hold the proletarian state to ransom by use of its near monopoly in grain. Kamenev's warning gave rise to a lively debate during 1925 in which it was shown by others that he had overreacted, and that TsSU figures were inaccurate. However despite the criticisms of the figures (which will be discussed in detail in Chapter 3 below), the debate revealed a continuing underlying concern over class differentiation within the party.

The issue was to arise again in 1927, when the *Platform of the Left Opposition*, which included Preobrazhenskii among its signatories, declared that 'in recent years the rural districts have gone far in the direction of capitalist differentiation', citing as evidence various data on inequalities in the distribution of means of production in peasant farming (*Platform . . .* 1927, 28–30). For the Left, the solution lay in the promotion of large-scale socialized agriculture, which, they argued, would require much greater investment in the plant and technology of agriculture than was possible on the Soviet industrial base of the 1920s. They therefore opposed Bukharin's ideas of basing industrial development on the needs of agriculture. As a result, in the bitter debates that followed the splits in the CPSU during the 1920s, the Left have often been characterized as anti-peasant and pro-industralization at the expense of the peasantry. However, although they were clearly in favour of industrialization, they nevertheless argued that such a policy was in the long-term interests of the peasants, and that it should be pursued in a way which preserved the *smychka* (alliance) between the peasantry and the proletariat which the NEP had established.

Perhaps the member of the Left to take the latter argument furthest was Trotsky. While very critical of Bukharin's plans for the development of co-operatives and other inducements to greater production for all strata of the peasantry, including the *kulaks*, Trotsky was also critical of the way industrial development was adversely affecting the peasants' interests. He went so far as to argue that, given shortages and inflation in prices of goods in the countryside, consumer goods for the peasants should in some cases be imported in preference to some home-based heavy industrial developments. As Day has shown, while Trotsky attacked Bukharin's plans for the encouragement he thought they would give to the class differentiation of the peasantry, he nevertheless considered that some degree of differentiation was permissible and necessary in the terms of the NEP compromise, and that 'concessions to the *kulak*, assuming the growth of state industry continued without interruption, would not pose the threat of . . . "a sharp turn to capitalism" ' (Day 1981, 62).

Despite the bitterness of the political debates of the 1920s, there was, then, general agreement about certain key points until the adoption of Stalin's policy of forced collectivization in the late 1920s. All agreed, it seems, on the necessity of the *smychka* and, with it, the necessity of some degree of differentiation of the peasantry. Furthermore, all agreed that, given control over the 'commanding heights' of the economy (industry, finance, and foreign trade) by the socialist state, differentiation posed no short-term threat of a strong resurgence of capitalism in the Soviet Union. There was however growing disquiet on the left of the Party about the policies advocated by Bukharin and the Right.

It is ironical therefore that, when the centre of the Party under Stalin finally came to recognize the importance of the differentiation question in the late 1920s, their reaction was to bring the NEP compromise altogether to an end. In response to further recurrence of problems in securing an adequate supply of grain, the government defined the problem as one of hoarding by *kulaks* and strong peasants who were using their hold on grain surpluses as a weapon against the socialist state. First compulsory requisitioning was reintroduced, and then, at the very end of the decade, the fateful decision was taken in favour of a rapid and forced collectivization of peasant farming.[24]

It was in the context of such debates and shifts of policy that growing awareness of the existence of a problem of class differentiation of the peasantry gave rise to the development of research on the subject. A wide variety of studies were commissioned or encouraged by various government institutions in the second half of the 1920s, and among these, the body of research which was to become pre-eminent was that of Kritsman and his group. As Marxist researchers, engaged in the study of a subject of vital contemporary political importance, they were well rehearsed in the theoretical and political debates that had gone before. They developed their approach on the basis of the theoretical positions worked out by their predecessors which have been the subject of this chapter, and their innovations must be seen as developments in the context of the theory they inherited.

Essentially, the Agrarian Marxists' theoretical heritage was one which, despite hints to the contrary in Marx, tended to assume that inherent in the growth of commodity production in peasant agriculture was the necessary emergence of capitalist farming and, associated with it, the class differentiation of the peasantry. While, in the Soviet period, this view was modified to recognize that the Soviet state had the capacity to take measures to prevent such a development, nevertheless, the basic assumptions remained the same: that is, unless active steps were taken to counteract capitalist tendencies, they would necessarily follow from the growth of commodity production in agriculture. As will be suggested below, while in some ways Kritsman and his colleagues were able to break with this heritage, in other ways they were to remain bound by it.

In addition to the theoretical heritage, however, the Agrarian Marxists also drew on a long tradition of research methods which had been developed in social research on the Russian peasantry. The roots of the Agrarian Marxists in this research tradition is the subject of Chapter 2.

Notes

1. For a critique of Marx's views on agriculture in developed capitalism and a discussion of what have proved to be the more typical trends, see Djurfeldt (1981) and the ensuing debate: Winter (1982), Raikes (1982), Djurfeldt (1982), and Nelson (1983).

2. Marx often expressed himself in terms implying the inevitability of the processes he was decribing; for example see Marx (1865, 799).

3. This passage would seem to call into question the assertion by Hussain and Tribe that the 'concentration by Lenin on the peasantry as composed of increasingly antagonistic households has no direct foundation in *Capital*' (Hussain and Tribe 1981, Vol. 2, 48).

4. In many non-European parts of the empire, however, as well as in the

southern steppe, lower Voga, and north Caucasus regions, shifting cultivation was still common; see Davies (1980a, 18–23).

5. See for example Trotsky (1922, 12–13).

6. For a more detailed discussion of the pre-emancipation peasantry, see Blum (1971, Chs. 15–27).

7. On the emancipation and its effects on the peasantry, see Robinson (1932, Ch. 5); Volin (1970, Ch. 2); Atkinson (1983); Pavlovsky (1930); Kerblay (1968).

8. On the effects of the Stolypin reforms, see also Pallot (1982, 1984a, 1984b).

9. The definition of Russian Populism used here is that suggested by Lenin and largely adopted by Walicki, as characterized by: (1) 'Belief that capitalism in Russia represents a deterioration, retrogression', (2) 'Belief in the exceptional character of the Russian economic system in general, and of the peasantry with its village community, artel', etc., in particular . . . Lenin took the view that Populism . . . consisted in a combination of advocacy of a radical agrarian reform with "socialist dreams, with hopes of avoiding the capitalist path".' (Walicki 1969, 16).

10. On the basis of Marx's remarks on the Russian commune, Hussain and Tribe (1981, Vol. 2, 24) have gone so far as to suggest Marx was closer to Russian Populism than to early Russian Marxism, and that therefore the Populists should be seen as representing 'Marxist orthodoxy'. However, it seems to me that this overlooks Marx's views that developed socialism could arise on the basis of the commune only given the support of an already socialist industrialized West. The implication in Marx's remarks is surely that, in the absence of this factor, the effect of the growth of a commodity economy which he had already discussed in previous works would be increasingly obvious in the Russian countryside, leading eventually to the undermining of the commune as a possible base for a direct transition to socialism. Since in the 1890s the autocracy had not been overthrown and there had not been a socialist revolution in the West, the Russian Marxists were surely on strong ground in basing their theories on Marx's wider economic analysis rather than exclusively on a few brief remarks on Russia in the early 1880s.

11. This was the pseudonym used by the liberal populist N. F. Danielson, who was the translator of Marx's *Capital* into Russian.

12. See for example Voronstov (1882). Lenin's critique was developed in a series of works (Lenin 1893a, 1893b, 1894a, 1894b, 1897a, 1897b, 1899).

13. For Lenin's evidence of growing specialization, see 1899, Chs. 4–7, and for his evidence of the growth of capitalism in agriculture, see 1899, Chs. 2, 3. For a discussion of his methods of analysis and results, see Chapter 2 below.

14. Lenin also tried to develop further his analysis of the political significance of agrarian development. Returning to his theme of the two paths of capitalist development in agriculture, through changes in the estates and through peasant class differentiation, he stated a clear preference on political grounds for the path which led through the differentiation of the peasantry. On the one hand, if the predominant path lay through development of the estates into capitalist enterprises, then this would support the continuation of the large landowners and the existing state apparatus; while on the other hand, if, as a result of a revolution which overthrew the monarchy and the landowners, the predominant path of capitalist development lay through the differentiation of the peasantry, this would establish the conditions for 'the speediest and freest development of the productive forces on a capitalist basis' and the most favourable political 'conditions for the further accomplishment by the working class of its real and fundamental task of socialist reorganisation' (Lenin 1907, 33). For further discussion of Lenin's thinking on political strategy in relation to the peasantry after 1905, see Kingston-Mann (1980).

15. For a more detailed discussion of the various changes in Lenin's analysis of the revolution during this period see Harding (1981, Chs. 8–10). In particular, considering the implications of the adoption of the dictatorship of the proletariat, Harding argues:

> In all essentials, Lenin's class analysis of the dictatorship of the proletariat revives his arguments of 1905 and these in turn . . . can be traced back to 1894. Lenin now reverted to his old argument that the proletariat could only establish its pre-eminence by becoming the political vehicle and vanguard of all Russia's exploited. Only through an alliance with the poor peasantry and wage-working artisans could the proletariat achieve a radical democratic revolution. Only by splitting the peasantry, by organising the poor peasants under the leadership of the proletariat, would it be possible to establish and maintain the dictatorship of the proletariat and prepare the foundations of socialism.
>
> (Harding 1981, 208)

16. On the *kombedy* see Carr (1966, Vol. 2, 161–4); Atkinson (1983, 191–6).

17. For greater detail on these measures and their effects, see Carr (1966, Vol. 2, Chs. 16a, 17a, 18a); Nove (1972: Chs. 2–4).

18. Lenin specifically refered back to, and quoted, excerpts from his article (1918a) quoted above.

19. E.g. the official view represented by a report to the 15th Party Congress held that:

> The peculiarities of that differentiation are a result of altered social conditions. These peculiarities consist in the fact that, in contradiction to the capitalist type of development, which is expressed in the weakening of the middle peasantry, while the two extremes (the poor and the rich farmers) grow, in our country it is the reverse. We have a process of strengthening the middle peasant group, accompanied, so far, by a certain growth of the rich peasants from among the

more well-to-do middle peasants, and a diminution of the poor groups, of which some become proletarianished while others—the greater part—are gradually transferring to the middle group.

(*Report* . . . 1928, 362)

20. For further discussion of this point, see for example, Lewin (1968, 139).

21. For Bukharin's main discussion of this idea for a policy of socialist development, see Bukharin (1925b). For further discussion of Bukharin, see Lewin (1968, 1975); Cohen (1974).

22. Under Lenin's influence, Preobrazhenskii's theses were not put to the Congress for discussion. Instead, Lenin suggested setting up a commission to evaluate practical experience of cooperation only (Lenin 1922, 193). Lenin's philistine reaction is surprising in view of his consistency, in earlier writings on the peasantry, in stressing the dangers of differentiation, attempting to develop practical policies on the basis of a theoretical analysis of the question. Presumably fears for the fragility of the NEP compromise led him to accentuate pragmatic issues and to discourage theoretical analysis at that time. In doing so, however, he was to contribute to the relegation of deep critical analysis of the social relations of the NEP period from the higher levels of the Bolshevik party later in the 1920s.

23. For further discussion of Preobrazhenskii, see especially Filtzer (1978, 1979).

24. For further discussion of these developments, see Lewin (1968, Chs. 16, 17); Davies (1980a).

2

The Development of Empirical Research on the Differentiation of the Russian Peasantry

1 Research Methods in the Study of the Russian Peasantry

From the 1870s, a tradition of detailed research developed in Russia on a scale, and to a degree of sophistication, that is unique among societies with large peasant populations. Few other peasantries have attracted so much interest from the intelligentsia of their society, and few have approached the study of the peasantry with the rigour and scientific outlook of the Russian intelligentsia. The Russian research included a variety of different types of approaches, including a strong tradition of descriptive monographs on aspects of rural social conditions and ways of life. However, as far as the question of the differentiation of the peasantry was concerned, the most significant and most used forms of research were surveys and censuses of various kinds, especially those carried out under the auspices of the *zemstvo* (local government) statistical bureax.[1]

The *zemstvo* surveys were usually carried out at local *uezd* level. On the whole their distribution across the country was very uneven, so that generalization from their results was very difficult. Nevertheless, they were to be the main source of information in the debate on the differentiation of the Russian peasantry, and the research methods developed by *zemstvo* researchers formed the basis of the research approach to be developed by the Agrarian Marxists in the 1920s. Overall, the range of information produced was quite wide, although the surveys varied in the data they collected and the headings under which they categorized it. The topics investigated by at least some surveys included literacy, craft activities, provision of farm buildings, implements and machinery, animals and land, patterns of land use and of the renting and leasing out of land, the hiring of workers, sale and purchase of agricultural produce, and the provision of credit (Svavitskii 1961, 72–114).[2]

While most *zemstvo* research used household surveys based on a simple and relatively short questionnaire, aiming to cover all the households of a selected *uezd*, a second type of survey, the budget survey, was also developed by *zemstvo* researchers. Using a selected sample of the households in a given area, budget surveys involved more detailed and specialized analyses of all aspects of income and expenditure of a household than was possible on a mass scale with the household surveys. Sometimes budget studies were combined with household surveys, using their more general data to construct a suitable representative sample for further detailed budget research (Korenevskaya 1954, 4; Chayanov 1929a, 26).[3]

Having carried out a survey and collected the information, whether by household or by budget survey, the data then had to be organized and tabulated. This was one of the most debated areas of concern among the *zemstvo* researchers because it determined how the information collected could be used, and precluded certain ways of using it. Depending on the purpose of a study, and on the preconceptions of the researchers, the information of a survey would be published in tabular form and generally would have been available to other researchers only in such a form. In particular, those concerned with questions of the differentiation of the peasantry (eg. Lenin 1913, 84–5) were constant critics of the way the *zemstvo* researchers presented their data. The predominant view among researchers until the twentieth century was based on the idea that it was meaningful to discuss an average type of peasant household, rather than seeking to distinguish between different types of household in terms of their degree of wealth, or their production organization.

Depending on the purpose, and on the degree of sophistication of the data, two forms of tabulation were employed (although a lot of data were never processed at all). The first approach involved the organization of data in 'simple group tables' (*gruppovye tablitsy*) where households were put into different categories on the basis of a single indicator and all further information about the households was presented within such categories. The group tables were the most common form of presentation of data, although as time went on a second approach became used more often. This was the more complex 'combination table' (*kombinatsionnye tablitsy*), which used a number of different indicators to categorize households. First, a major grouping would be established on the basis of one indicator, and then each group would be divided into a series of sub-types on the basis of successive indicators, providing a complex and wide range of different types of household. In analysing the combination tables, researchers would often then 'condense' the results to form a smaller number of synthetic types, each defined in terms of a combination of different indicators rather than a single indicator.

2 Research on the Social Stratification of the Russian Peasantry before the Revolution

To the extent that the differentiation of the peasantry became a concern of researchers before the revolution, it was mainly conceived in terms of inequalities between households in the distribution of certain key variables or, in other words, was seen in terms of social stratification. Households were placed higher or lower on a scale depending on the extent of their provision with chosen factors of production. According to the particular study, data were then organized into either single-indicator group tables or combination tables in order to classify households into separate strata. For classifications using a single indicator, the most common indicator in the 1870s and 1880s was the size of allotment land. However, since a household might add to its land by renting or buying, and since some members might be employed elsewhere than on the household land, it was increasingly argued that size of allotment was not a good indicator of a household's economic strength. During the 1880s various alternatives were tried including total arable land of a household, total numbers of working cattle per household, and size of family. However, one of the most influential approaches was that of K. A. Verner in Taurida *guberniya*, who adopted the total area sown with crops by a household as his indicator. This, he argued, would offer the best reflection of cultivation by households on all the land at their disposal, however it had been acquired (Svavitskii 1961, 204–9). It was the work of Verner and the Taurida *guberniya zemstvo* that attracted the attention of V. Y. Postnikov, who used their work in his book, which in turn was an important influence on Lenin. During the 1890s sown area was adopted as the main indicator of differences between households by several other *zemstva* and by the turn of the century it had become the most commonly used.

Postnikov's study, *Yuzhno-Russkoe Krest'yanskoe Khozyaistvo* ('South Russian Peasant Farming'), published in 1891, marked a major step forward in the use of *zemstvo* data to study inequality within the peasantry, since, unlike many of the *zemstvo* statisticians, he explicitly recognized its existence and made it a major concern of his work. Furthermore, whereas most *zemstvo* studies related to only one local area at a time, Postnikov attempted to bring together the results of all the studies of southern Russia to come to some more general conclusions.

In his study, Postnikov identified six strata according to their extent of sown area, and found that the mass of the peasants were distributed in the middle strata, with smaller numbers in extreme groups at each end of the scale. Postnikov went on to describe the different characteristics of households in the different strata. For example, he produced tables showing how each stratum, defined by extent of sowing, also differed in terms of family size and composition, extent of renting of land, provision with animals and various items of stock, and the extent of sale and hire of labour power. The main aim of the study was to investigate the significance for their production of differences in the distribution of factors of production between different households in different strata.[4]

Although Postnikov and other researchers claimed good results using sown area as their main indicator, there were a number of problems with it in the study of peasant differentiation. First, while it appeared useful for areas of extensive cultivation, it was more misleading in relation to intensive cultivation, where yields and profits might be high from relatively small areas of land. Second, it was not particularly useful for making comparisons between areas where, for example, soil fertility, weather, transport, or market conditions would make for different levels of productivity of the soil. Third, sown area accurately indicated wealth, and the rate of return on investment of labour and capital, only if it could be assumed that all the various factors of production were relatively easily available to a farmer. If some peasants were forced to pay very high rates for the labour, land, or stock they required, then their sown area would not represent such a degree of well-being as if they had all these factors easily and economically available.

If, for the above reasons, there were problems with using sown area figures to study the differentiation of the peasantry, other single indicators also entailed their own problems. The next most popular indicator was the number of working animals available to a household. To begin with, this was probably of less use than sown area, since it represented not the outcome of the productive activities 'of farms, but one factor of production necessary for production to be carried out. Different crops would require draught animals to greater or lesser degrees relative to other factors of production. Furthermore, even with the same crop, local factors could again intervene to decrease the value of this indicator for studies comparing different areas. Factors such as the heaviness of the soil could alter the number of animals required to make a full plough team. Where the soil required a large plough team, ownership of several draught animals would not necessarily be such a good sign of wealth as it would be where only a small plough team was required.

Such considerations were aired in the course of various debates on methodological issues between *zemstvo* statisticians during the 1890s and the early years of the twentieth century (Svavitskii 1961, 218–22). Further problems raised included the question of how to measure the wealth or performance of households whose main activity or source of income was not from field cultivation at all, or where subsidiary activities other than field cultivation substantially affected the level of well-being of a household. Included here, for example, were animal breeding, dairy farming, and market gardening, as well *promysly*,[5] the various non-agricultural trades and crafts engaged in by the Russian peasantry. Indices of sown area or any other single indicator were clearly inadequate to take account of such activities and sources of income.

As an alternative, therefore, some *zemstvo* research developed the use of combination tables of different indicators for studies concerning peasant differentiation. Such work was pioneered in the 1880s by, for example, A. P. Shlikevich in Chernigov and N. A. Bazilevich in Poltava, and developed further in the research of F. Shcherbina. These studies raised some interesting methodological issues which were to become important in the research of 1920s. First was the question of the interrelation of indicators based on different scales of measurement, such as desyatins of land owned and head of cattle owned. The usual practice was to take one main indicator to delineate different groups of households and then use further indicators to produce series of sub-groups for each main group. However, a novel feature of the research of Bazilevich involved an attempt to make these different measures commensurable, enabling the classification of households into groups on a single scale of measurement. While, theoretically, the money value of each factor used as an indicator could have been used, given the uneven spread of commodity relations in the Russian countryside, Bazilevich developed an alternative 'points system' as approximate measure of the relative values of each indicator.

A further problem arose, however, over the use of indicators that could not be easily measured. For example, while the hire and sale of labour or the renting of land might be useful indicators to distinguish different groups of peasants, much of the available data from *zemstvo* surveys only recorded whether such transactions occurred, rather than measuring their extent or value. For some researchers of the time it was only legitimate to use 'quantitative' indicators, because only these had any objective value in identifying economic differences between households. By contrast, non-measurable or 'qualitative' indicators, it was argued, reflected the subjective impressions of researchers. In the study by Shlikevich, however, a qualitative indicator, whether a household rented or leased out land, was used alongside three quantitative indicators: extent of land owned, numbers of working cattle owned, and the number of adult working men in a household.

This issue was carried further by Shcherbina, who stressed the importance for differentiation studies not only of measures of inequality between households in their access to different factors of production, but also of indicators of the social relations that households were involved in. For Shcherbina, therefore, whereas the amount of land and cattle owned could indicate the degree of wealth or economic strength of a household, classification could also be made into social types on the basis of qualitative indicators such as whether a household bought or sold agricultural labour, or whether it was involved in non-agricultural activities, and if so, what relations this involved (Svavitskii 1961, 181–90).

By the turn of the century, as a result of studies like those described above, the issue of differentiation had become of greater concern to *zemstvo* researchers and non-Marxist students of the peasantry in general. Among such writers, however, differentiation was still not understood in terms of the peasantry splitting into separate classes, but rather in terms of differences in wealth, or in the ownership of key means of production between households who basically shared the same class position and way of life despite their different positions on a scale of stratification.

In the early years of the twentieth century, among those researchers sharing such an understanding of differentiation, the main issues were to explain its causes and to investigate its nature and extent. The main development in such research came from a series of studies, known as 'dynamic surveys' (*dinamicheskie perepisi*). They were given the name 'dynamic' because, unlike most surveys, they did not simply record the extent of inequality at a given point in time, but attempted to follow through with a further survey of the same sample some years later to find out what changes had taken place in the position of each household.

Various studies of this kind were undertaken, notably by N. N. Chernenkov, who compared data on over 17,000 households in a *uezd* of Saratov *guberniya* in 1894 and 1897, G. A. Kushchenko in Chernigov *guberniya* in 1882 and 1918, A. I. Khryashcheva in Tula *guberniya* in 1899 and 1911, and P. A. Vikhlyaev in Moscow *guberniya* in 1900 and 1910. The results of such surveys showed that, even where the overall proportions of different strata in a population had stayed roughly the same, there was a high degree of movement of farms up or down a stratification scale, as well as the disappearance of some farms and the emergence of new ones. Thus, while figures for the overall numbers of households in different strata might, for example, show an increase in differentiation over a given period, with the growth of extreme groups and the decline of middle groups, the membership of all groups would be radically different.

Such results attracted a great deal of interest among non-Marixst circles of the time because they seemed to contradict the idea of a progressive differentiation or dissolution of the peasantry as a result of growing inequalities between rich and poor. From the results of the dynamic studies, it seemed that households could expect to be both relatively rich and relatively poor at different times, and the idea seemed confirmed that differentiation was therefore a characteristic of peasant society, internal to it and not a reflection of forces undermining it.[6]

(A particularly influential version of this interpretation was put forward by Chayanov and his colleagues in the Organization and Production School. While they began their work before the revolution, their ideas on differentiation were further developed in the 1920s. Their work will be discussed in Section 4 below.)

By the time of the revolution, research on inequality in Russian peasant society had taken on a clear form and character which was to continue in the 1920s. It had been established that inequalities existed in levels of consumption and production capacity, and it was thought that sown area was probably the best single indicator of differentiation. The predominant interpretation of such inequality was that it was an intrinsic feature of peasant society rather than a threat to it, and that, in any case, the level of any particular household on a scale of stratification was likely to fluctuate, thereby reinforcing a common outlook and experience among all peasants rather than serving to promote sectional interests within the peasantry.

However, such a view did not go uncontested. From the 1890s onwards a few writers began to attempt to use the growing body of empirical research on the peasantry as support for an alternative analysis, which saw the basic process in the Russian countryside as differentiation into the classes of a capitalist society. This involved the idea that the differentiation of the peasantry was not simply resulting in the emergence of different strata with access to more or less of particular factors of production, but that it also implied the emergence of different social classes defined by different relations of production, and therefore different material and political interests. At first, in the 1890s, studies such as those by Lenin and Gurvich concentrated on the reinterpretation of existing *zemstvo* research figures from the various types of survey discussed above. Then, in the early years of the twentieth century, there were some isolated attempts by researchers such as Groman and Baskin to actually devise surveys to tackle more directly the question of a class analysis of the peasantry as distinct from the study of inequality between peasant farms. As such, these various writers were the direct precursors of the Agrarian Marxists of the 1920s, and it is to their pioneering work that the following section is devoted.

3 Attempts at a Class Analysis of the Russian Peasantry before the Revolution

The most comprehensive analysis of the existing data on the Russian peasantry before the revolution was that of Lenin, especially in his book *The Development of Capitalism in Russia (1899)*. His approach was to take all the existing evidence on inequalities between households and use it in support of the argument that the existing differentiation represented the first stages of the emergence of an agrarian bourgeoisie and proletariat. His information consisted of data on sown area for Taurida and Perm, and on the distribution of working animals for Saratov, Samara, Orel, Voronezh, and Nizhni-Novgorod. Using these measures, he divided the peasant population of each *guberniya* into groups of rich peasants (e.g. in Taurida those sowing above 25 desyatins of land, in Samara those owning 5 or more head of working animals), middle peasants (in Taurida 10–25 desyatins of sown area, in Samara 2–4 head of animals), and poor peasants (in Taurida up to 10 desyatins, in Samara those with none or one working animal).

The most detailed case of this kind which Lenin was able to make was for Taurida *guberniya*, using Postnikov's figures. Here, Lenin argued, there were a number of signs of the beginnings of capitalist farming. First, it was clear that cultivated land was concentrated in the upper groups. Second, on the basis of Postnikov's estimates of the proportions of cultivation which went to satisfy the food, fodder, and service requirements of the household and farm, it was clear that the remainder, which was the marketable surplus, was larger in the upper groups, showing a greater orientation to commodity production. Third, it was clear from Postnikov's estimates of family-labour norms (i.e. the amount of land which a family can cultivate with the labour of its own members only) that farms in the upper group, with their higher concentration of cultivated land, would need to hire labour in order to farm; on the other hand, from estimates of the income that the poorer groups would be likely to receive from cultivation, it could be seen that they would need to sell labour power. Fourth, figures showing the concentration of various farm implements among the upper groups, and the greater efficiency of each labour unit on the larger farms, indicated that different techniques of farming were being employed on the better-off farms. All this, for Lenin, suggested that the differences shown by the sown area figures were increasingly not simply differences between strata, but emerging class differences between bourgeois and proletarian elements (Lenin 1899, 72–5).

For other *guberniyas* Lenin did not have the benefit of detailed calculations such as those of Postnikov on family-labour norms, the proportions of produce to be marketed, or the likely income from cultivation of different groups. As a result, Lenin's evidence for class differentiation was even more circumstantial. For example, in Samara *guberniya* he pointed to the concentration on better-off farms of cultivated land, improved agricultural implements, and working cattle, and also to the greater extent of hiring labour among better-off farms and selling labour among poorer farms. All this suggested, he argued, that methods of farming were becoming increasingly different on richer and poorer farms, and that class differences were emerging between them (Lenin 1899, 87–92). Similar evidence and argument was presented for the rest of the data available to him (Lenin 1899, 94–129). In all these cases, Lenin's information showed growing concentrations of means of production among the better-off peasants and, in some cases, a greater tendency to rent land and hire labour among this group, but he was unable to provide the detailed reasoning, using family-labour norms, linking such concentrations to growing commodity production and commercial orientation which had been possible for Taurida *guberniya*.

Having established the existence of differentiation, and having argued for the likelihood of its being class differentiation for each case separately, using data organized by different indices, Lenin then attempted to compare the data in order to produce a more general picture for European Russia. His method was to compare the figures for the various *guberniyas* not in terms of the three class groups he had devised, but by taking equal percentages of the top and bottom ends of each of the scales of stratification he had used. Taking the top 20 per cent and the bottom 50 per cent of each of the sets of data available, he compared them across a range of variables which he took as the most significant ones for the differentiation process. Taking such indicators as land of various categories per household, working animals, farm stock, employment of hired workers, and involvement of family members in various off-farm work per household, he calculated the share of each factor going to the top group and the bottom group, so that it was possible to see the general picture of differentiation for 21 different *uezds*, giving a sample of over half a million peasant households, or over three and a half million people.

In each *uezd*, despite geographical and economic differences, and despite the different methods by which the data had been organized, the pattern of differentiation between top and bottom was quite similar. For all the variables, the same kind of differentiation emerged. Moreover, even though better-off households tended to be larger ones, when the distribution of the variables was calculated per person instead of per household, the better-off peasants still had much greater concentrations of land, animals, and stock, including improved implements, and still tended to rent more land and hire more labour than the lower group. The lower group, on the other hand, tended to sell more labour and lease out more land than the top group (Lenin 1899, 129–43).

In this way Lenin attempted to use the available data from *zemstvo* household surveys, and make the various indicators commensurable, in order to show a general comparative picture of the differentiation of the Russian peasantry.[7] In so doing he recognized the inadequate nature of his data for identifying the characteristics of different emergent social classes, but nevertheless presented his analysis as an accurate picture of the Russian peasantry. More detailed budget data would have produced a more satisfactory picture of differentiation in the relations and organization of production characteristic of different classes, but for the most part this was not available.

One exception, however, was a study of 67 peasant budgets in Voronezh *guberniya* by Shcherbina. This offered information not only on standards of living, but also on degrees of involvement in market relations. In particular, the study showed that both in poor households without horses and in well-off households with five or more horses, the cash part of both income and expenditure was much larger than in households in the middle of the range owning between one and four horses. To Lenin, such figures indicated a differentiation into a proletarian group, obliged to sell their labour, and a capitalist group, selling commodities produced through the employment of wage labour (Lenin 1899, 156–7).

In this way Lenin used both household and budget surveys to argue that the growth of a commodity economy was bringing about the class differentiation of the Russian peasantry. In the manner of his presentation, he gave an impression of great confidence that his analysis of the available data supported his conclusions. However, as noted in Chapter 1, there were a number of problems with his conceptualization of the issue which led him to overestimate the extent of differentiation at various times. There were also problems with his data and the methods he used to analyse it.

First, there was a problem concerning the nature of the data. Although Lenin was very critical of *zemstvo* research in general, attacking both the way a lot of information was left unanalysed and the way the most appropriate information for questions of class analysis was often not sought by *zemstvo* statisticians,[8] he nevertheless seemed confident that classification of households into strata did provide a suitable basis for analysis of the development of class relations. He supported Postnikov's approval of sown area as the best indicator in areas of extensive cultivation, and seemed content to use ownership of draught animals as his main index of stratification where sown area figures were not available.[9] However, in accepting such indicators, Lenin was accepting not only the problems and blind-spots they entailed for an adequate study of the kinds of inequalities existing in Russian peasant society which had been discussed by the *zemstvo* researchers, but also the extra problems created by the use of stratification categories for research on class relations.

Lenin's method of using such data was to pick out certain characteristics which would be present in the development of capitalist agriculture and find out how far they were present in the different strata of the Russian peasantry as defined by *zemstvo* research. What he was able to show was the statistical probability that better-off groups, in terms of sown area or possession of draught animals, were in general concentrating land and means of production in their hands to the point where, it could be assumed, they needed to hire labour in order to use it all effectively, and that poorer groups were suffering from shortages of land or other means of production so that, Lenin assumed, they were obliged to seek wage work in order to survive. In some cases Lenin was able to supplement this by producing figures showing that better-off peasants tended to hire labour and rent land more than the strata below them, while poor peasants tended to sell labour power and lease out land which they did not have the stock to cultivate to a greater extent than the strata above them. However, the data of the household surveys did not actually provide detailed information on individual farms to identify some of them clearly as capitalist or proletarian. In the end, Lenin could only identify strata with certain predominant characteristics. His data did not allow the identification of classes in the Marxist sense.

In short, the information available was, at best, tangential to Lenin's needs. He had to resort to round-about methods of interpreting it. With the exception of small amounts of mainly inadequate information on the hire and sale of labour and the rent and lease of land, there was no direct evidence available on the extent of relations of exploitation through which an emerging agrarian bourgeoisie would be able to build up a surplus at the expense of an emerging proletariat; and, given the way *zemstvo* research was presented, there was no way of classifying households by such information. Moreover, apart from evidence of the concentration of ownership of land and farm stock, there was no evidence available for the extent of accumulation of capital by well-off peasant farmers, or for the patterns of investment of the capital of rich peasants either inside or outside agriculture.

A further problem with Lenin's approach was that he had no way of studying in detail the situation of the middle peasantry. According to his theory, this group consisted of those households least affected by the growth of commodity production. They came closest, it would seem, to resembling the hypothetical independent peasantry of a pre-capitalist natural economy. Yet, on the other hand, they were also a product of a petty-commodity economy, a transitional group destined to disappear with the development of capitalism (Lenin 1899, 183–4).

The problem with this approach was, first, that the evidence was slim and, second, that the middle peasantry were only vaguely conceptualized. Given the lack of relevant budget survey data, there was little direct evidence that they were less involved in commodity relations than rich or poor peasants. While it was quite possible that they produced less for the market than rich peasants, and sold their labour less than the poor peasants, in a sense this could well have been a false way of describing them. It might also have been found that the middle peasants, on average, sold their labour more than the better-off, and produced for the market more than the poor. Furthermore, the preconditions and details of the modes of operation and reproduction of the middle peasants went unanalysed. As far as Lenin's information was concerned, they could only be pointed to as the group in the middle. In particular, because of his method of contrasting the top and bottom strata of the peasantry, the middle peasants often seemed like a relatively unimportant residue in his analysis.

In periods when Lenin seemed most assured of the rapidity of the class differentiation of the peasantry, it was possible to see the middle peasants as relatively unimportant. Yet, at other times, such as after 1905, or during the period of the NEP, the middle peasants were credited with a more stable existence, at least in the short term. In the 1920s they became a major focus of government policy in the countryside. The problem was, however, that they had not been subjected to a Marxist analysis in their own right, and Lenin's approach to the use of figures on the peasantry was particularly unsuited to analysing them in depth.

In general, the main problem with Lenin's analysis was that his evidence was too indirect and circumstantial, dealing with inequalities that could only be assumed to reflect class differences. This meant that his empirical work, despite its breadth and thoroughness, could neither fully support nor directly challenge his assumptions (discussed in Chapter 1) concerning the necessary class differentiation of the peasantry once pre-capitalist relations had dissolved into commodity production. However, given the assuredness with which Lenin stated his conclusion, the impression he gave to succeeding generations of Marxists was that his analysis of the figures had proved that a full class differentiation was beginning to develop in Russia before the revolution, and that the use of data on inequality between households was adequate for such analysis. For the most part, the theoretical assumptions continued to be accepted by later Russian and Soviet Marxist researchers, but to some extent alternative approaches to the analysis of differentiation were already being developed at the same time as Lenin produced his own analysis.

For example, in the 1890s, at roughly the same time as Lenin's first writings, I. A. Gurvich produced an analysis of peasant farming in Voronezh *guberniya*, based on the budget research of Shcherbina. In his study Gurvich classified households into three groups using the balance of income and expenditure of households as his indicator (Gurvich 1896, 73–85). The three classes were:

1. households with sufficient income, from agriculture or outside it, to cover all expenditure, so that they did not need to hire out the labour of their members;

2. households engaged in farming but also selling labour power in order to balance their expenditure. Gurvich described this group as semi-cultivators and semi-workers. He further divided it into two sub-groups, made up of households who
   (a) sold labour power in order to cover small debts,
   (b) sold labour power in order to earn enough to survive;

3. proletarian households, no longer farming a plot of their own, surviving by selling their own labour power, sometimes also hiring someone else to work on their own small plot.

In contrast to Lenin, Gurvich did not distinguish any separate group of agrarian bourgeoisie distinct from the self-sufficient peasant households who might, in some cases, hire extra labour. At this 'embryonic stage' of its development, he thought, capitalism was marked by a variety of transitional and contradictory forms. Contradictory class relations might be found in one and the same household, in that some members might sell their labour while others worked on the family farm (Gurvich 1896, 71–2). In this, Gurvich was clearly concerned to approach the question more tentatively than Lenin. However, it is not clear why he made no distinction in class 1 between households with a sufficient income to cover expenses and those with a surplus of income over expenses. Without this, no judgement could be made about tendencies towards the emergence of an exploiting group in the countryside, however slight such tendencies were.

Perhaps the main significance of Gurvich's approach was that he showed the possibilities of budget data for using more sophisticated indicators of potential class characteristics than was possible with the data available to Lenin from the household surveys. Nevertheless, his indicators were still indirect, like Lenin's, in that they did not represent either the processes of extraction or accumulation of a surplus.

The next step was for *zemstvo* researchers to actually devise budget research specifically to yield information on class differentiation in the forms of more direct indicators of class characteristics. Although few *zemstvo* statisticians were disposed to do this, there were two examples of such work in the early years of the twentieth century.

The first researcher to make such an attempt was V. G. Groman. As director of the statistical bureau of Penza *guberniya zemstvo*, Groman carried out a study of Mokshanskii *uezd* in 1913, in which he used hire and sale of labour as his main indicators of developing capitalist relations of exploitation. His approach was to calculate the relation between the total amount of a household's labour and the amount it hired and the amount it sold. Such an approach yielded a classification of households into entrepreneurial groups with a significant proportion of hired labour, an independent group neither hiring nor selling labour, and groups of 'hired workers' which sold significant amounts of labour power (Nemchinov 1927a, 82–3).

Groman's research was one of the first attempts to use a direct indicator of the extent of exploitation between households as a means of determining whether class differentiation was taking place. However, his results were unable to show any clear emergence of classes in the Penza countryside at the time. Rather more successful was the work of G. I. Baskin, who combined use of the hire of labour as an indicator with data on various non-agricultural sources of income, and also used data on temporary forms of the hire of labour, by the day or on piece-work, as well as hire by the year or the season. Using this approach, Baskin identified an entrepreneurial class employing regular hired labour (2.3 per cent of his sample), a proletarian class which did not cultivate any land of their own and were assumed to be selling their labour (8.5 per cent), and middle groups, which either employed temporary labour or cultivated using family labour only (31.5 and 56.9 per cent, respectively)[10] (Nemchinov 1927a, 71–2; Chayanov 1929a, 303).

Despite their methodological advances, compared with research based only on inequalities of distribution of factors between households there were various problems with the work of Groman and Baskin. While Baskin had used a more sophisticated combination of indicators, and had as a result uncovered some degree of differentiation, his approach involved only qualitative indicators, so that the extent of exploitation could not be measured. On the other hand, while Groman used a measure of the significance of hire and sale of labour, this indicator by itself had not enabled him to identify any significant differentiation. Furthermore, it is questionable whether in fact transactions in labour power were the main relations of exploitation between peasant households at the early stage of capitalist development that both researchers were studying. Perhaps if they had turned their attention to other forms of the extraction of a surplus, as the Agrarian Marxists were to do in the 1920s, Groman might have uncovered more significant differentiation and Baskin's large middle groups might have become a little smaller.

Nevertheless, despite such reservations, the work of Groman and Baskin, as well as Gurvich before them, while not as influential as that of Lenin, helped to pioneer a more complex and sophisticated approach to the study of peasant class differentiation. Along with Lenin, they must be seen as part of the heritage on which Kritsman and his colleagues were to draw.

4 Research on the Differentiation of the Peasantry in the 1920s

In the early Soviet period, however, prior to the emergence of the Agrarian Marxist school, the main influences on thinking about peasant differentiation were either Chayanov and his colleagues, or Lenin. The Chayanov group set up a centre for research on agronomy and agricultural economics at the Timiryazev Academy in Moscow, and continued to develop their earlier ideas on the specific nature of the peasant economy and the importance of cyclical social mobility within it. At the same time, the collection of agrarian statistics was organized centrally in a newly formed Central Statistical Board (TsSU), under Marxist statisticians such as Popov and Khryashcheva, who continued along lines developed before the revolution, combining an interest in the dynamic survey approach with a method of analysis based on Lenin's use of sown area figures as the most appropriate measure of class differentiation.

Under the influence of Khryashcheva, dynamic household and budget studies were begun again, collecting information on living standards and production organization similar to those collected in the earlier years of this century. Similar approaches to the processing of information were also continued. For the classification of households into socioeconomic groups, sown area retained its popularity as the preferred indicator in the early 1920s, with some classifications also made on the basis of ownership of working animals and other items of farm stock.

Khryashcheva was also the leading figure in the interpretation of the results of the new empirical research. In a series of articles (Khryashcheva 1924a, 1924b, 1925a, 1925b, 1925c) and in a major book (1926), she developed interpretative analyses of the TsSU statistics covering various aspects of peasant farming, and in particular the group and class structure of the peasantry.

While in general she defended the use of sown area as the basic indicator of differentiation, Khryashcheva also accepted the conditional nature of the figures she was using, and stressed the subjective element involved in translating membership of a sown area group into membership of a social class. Part of the problem could be overcome, she thought, by increasing the reliability of the data and by extending data-gathering to all areas of the country. The reliability of the exercise could be increased further by making it sensitive to regional differences in agriculture whereby a given sown area could have a different significance for a farm's social position in one region compared with another. To resolve this problem, Khryashcheva worked out the formula shown in Table 2.1. Such figures, she hoped, would be sensitive on the one hand to the extent of production required in different regions to avoid being in a weak position in relation to other farms, or on the other hand to the production required to qualify for being in a strong position. These relations would be affected in different regions by the extensiveness or intensiveness of cultivation and by the degree of productivity. Such a formula still produced figures of a conditional nature, but she held that they would be more reliable than figures produced using alternative indicators such as ownership of draught animals, which had even more variable significance (Khryashcheva 1926, 90–1).

Table 2.1

Grouping of the Households by Sown Area
(in desatyins)

| Regions | Classes | | | | |
	Small	Weak	Middle	Well-to-do	Rich
Consumer zone	up to 1	1–2	2–4	4–6	more than 6
Producer zone	up to 2	2–4	4–6	6–10	more than 10
South-East and Siberia	up to 4	4–6	6–10	10–16	more than 16

On the basis of her approach, Khryashcheva argued that it was possible to identify a process of levelling of inequalities in the period 1917–20, followed by a slight growth of inequalities thereafter. However, unlike the pre-revolutionary period, the trend in the 1920s was characterized by a decline of the size of the bottom groups, accompanied by a growth of the middle and top groups (Khryashcheva 1926, 82–91; Cox 1983a, 183–7).

Khryashcheva's conclusions concerning class differentiation in the 1920s were that the old forms of class relations could no longer emerge in the Soviet countryside. There was, she argued, no longer any private property in land, and therefore no basis for large farms exploiting wage labour to the extent possible before the revolution. Most peasant farms in fact were small, and in this new situation, neither absolute ruin and proletarianization of one stratum, nor great enrichment of another exploiting stratum would be possible on any large scale (Khryashcheva 1926, 120).

The new situation created by the NEP was for Khryashcheva a complex one. Analysis of it could proceed only by taking into account the interaction of various factors, including the specific characteristics of small peasant farms on the one hand and the economic and political change brought about by the revolution on the other. As a Marxist, Khryashcheva accepted that the reintroduction of a petty commodity economy under the NEP would encourage competition and differentiation among the peasantry, but, given the small size of nearly all farms after the redistribution of land following the revolution, the base on which such differentiation could build was very narrow.

The factors that would be conducive to class differentiation were the development of rent relations in the Soviet countryside, the continued existence of private trading capital, and the lack of any collective control over the means of production in agriculture, which meant that households without key items of stock, or with insufficient draught animals, were placed in a dependent situation. On the other hand, Khryashcheva discussed certain factors which would help arrest any process of differentiation taking place. These included the fact that there could be no private property in land and the fact of state control over the economy, so that trade, taxation, and industrial production could be regulated to take into account the interests of small peasant farmers.

Khryashcheva also discussed a further factor whose effect was more complex. In the industrialization of the Soviet economy under state sponsorship, she saw an important factor which could help arrest the development of class differences in the countryside. As long as industry could be expanded, there would be a growing demand for labour which would find a response especially from those peasants who were too poor to cultivate their farms successfully. Thus, although as a result of the various factors mentioned above a process of differentiation would be slowly taking place, it would not have the effect of creating an agricultural proletariat in the countryside. However, to the extent that industry was unable to provide opportunities for poor peasants to leave the countryside, and such was the situation at the time of her writing in the mid-1920s, then industrialization policy could also be mentioned as a factor encouraging differentiation by allowing the development of an agricultural proletariat (Khryashcheva 1926, 121–4).

Such an analysis was clearly offered as an explanation for the trend shown by the figures of the 1920s of a decline of the bottom sowing groups and a rise of the middle and, to some extent, the upper groups. Khryashcheva's views were also probably influential on the dominant opinions within the Party in the mid-1920s, where a somewhat similar interpretation of the differentiation of the peasantry was put forward. This can be seen, for example, in the theses to the 15th Party Congress discussed above in Chapter 1.

Implicit in the views of both Khryashcheva and the Party was a perception of the situation in the 1920s as one where the middle peasantry could flourish as independent producers. The removal of the domination of capitalism at the levels of state and national economy were thought to have provided the basis for a new pattern of development, unlike the pre-revolutionary capitalist development, where there would be no large sector of proletarianized peasants (because of the influence of industrialization as well as state policies in the countryside) and no major threat of a large capitalist farming sector (again, as a result of state policies). It followed, therefore, that the focus of interest should be on the independent peasantry, small and middle, who from now on would dominate the countryside for the foreseeable future.

Such a view found further support, no doubt, from the results of the new dynamic surveys undertaken by the TsSU in the 1920s. Their early results suggested a re-emergence of the same patterns of social mobility that had been revealed by the pre-revolutionary studies. While the largest proportion of households remained in the same strata (defined by sown area), there was nevertheless a substantial movement of households between strata, even over the one-year period 1924–5.

For Khryashcheva, the explanation of such patterns lay partly in the workings of a commodity economy, but also in the specific features of the peasant farm which, unlike a capitalist enterprise, was shaped as much by non-economic factors as by economic rationality. The evolution of households, she argued, had a 'dual character', resulting from the interaction of pressures of economic development and the tendencies of households to undergo 'substantive changes' (*organicheskie izmeneniya*) such as splitting up or merger. While economic development could promote the growth of households, the strongest tended to split up into weaker units, while the weakest sometimes merged to form stronger units. The end result was extensive social mobility (Khryashcheva 1925d, 60–1; TsSU, 1927, 66–7; Cox 1983a, 180; Shanin 1972, 99–101).

However, Khryashcheva's was only a partial explanation since, as Shanin has noted, it could not explain mobility which did not result in substantive changes. The main attempt at a more comprehensive explanation was provided by Chayanov and his colleagues in the Organization and Production School (Shanin 1972, 112).[11]

For Chayanov, the explanation also lay in the specifics of peasant society, in the composition of the household. More specifically, he argued that the ratio of workers to consumers in a household, by determining both its consumption needs and its productive capacity, determined the level of production and the extent of sown area. Building on his work before the revolution, he developed a more general theory of the peasant economy, illustrating how its specific features, including multi-directional mobility, could be explained by his theory.

In his review of the evidence of dynamic surveys, Chayanov suggested that, although it could not account entirely for all the patterns of mobility discovered, the main factor determining them was the composition of the household:

Farms may increase and decline with unchanged family composition due to *purely economic causes*. Apart from this, favourable and unfavourable market situations as regards the general economy can make it considerably easier or more difficult for the family to develop its activity in accordance with its own growth. There is, nevertheless, no doubt at all that demographic causes play the leading part in these movements.

(Chayanov 1925, 249)

The way in which family composition could explain social mobility could be made clear if the ratio of its labour and consumer units were charted over the years of the family's generational cycle. A family would start off as a married couple and gradually grow. With the birth of each child and with children growing up, and able to help with work on the farm, the labour-consumer ratio would regularly change. The balance would be at its most onerous in about the fourteenth year of a nuclear family's existence (assuming no children when it came into being, and the birth of one child at regular intervals), and thereafter things would gradually improve as more and more labour became available as children grew up. During this period it would be possible to expand production and build up a surplus. However, in turn, this situation would not last. As a result of marriages of older children, either the family would split up, thus weakening the position of the various resulting smaller families, or the inclusion of more pregnant wives and children into an extended family, possibly with the grandparents becoming less able to work, would again cause the consumer–worker ratio to grow, placing more burdens on the family's resources (Chayanov 1925, 67).

As a result of such 'demographic factors', as Chayanov chose to call them, the peasantry was seen not as permanently 'polarizing', but as experiencing cycles of mobility. Furthermore, as long as the countryside was dominated by a small independent peasantry, then, for Chayanov, such particular trends and characteristics of a peasant society, distinct from capitalism, would still apply. Such a peasant society, he thought, still prevailed in the Soviet Union of the 1920s, and he made it clear that his hope was not to see any significant growth of capitalism in agriculture but that, with support of co-operative organizations, peasant farming 'will be able to defend its positions against large-scale, capitalist type farms as it did in former times' (Chayanov 1925, 256).

However, as noted above, Chayanov also accepted that economic factors could be responsible for some degree of differentiation. For Chayanov, there were different kinds of differentiation taking place, and, given the pressures of a growing commodity economy, class differentiation did exist (Chayanov 1925, 249–50). The important point for Chayanov, therefore, was not to argue for 'demographic differentiation' to the exclusion of class differentiation, but to clearly distinguish the two, and not confuse evidence of demographic differentiation with the evidence required to pass judgement on the extent of class differentiation. In this sense, he seemed to suggest, his own research approaches were of continuing relevance in the Soviet Union of the 1920s, and in a sense were complementary to those being developed by Marxists[12] (Chayanov 1925, 255).

The theme of a variety of types of differentiation was the issue that Chayanov particularly explored in his contribution to the major debate on the differentiation of the peasantry which was held at the

Timiryazev Academy in 1927.[13] In his contribution, Chayanov outlined five possible meanings of the term 'differentiation', corresponding to five theoretically possible types of differentiation process. There was, first, emergence of large enterprises from a mass of small ones, second, the emergence of capitalist farms as distinct from peasant family farms; third, the separation of trades and crafts from agriculture; fourth, the specialization of some farms in particular crops or activities; and fifth, the 'demographic differentiation' about which he had already written in previous works (Chayanov 1927, 109–18).

For Chayanov, in any concrete situation all five types would be interlinked in different ways in different geographical regions and historical periods. However, in order for differentiation to be studied, each type had to be examined separately, and the most appropriate indicators and means of measurement had to be found for each. One of the main problems with the whole debate on differentiation, Chayanov thought, had been the inability of many writers adequately to distinguish between different types of differentiation and find the most appropriate indicators of each (Chayanov 1927, 119).

The theme of different types and meanings of differentiation was also taken up by other contributors to the same conference who were also members of the Organization and Production School. For Chelintsev, a distinction had to be made between the potential for differentiation (*differentsirovanost*) which was revealed by statistics on inequality between households, and the actual process of differentiation. Not all evidence of inequality between sizes of farms should be interpreted in terms of differentiation, he argued, because in many cases different sizes of farm were connected with different types of farming with different forms of organization and relation of technical factors. Some would be more extensive, some more intensive in their patterns of land use (Chelintsev 1927a, 114–5).

Furthermore, for Chelintsev, as well as for Makarov, in another contribution to the same debate, economic indices would have different meanings according to the wider economic context of the particular region of the country they related to. Thus, another aspect of the problem was differentiation between different regions, and this factor again was intertwined with class differentiation and differentially affected the likelihood of inequalities leading to class differentiation. For example, looking back to the period before the revolution, Chelintsev argued that significant differences could be seen between (1) southern Russia, where differentiation grew along with more extensive land use, (2) the central black earth region, where differentiation was much weaker, and where, instead, a stratum of non-capitalist family of 'a small producer (*prodovol'stvennyi*) type' predominated, and (3) the central non-black earth region, where, again, differentiation was weak, in this case as a result of the growth of capitalist industry in the cities (Chelintsev 1927a, 120–1).

Basic to the ideas of all the Organization and Production School contributors was the view that peasant family farms remained a clearly distinct type, and, in areas where differentiation had not undermined them, were becoming neither capitalists nor proletarians; furthermore, they were able to take part in a struggle with capitalist farming and actively to resist its growth.

This position was brought out most clearly by Makarov in his contribution to the 1927 debate. The basic theme of Makarov's paper was that the problem of differentiation hinged on 'the struggle of capitalist and non-capitalist farms in the process of the evolution of agriculture. The objects of struggle are land and labourers' (Makarov 1927, 103). The forms of this struggle would differ according to the prevailing conditions of agriculture in different regions of the country. Where extensive field cultivation predominated, and where, consequently, large farms would need to hire extra labour, non-capitalist farms would pursue the struggle by not giving up their labour to capitalist farms. On the other hand, where farming was intensive and density of population high, and where, consequently, there was great demand for land, capitalist farming could be kept out by peasant households being willing to accept higher land values than capitalists would find profitable to pay. In general, Makarov argued, peasants could undercut capitalist farming by accepting higher costs of factors of production and lower prices for their produce. They could do this because they did not have to make a profit and could, within limits, adjust their consumption levels and deprive themselves in order to keep their farms going (Makarov 1927, 103–4).

As for the actual position of differentiation in the 1920s, Makarov agreed with Marxist writers that the relevant data were not being collected. He accepted that class differentiation would not be revealed by examining sown area statistics, and that an examination of the extent of relations of exploitation was required. However, exploitation did not always signify capitalist development. The possibilities of capitalist development depended on the possibilities available for peasant farms to struggle against it, and both of these depended on the specific features of the national and regional economies of different parts of the Soviet Union. Thus, although figures for the rent and lease of land, and for the hire and sale of labour, were available, albeit of poor quality, the significance of such phenomena had to be treated with care.

To take Makarov's main example, the available figures for renting land showed a general increase in the years up to 1925, including both areas of more intensive farming in the Central Agricultural Region, and areas of more extensive farming in the outlying territories of the south, the Urals and Siberia. However, for Makarov the social meaning of these rent relations could well be different in different regions. While they probably represented a growth of capitalist tendencies in the areas of extensive farming, in the Central Agricultural Region they probably reflected renting by small peasant farms at unprofitable rates for capitalist farming (Makarov 1927, 108–11). Thus, for Makarov, by taking into account the regional differentiation of the Soviet Union, and making judgements about which regions would be most likely to have the potential for capitalist development, it was possible to make more reliable interpretations of the available figures. His approach fitted well with the general orientation of the Organization and Production School of seeing differentiation as consisting of different types, each of which needed to be examined both separately and in its relation to others.

The research of Makarov, Chelintsev, and Chayanov on the differentiation of the peasantry confirmed them in their view that, while class differentiation was developing slowly in some areas, most differentiation was of other kinds and was of a more transitory nature, occurring within the peasantry, and not basically undermining the specificity of peasant society. On the basis of these views, the policies they proposed were for the treating of different strata differently without basically discriminating against any stratum in particular. Different co-operative organizations could help develop different strata of peasant farms in their own ways, but the basis of agricultural development should be the peasant family farm.

The ideal for us would be the peasant family farm, which would have deleted from its organisational plan all those branches of farming in which large-scale production is superior to small-scale production and which would have organised these in varying degrees of scale in co-operatives.

(Chayanov 1922; quoted in Solomon 1977, 73)

The ideas of Chayanov and his colleagues were perhaps the most comprehensive attempt to theorize broadly about the nature of peasant society and peasant production. Their work attracted many supporters until its supression in the Soviet Union at the end of the 1920s, and has given rise to extensive debates in the West in recent years. Their ideas have also attracted much criticism, however. Chayanov's argument for a specific type of peasant economy operating according to its own laws of development has been met with scepticism from writers of various persuasions.[14]

Specifically, on the issue of the differentiation of the peasantry, the views of Chayanov and his colleagues have attracted a number of criticisms. Although the existence of class differentiation was recognized, and although Chayanov argued for a number of different types of differentiation, all mutually affecting each other, the nature of his method of abstraction of demographic differentiation virtually precluded any serious consideration of how growing commodity relations and the formation of separate class interests might undermine and basically change the kind of society where demographic differentiation was a dominant feature.

At a theoretical level, a concern with class interest and exploitation would have been difficult to combine with the basic assumptions of Chayanov's approach concerning the specificity of peasant society as basically homogeneous in its systems of production and its political relations. However, it is also important to note that, in practice, in the conduct of their research, the Organization and Production School writers were constrained in dealing with concepts of class and exploitation by the problematic of stratification on which their research was based.

Although Chayanov's preference was to classify households into groups in terms of family composition, and although he and his colleagues polemicized against giving too much weight to extent of cultivation as a determinant of the economic strength of farms, in practice, they still saw differentiation in terms of strata defined by inequalities in the differentiation of key values, and they still accepted the convention of using indices such as sown area in their work. While they paid lip service to, and were perhaps even genuinely interested in the possibility of, identifying classes by direct indicators, as is suggested by their more general and theoretical comments at the 1927 conference, in their substantive work on differentiation they were unable to move away from seeing it in terms of strata.

This was most obvious from Makarov's contribution, where it was assumed that renting of land by small farms must have been of a non-capitalist type, rather than a sign of exploitative relations and potential capitalist development, whereas it was assumed that renting by large farms was more likely to be of a potentially capitalist nature. In proposing such a hypothesis, Makarov was falling into the standard trap of assuming that larger farms are more likely to have capitalist tendencies than smaller farms. Such an assumption ignores the possibility that capitalism might develop in the countryside based on intensive cultivation of crops other than grain, or in areas other than field cultivation, and would therefore bear little relation to the extent of sown area of a farm.

More basically, Makarov's assumptions reveal the extent of the problem of using stratification data as indicators for research where the issue of class differentiation is at stake. Although it is recognized as a convenient device rather than as a means of directly uncovering class relations, once adopted, it takes on a logic of its own. Thus, not only the Marxist statistical establishment of the 1920s, but also the Organization and Production School helped perpetuate research approaches to peasant differentiation using inappropriate data.

Despite the development of the Agrarian Marxist research, and the growing interest in it among agrarian researchers towards the end of the 1920s, the 'stratification' approach never finally lost its popularity. Although sown area was increasingly rejected as an indicator,[15] the 'stratification' approach survived, especially in schemes based on the use of what were described as 'value indicators' of differentiation. Among Agrarian Marxist writers, Nemchinov was to display an interest in such indicators, using the total value of household means of production in his analysis of TsSU survey data, and a similar approach lay at the basis of Strumilin's influential studies where a measure of total farm income was used.[16]

The challenge to all such approaches by Kritsman and his group, and the alternatives they devised, form the subject of the following chapters.

Notes

1. For further information on the statistical bureaux and on the statisticians who worked in them, see Johnson (1982).
2. The main reasons for the commissioning of the *zemstvo* surveys were to make assessments for tax purposes, and also to investigate poverty and various aspects of peasant living conditions. By 1913 *zemstvo* bureaux had carried out censuses of 378 *uezds* in European Russia (i.e. about three-quarters of all *uezds*). (Svavitskii 1961, 54, 61, 66; Johnson 1982, 345). To begin with, they were concerned mainly with surveys of peasant houeholds, valuation of their land, and assessment of their profitability, but later some of the surveys became increasingly detailed and increasingly concerned with providing agronomic analysis of peasant agriculture (Svavitskii 1961, 41; Lenin 1960, 512).
3. Although the first budget studies were carried out as early as the 1840s, they were developed and refined towards the end of the century, especially under the influence of F. Shcherbina (1900). Then in the early twentieth century they were adapted by Chayanov and others for the study of peasant production. Reflecting the increasing commoditization of Russian peasant agriculture, it was hoped that budget surveys would provide a more detailed impression of all the operations and transactions of a household farm. For descriptions of the main data sought by budget studies, see e.g. Lenin (1913, 82–3); Shanin (1972, 66).
4. For further details of Postnikov's study, see Lenin (1893a, 21–36).
5. For different interpretations of the meaning of the term *promysly*, see Shanin (1975, 224–5), and Smith (1975, 489–90). For Smith, *promysly* were 'any trade producing an income. . . . Thus, it is scarcely surprising that by the 19th century a further extension should have taken place in the meaning of the term so that it then included wage labour as an item producing income for the peasant' (Smith 1975, 489–90). It was because of this latter meaning of the term that Marxist writers found its use by *zemstvo* researchers misleading. For the purposes of assessing whether proletarianization of the peasantry was taking place, it was necessary to know the extent of a household's involvement in wage labour, but in *zemstvo* usage evidence of this was hidden within a wider category of data on *promysly*, including all sorts of other crafts and trades which may have involved indepedent economic activity, or even the exploitation of the labour of others. For this reason Lenin was critical of the usefulness of a category of *promysly* in *zemstvo* research, and Kritsman repeated similar criticisms of its use in TsSU statistics after the revolution.
6. For illustrations of the results of selected dynamic surveys, see Chayanov (1925), Shanin (1972).

7. A rather different account of Lenin's procedure in developing this argument is given by Hunt. According to him, Lenin's starting point was to take the top 20 per cent and the bottom 50 per cent and compare them with reference to the variables mentioned above, so that 'this relational analysis produces a descriptive characterization of the social structure as a three class system'. Then, as a result of examining the gap between groups quantitatively for various factors, Hunt argues that it was possible to draw class boundaries more accurately and less arbitrarily than to begin with:

The certainty of the demarcation is increased when a qualitative transition can be shown to coincide at the same point with reference to a number of different variables. Lenin then proceeded to establish the most readily available method of identifying the three classes by the selection of the criterion which most directly correlated with these groups. . . . The criterion he utilised was the ownership of draught animals. . . . The end result is that Lenin, rejecting the arbitrary differentiation of the *zemstvo* statistics, proceeded to a much higher level of analytical sophistication, and thereby returned to a relatively direct tool for identification which gave effect to the general objective of a class analysis of rural Russia. (Hunt 1976, 16–17)

This seems to me to be a highly misleading account of Lenin's approach. First, on a straightforward point of fact, ownership of draught animals was chosen not because it was 'the criterion which most directly correlated with' Lenin's chosen groups, but because it was the only one available. Indeed, where possible, as noted below, Lenin preferred to use sown area as his indicator.

Second, Lenin's class grouping did not arise as clearly from his examination of the evidence as Hunt suggests. As I hope to have shown above, Lenin's class groups were deduced from his theory of the transition to capitalism in Russian peasant society. Given the nature of the data available to him, his only possible approach was to interpret it by taking strata defined in terms of inequality as rather arbitrary approximations of class groups, and then demonstrating statistically that each of the class tendencies suggested in his theory were more likely to occur in the stratum he had approximated them to than in other strata. In this way he rather arbitrarily identified class groups separately for each *guberniya* and his device of taking a top and bottom group in percentage terms in order to make comparisons between them was only a further elaboration of this method, and not the starting point, as Hunt claims. Furthermore, Lenin did not proceed from there to remove the arbitrariness of his grouping by clearly identifying the boundaries of separate class groups where the gaps between strata were most marked. Even if he had carried out such an exercise, it is difficult to see how he would have arrived at the identification of classes by such a method. It would still have involved arbitrarily assuming that the boundary between classes occurs where inequalities between strata are greatest.

Basically, despite Hunt's assumptions, there is no way of translating strata directly into classes, and moreover, there is no basis for thinking that Lenin aimed to do this. Being more of a realist, he accepted the limitations of the data available to him and made the best use of them that he could for the purpose of his argument.

8. Even where the information was gathered in such a comprehensive way that everything required for a class anaysis had been recorded, it was very unlikely that it would be tabulated and available to researchers in an appropriate form. In this way much useful information must have been lost. Lenin railed at this waste:

> The whole point is how the excellent data will be *tabulated*. . . . Herein lies the weakest spot of our *zemstvo* statistics, which as far as thoroughness and care for detail are concerned, are splendid. . . . To be *rationally* compiled, such tables must first of all enable one to trace the process of development of capitalism in all its ramifications and forms. (Lenin 1913, 84–5)

9. In the case of the budget survey of Voronezh, Lenin admitted that classification by ownership of horses was not suitable for this locality, where a large role was played by non-agricultural occupations in both top and bottom groups, but he decided to use it in order to be able to make the budget data directly comparable with household survey data he had already used (Lenin 1899, 151).

10. There was also a small group that did not cultivate land, but ran trading or industrial enterprises only; they made up 0.3 per cent of the sample.

11. An alternative approach, also aiming at a comprehensive explanation of the mobility revealed by the dynamic surveys, has been put forward more recently by Shanin (1972, Chs. 3–7). For an outline and critique of Shanin's thesis, see Cox (1979b).

12. In this context it is difficult to understand Shanin's characterization of Chayanov's theory as 'monistic' biological determinism (Shanin 1972, 101–5). Indeed, Harrison has suggested that Chayanov and his colleagues saw Marxist research on class differentiation using direct indicators not only as complementary to their own work, but as a 'vindication of their own theories: social relations were not a function of differences in the size of farms, but existed and had to be measured in their own right' (Harrison 1974, 266). This point relates to the polemic between Chaynaov and those who argued that size of holding determined family structure and composition rather than vice versa, as Chayanov argued.

13. A rather misleading account of this debate appears in Solomon (1977, Ch. 7). Solomon concentrates on the element of polemic between the Organization and Production School and the Agrarian Marxists to the point where she omits to discuss in any detail the interesting substantive work that was presented in the leading papers at this conference.

14. For discussion and critique of the work of Chayanov and his colleagues, see, e.g., Harrison (1974, 1975, 1977a, 1977b, 1979); Thorner *et al.* (1966); Millar (1970); Kerblay (1971); Littlejohn (1977); Ennew *et al.* (1977); Shanin (1972, 1973); Solomon (1977); Danilov (1977); Danilov and Slavko (1972).
15. A few studies published in the late 1920s persisted with sown area and ownership of working animals as the main indicators for grouping households. These include Gurevich (1925), Shulimov (1927), Voronov (1927), and Drozdov (1928).
16. Strumilin's scheme has been used in recent studies by Grosskopf (1976) and Bettelheim (1978). Using data on income collected for tax purposes, Strumilin distinguished between *bednyaks*, whose income would be the equivalent of the officially established norm for wages of agricultural workers (*batraks*); *serednyaks*, whose income was above the *batrak* norm but below the amount that could be earned by the labour of all members of the household; and *kulaks*, whose income was above such a level. For the tax year 1926–7, Strumilin's results showed proportions of 29.4 per cent *bednyak*, 67.5 per cent *serednyak*, and 3.1 per cent *kulak* (Strumilin 1928, 39–40, 53). There were various technical problems involved in the study, which Strumilin tried to resolve in his follow-up analysis of the 1927–8 tax figures (Strumilin 1929). However, neither study could really escape from the problem of the arbitrary nature of the delineation between classes. As with all other 'stratification' approaches to the problem of class differentiation, the results could show at best only a very approximate reflection of the class structure of the peasantry. For a more detailed discussion of Strumilin's studies, see Cox (1983a, 408–12).

3

The Development of the Agrarian Marxist Perspective

On the basis of both the theoretical and methodological developments described in the previous two chapters, a new approach to the study of the class differentiation of the peasantry was developed in the Soviet Union from the middle of the 1920s. At this time a group of scholars, who became known as the Agrarian Marxists, came together in a newly formed Agrarian Section of the Communist Academy in Moscow. Their main concerns were to develop and carry out research on agrarian issues and, to this end, to publish a new journal of the Agrarian Section, *Na Agrarnom Fronte*, whose first issue appeared at the beginning of 1925. The leader of the Section, and chief editor of the journal, was L. N. Kritsman, a Marxist economist who had already published a number of works on social and economic issues relating to the development of Soviet society, and who had held a number of posts in the service of the new Soviet state.[1] Around Kritsman were gathered a group of researchers representing the first generation of young Marxist scholars to emerge after the revolution. It is on the work of this group that the rest of this book is focused.

Section 1 will discuss the development of Kritsman's theoretical ideas which formed the basis of Agrarian Marxist research, while the remaining sections will be concerned with the group's critiques of rival approaches to the study of the peasantry in the 1920s.

1 Theoretical Developments

As noted in Chapter 1, by the mid-1920s a common set of ideas had been developed by Soviet Marxists concerning the major social trends in Soviet society and the place of the peasantry within them. Building on these ideas, and especially those of Lenin on the transitional nature of early Soviet society, Kritsman began to develop a less abstract and more detailed analysis of the peasantry and their class character. Although he did not publish any clear statement of the theoretical basis of the research he proposed prior to its commencement, an insight into Kritsman's theoretical approach can be gained from his paper to a conference at the Communist Academy in 1928. There he outlined the general theoretical context of Agrarian Marxist research, drawing explicitly on the earlier work of Lenin (1921a):

> The first question, of into what groups we place peasant farms, is a question about those classes or class-like formations which we attempt to distinguish by means of statistical grouping. We can answer this question, of course, only on the basis of an analysis of that society in relation to which the question is posed, for in various societies, clearly, various classes will be present. In our Soviet society there coexist several economic structures (*uklady*).

(Kritsman 1928a, 117)

Kritsman went on to repeat Lenin's list of five such structures (or 'elements', as Lenin had called them) and to add a sixth; for, as Kritsman pointed out, in some parts of the Soviet Union, especially in parts of central Asia, a sixth structure of feudalism could be added. On the basis of these concepts, he took Lenin's analysis a stage further by attempting to deduce the range of different social classes which would be present given the existence of various economic structures.

> If we proceed from these economic structures, each one of these gives us a known quantity of classes which we must take into account. If we take into account, for example, the capitalist economic structure, then it follows that we take account of two classes, the proletariat and capital. Also in relation to simple commodity society, and in relation to socialism (and the transitional form to socialism), in the conditions of their coexistence with other economic structures, it becomes necessary to take further classes into account: the petty bourgeoisie (independent commodity producers) and the proletariat of the Soviet state economy. If we take feudalism, there also we have to deal with two classes, the enserfed peasantry and the landlords. Finally come the combinations of economic structures, for example the co-operation of petty producers, or state capitalism. As a result we have a relatively large number of classes.

(Kritsman 1928a, 118)

The next step, in keeping with Marx's approach in *Capital*, was to abstract those particular classes whose relationships provided the key to the understanding of the particular aspects of the society which were under study. Of course, the particular aspects to be

abstracted would be decided not arbitrarily, but as a result of a
wider political analysis. Mistakes, thought Kritsman, had been
made by many researchers in studying the class nature of the
peasantry because of their failure to see the peasantry in a broad
enough context (Kritsman 1926a, 271).[2]

Of great importance among the wider political questions related
to the class structure of the peasantry was the whole question of the
nature of the revolution and the incomplete character of its results as
far as rural society was concerned. Kritsman had first discussed this
in his study of war communism (1925b) and then, more specifically,
in his article 'On the Question of the Class Stratification of the
Contemporary Countryside' (1925d).

For Kritsman, the revolution in the countryside could be
understood as comprising two stages. First there was the anti-
landlord revolution, the result of which was

the destruction of the feudal relations which were smothering the peasantry,
and which had been preserved in various forms, even in the transition to
capitalist agriculture on landlords' and merchants' farms: in practice [this
meant] the destruction of the unequal legal position of the peasantry and
their attachment to the commune [*obschchina*], the abolition of one-sided
hiring and renting arrangements, payment by labour, etc.

(Kritsman 1925d, Part I, 47–8)

In a sense, this first stage of the agrarian revolution could be seen as
a form of progress in so far as feudal relations had prevented the full
use of the productive forces of peasant agriculture. It enabled the
emergence of the middle peasants (*serednyaks*) as the main group
within the peasantry. They had been 'the specific object of feudal
exploitation', and the anti-feudal revolution, involving 'a transition
from feudal and semi-feudal to petty bourgeois relations', brought
about the rise in economic terms of such middle peasants, producing
for their own subsistence as well as for the market, for the most part,
it was thought, without becoming involved in the exploitation of the
labour of their neighbours (Kritsman 1926a, 273–4).

The first stage of the agrarian revolution, however, was intertwined
with the second stage, which was essentially an anti-capitalist
revolution in the countryside. This involved the poorer peasants in
seeking not only the redistribution of land seized from the
landowners, but also a redistribution within the peasantry, away
from those who had begun to build up large farms oriented to
commodity production before the revolution. According to

Kritsman, 'the extent and level of the peasant capitalist economy was not such that in itself it called forth the necessity of an anti-capitalist revolution', but, nevertheless, two other factors present encouraged events in such a direction. First was the general decline in production in Russian agriculture as a result of the war and the revolution, which meant that the proletarian or semi-proletarian elements were forced more into subsistence farming on their own account to ensure their survival. Second was the impetus provided by the urban revolutionary movement. The result of the second stage was a significant degree of levelling of inequalities, especially in respect of the distribution of arable land, and, for the period of the duration of the *kombedy*, the possibility of access to the scarce means of production for poor peasants (Kritsman 1925d, Part I, 48).

The interaction of the two revolutions within the one meant that the objective aims of neither were fully realized. The low level of development of the productive forces in agriculture and the political weakness of the party in the countryside helped to restrict the development of a fully socialist agrarian revolution, while the industrial and state powers of the proletariat prevented any easy or unhindered development of a strong trend towards capitalist agriculture (Kritsman 1926a, 271–3).

The complex pattern of interpenetration of the two revolutions resulted in the complexity of different co-existing structures within the overall social formation of the Soviet Union in the 1920s which Lenin had outlined. Unfortunately, Kritsman, like other leading Bolshevik theorists, did not produce a detailed concrete analysis of how precisely the different structures interpenetrated and affected each other. Lenin only bequeathed his outline of the structures and Kritsman, like Preobrazhenskii (1926), recognized it as an interesting topic, but never got round to tackling it before being overtaken by political events.

In general, however, it is clear that the path of development of Soviet society for Kritsman was to be understood as follows. First, as noted above, Soviet society was the complex result of the inter-penetration of various different structures or elements. Second, each in a pure form would have its own laws of motion which would presuppose a given mode of expropriation of the surplus, and a given pattern of class relations. In the interpenetration of structures, a number of different patterns of class relations would be theoretically possible, but the more dominant structures could be expected, in time, to undermine the weaker ones to impose a pattern of class relations more similar to those prevailing in the pure form of the dominant structure. This, however, would be a long-term development, and in the early stages of the development of a transitional society the patterns of class relations could be both very complex and quite fluid.

Prior to the Bolshevik revolution, Marxist theory would have automatically identified capitalism as the structure which would come to predominate in a transitional society with a majority peasant population. However, as noted above, the Bolshevik revolution had called for a revision of this notion of transition in the eyes of Lenin and the Bolsheviks. The revolution had introduced the possibility of conscious intervention in economic relations by the Soviet state in order to regulate and limit the growth of capitalist relations and to foster the growth of socialist forms of production and distribution. In other words, the revolution had made possible the new combined structure of state capitalism and its variant in the conditions of petty commodity production, co-operation. In this, Kritsman followed Lenin. The proletariat, he thought, not only had control over large industry and the state, but also controlled the links between the state and the petty bourgeois and capitalist sectors through organizations for credit, trade, and the co-operatives. However, as industrialization got under way, the economic power of industry, and therefore of the socialist state, would increase in the national economy as a whole. The state would be able to give greater support to socialized forms of agriculture, and as conditions of labour in this sector improved, the nascent capitalist farms would suffer in the competition for labour and their viability would be undermined.

As far as the fate of the peasants was concerned, transition could therefore mean different things. First, they might move into co-operatives as a first stage towards a more collectivized, socialist agriculture. Second, they might join co-operatives as a first stage to membership of some more capitalist venture. Third, they might undergo the classic pattern of class differentiation seen as the norm for the transitional period by Marxist theory. Thus, for Kritsman the development of capitalism in agriculture was a real possibility, but he doubted whether it could develop as the predominant element given the dominance of the Soviet state. Although first the policies of the NEP and then the further relaxation of hiring and leasing arrangements in 1925 meant the legalization of capitalism, with some form of class antagonism in the countryside, he did not consider that it would be necessary to expropriate the peasant capitalists from their farms or to force the peasants more generally into collectivized agriculture. Only in conditions of a renewed intervention by foreign capitalism, as had happened during the Civil War, would a strong threat from indigenous capitalism become likely (Kritsman 1926a, 272–3, 278–80).

Until the end of the 1920s, Kritsman consistently maintained this vision of Soviet social development. On several occasions he professed a belief in the power of state intervention to check capitalist tendencies in peasant agriculture, and to this extent he would seem to have had no quarrel with official government thinking in the debate on the class differentiation of the peasantry. At the same time, however, he was strongly opposed to any suggestion that the question of capitalist tendencies in agriculture could be ignored, as it seemed, for a while, was the tendency among some government figures. For Kritsman, class differentiation was an undercurrent determining all other relations in the countryside, and therefore focus on it was a necessary starting point for the study of all aspects of the social structure of the peasantry. It was important, therefore, to have accurate information on both the rate and the specific forms of capitalist development if effective policies were to be devised to counteract them.

In this lay the crucial importance of research on the class differentiation of the peasantry. It should not be the only topic for research. Others should include co-operation, the collective movement in agriculture, and state farms, but none of these could be studied in isolation from an understanding of the basic tendencies going on in the majority sector of petty commodity peasant production. Effective policies for the promoting of co-operatives or collective farms could be devised only on the basis of knowledge of the extent of exploitative relations among the peasantry and the degree to which different economic groups within it were consolidating. For Kritsman, the current reality was that the peasantry were a 'petty bourgeois mass', but the main point of research on differentiation was to establish how far this mass was retaining its homogeneity, and how far it was being split into different groups developing the beginnings of different class interests (Kritsman 1926a, 270; Kritsman 1928a, 114–17).

Equipped with this understanding of the peasantry, the task which Kritsman and his colleagues set themselves was to develop a more detailed and concrete understanding of the peasantry, their internal dynamics, their relations with other classes, and their significance for policies of socialist construction. In particular, and as a first priority, it was necessary to specify more exactly the class nature of the peasantry, and to distinguish more clearly the character and boundaries of the class groups into which it was likely to split.

For the latter task, empirical research was required which would adapt and transform the research methods already developed by Russian agrarian statisticians to make them suitable for answering the new questions raised about the peasantry by recent Marxist theory. As a prelude to carrying out research of their own, therefore, the Agrarian Marxists had to concern themselves with the nature of agrarian economic thought and agrarian statistics as they existed in the Soviet Union in the early 1920s, and to develop critiques of them in order to determine how they should be transformed. This involved critiques both of the dominant non-Marxist school of theory of the peasantry, the work of the Organization and Production School, and of the statistical ideas of the leading figures in the TsSU.

2   The Agrarian Marxist Critique of the Organization and Production School

When the new Agrarian Section of the Communist Academy was set up in 1925, based in offices at the Timiryazev Academy, one of its first tasks was to develop a critique of the hitherto dominant arguments of their neighbours at the Timiryazev, the Organization and Production School. Many of the new group had also been students of Chayanov and his colleagues.[3] In 1925, in the first few issues of the newly founded journal of the Agrarian Section, *Na Agrarnom Fronte*, several articles appeared developing various aspects of a critique of Chayanov and his colleagues, thus initiating a debate which was to continue until the end of the 1920s. However, the first criticisms from Kritsman had already been published slightly earlier, in 1924.

In the foreword to Chayanov's collection of essays (Chayanov 1924b), Kritsman set down a number of criticisms, some of which were to be developed further by other writers in later years. Although critical, Kritsman's tone was respectful; he found some of Chayanov's ideas interesting, and recognized his work as a serious attempt at a general theory of peasant society (Kritsman 1924b, 3–4). However, in the way Chayanov conceptualized both capitalist and peasant economy, and in the particular abstractions from complex reality that such conceptions involved, Kritsman thought Chayanov's theory had some serious problems. For Kritsman, Chayanov's understanding of capitalist farming was faulty in that it was seen as largely the same as peasant farming, involving a family working their own farm with the same forms of technology and organization, except that capitalist farms used more hired labour in order to cultivate more extensively (Kritsman 1924b, 6–7).

Such a faulty understanding of capitalism, Kritsman argued, was linked to a number of other misunderstandings. First, it supported a view of peasant economy which ignored the forces and relations of production. It stressed the determining role of 'natural' factors of consumption and labour as opposed to the influence of technical factors, or the forces of production. This was revealed most explicitly for Kritsman in Chayanov's (1924c) essay on the significance of machinery in different kinds of agriculture. Here Chayanov was led by his theory to examine peasant agriculture and the influence of its organizational structure on the use of machinery with a view to establishing the best ways in which machinery could be used in peasant farming. Such an approach, Kritsman argued, produced a blind spot which meant that the effect of the introduction of machinery on peasant farm organization was not examined in turn. In other words, Chayanov had developed a theory which abstracted from technical progress and the development of the productive forces. This enabled him to assume that the chief sources of change in peasant agriculture were natural factors rather than factors that had been socially constructed (Kritsman 1924b, 4–5).

Second, Kritsman argued that Chayanov's lack of understanding of the nature of capitalist agriculture, and the differences in its social relations and patterns of organization from peasant agriculture, allowed him and his colleagues to see peasant agriculture as a distinct independent type of farming which not only could success-fully compete with capitalism (as Makarov (1927) was to argue),[4] but also was able to protect itself from being undermined by capitalist class differentiation. In other words, he did not understand how increasing involvement in a commodity economy would slowly transform the relations of peasant farming, giving rise to new forms of exploitation and new class interests.

All this had repercussions for Chayanov's understanding of the differentiation of the peasantry. According to his theory, it was natural factors, particularly the ratio of labour units to consumer units of the peasant household, which were the main determinants of differentiation, rather than social factors. According to Kritsman, Chayanov was therefore predisposed to choose evidence in the results of surveys which supported his theory. In particular, suggested Kritsman, Chayanov had organized some pre-revolutionary survey data so that the boundaries between strata within the peasantry were confused. This had helped produce results showing smaller differences between strata than Kritsman thought there should have been. By adopting too low a boundary between rich and middle peasants, Chayanov had included many households which were in fact middle-peasant in his top stratum. He had then proceeded to make a number of generalizations from these data about the extent of purchase of land and hire of labour in different strata showing little differences between them. Drawing on figures from Lenin (1899), Kritsman showed that, if a higher boundary in terms of sown area between rich and middle peasants were chosen, thus isolating the really big farms, then quite significant differences could be found, suggesting for Kritsman the misleading nature of Chayanov's interpretation of the figures (Kritsman 1924b, 9–11).

In conclusion, Kritsman argued, Chayanov's theory suffered from a lack of dialectical method. It had no sense of the location of peasant farming in historical development, or of its relations with other sections of society. It was neither a proletarian nor a capitalist theory, but a 'petty bourgeois political economy, not oriented to the real conditions of the contemporary peasant economy'. It was an idealized and idealistic view of the peasantry (Kritsman 1924b, 16).

Kritsman's work was followed in 1925 by articles in *Na Agrarnom Fronte* by G. Meerson and G. Raevich. Raevich took issue with what he saw as Chayanov's stress on the subjectively determined consumption needs of households as the chief determinant of their levels of productive activity. Instead, he argued, drawing on an analysis of pre-revolutionary survey material from Smolensk and Penza *guberniyas* in 1911 and 1913 respectively, that it was impossible to identify a single determinant of productive activity, or of the degree of 'drudgery' of labour which would deter peasants from extra efforts, or of the relation between family labour and hired labour on a peasant farm, all of which Chayanov had sought to explain as responses to the level of consumption needs recognized by peasant households. Furthermore, Raevich felt that the pattern of determination of these phenomena varied between different social groups within the peasantry. In his conclusion, Raevich put forward an argument which was to become common in the work of the Agrarian Marxists in the following years:

Research on the labour organization of peasant agriculture must always have in mind, not peasant agriculture as something unified, but various social groups of farms, not only these fully formed as capitalist or proletarian, but also formations of a transitional character. In fact, we see that, for various social groups of peasant agriculture, there are not only various [patterns] but also directly contradictory patterns.

(Raevich 1925, 34)

The stress in Chayanov's work on the determination of the organization of peasant agriculture by consumption needs was also attacked by Meerson, whose approach was to argue that Chayanov's work involved an idealization of the history of Russian peasant agriculture. Drawing on information available on farming in fifteenth-century Novgorod, Meerson argued that Chayanov's theory of peasant economy was based on assumptions which not only did not hold true for the early twentieth century, but were also ill-founded for Russian peasant agriculture before the development of a commodity economy (Meerson 1925).[5]

The criticisms developed by the Agrarian Marxists touched on a number of different aspects of Organization and Production theory which, for the purposes of developing a more comprehensive critique, could have done with further elaboration and study. However, in the context of the political debates of the 1920s, and in terms of the theoretical concerns of developing a Marxist approach to the study of the peasantry, the chief area of immediate interest for Kritsman and his colleagues was to be the question of the class differentiation of the peasantry. In opposition to Chayanov and his colleagues, the Agrarian Marxists wished to argue that class differentiation was not just one minor form of differentiation, but the most significant form, which, if it did not receive sufficient political and theoretical attention, would increasingly threaten to undermine other processes at work in Soviet society.

With such priorities in mind, Kritsman and his colleagues did not develop their general criticisms of their rivals any further at this stage, in the mid-1920s. Nor did they attempt an alternative comprehensive Marxist theory of the peasantry to put in the place of Chayanov's theory, as, for example, Solomon has recently suggested they should have.[6] Instead, their priority for political reasons, in keeping with Kritsman's analysis of the contemporary situation, was the study of the class differentiation of the peasantry. For this it was necessary to move on from criticisms of Chayanov and his colleagues to a critical review of the evidence of class differentiation and a critique of the assumptions and methods which had helped construct that evidence. A more immediate priority, therefore, was a critique of the established views in agrarian statistics and especially the way pre-revolutionary approaches had been adopted by Khryashcheva and her colleagues at the TsSU.

3   The Critique of Soviet Agrarian Statistics

By the mid-1920s, dissatisfaction with official agrarian statistics was being voiced increasingly widely in the Soviet Union. Discontent was expressed not only by researchers but also by political leaders, whose policy judgements were based on data provided by the TsSU.

The main source of theoretical and methodological criticism was Kritsman. His general view can be seen from a slightly later piece of work (1928c), in which he attempted to outline a sociology of Russian agrarian statistics seeing the changing approaches of the statisticians as reflections of changing social relations with the development of capitalism in Russia. According to Kritsman, Russian agrarian statistics had consistently lagged behind social development, thus making it unable to cope with the requirements of contemporary problems.

The first attempts of the *zemstvo* statisticians to classify the peasants into groups bore the impression of feudal society, classifying households by the basic elements of feudal relations, that is, by ownership of allotment land and by number of units of labour with draught animals (*tyaglo*). Quoting Svavitskii (1924), Kritsman showed that in the 1880s more than three-quarters of the groupings in combination tables by *zemstvo* statisticians used such indicators. Feudalism also influenced the concepts that informed *zemstvo* research. This was reflected, for Kritsman, in the stress on the idea of peasant economy as a natural economy, self-sufficient and isolated from the rest of society, a view which, Kritsman thought, helped to mystify the class contradictions of Russian society of the period.

However, beginning in the 1890s, criticisms of feudal ideas in the *zemstvo* statistics were developed, notably by Lenin, who sought to show that grouping by ownership of allotment land hid differences within the peasantry; because it could not show whether land lay unused, or how much land was rented or bought, it was not a true measure of farm size or strength. Groupings on the basis of land ownership reflected juridical rather than economic relations. It was for this reason, thought Kritsman, that sown area was adopted as a more suitable indicator in the 1890s, gradually becoming the most common single indicator in the early twentieth century. Meanwhile, in combination tables, landownership and *tyaglo* were replaced by sown area, ownership of working cattle, and income from *promysly*. This combination more accurately reflected the economic dimensions of peasant farms and, sociologically, indicated a shift from a concern with characteristics of feudal society to a concern with those of bourgeois society (Kritsman 1928c, 305–6).

To some extent, however, the trends were contradictory. Especially after 1905, use of family size as the chief indicator became more common, reflecting the influence of the Organization and Production School and, for Kritsman, marking a step backwards in the ability of agrarian statistics to reveal the most significant relations in peasant society. Furthermore, even groupings based on sown area, working cattle, and *promysly* could not necessarily help uncover the contradictions of capitalist development. Only for certain agricultural conditions, and only in the hands of a handful of researchers, had sown area data yielded useful information for class analysis. Even then, Lenin (for example) only used sown area as his indicator because he had to in the absence of anything better; where possible, he also used a range of other indicators depending on the given region and its predominant type of farming. Similarly, data on income from *promysly* were usually presented by *zemstvo* and Soviet statisticians in such a way that it was impossible to tell the class character of the relations involved. In fact, for the most part, the new indicators had been more conducive to theoretical tendencies such as those of Struve and Legal Marxism, with their concern with the evolutionary development of the productive forces, than with the concerns of uncovering class contradictions (Kritsman 1925c, 306–7; 1925g, 322).

In the post-revolutionary period, when sown area became the predominant indicator in agrarian statistics, its suitability for making judgements about class differentiation became even more questionable. In particular, criticisms were expressed in the course of two different areas of debate: on the one hand among researchers studying the issue of class differentiation in its own right, and on the other hand, developing in parallel with such work, among those concerned more directly with policy issues for which judgements on the different interests and influence of different groups within the peasantry were needed. Indeed, the latter criticisms were probably helpful in supporting the idea of research into alternative approaches to the study of differentiation which were to be developed by Kritsman and others. Each of these areas of debate will be discussed in turn.

In developing his criticisms of existing Soviet official statistics on peasant differentiation, Kritsman attempted to show that they had in fact created a false impression. According to sown area figures, the conclusion seemed to be that a levelling process had taken place as a result of the revolution. However, Kritsman pointed out that there had been nothing like the same equalization in the distribution of working animals. In fact, the proportion of farms sowing grain despite a complete lack of their own working animals had risen from 11.1 to 19 per cent in 1920. For Kritsman, such farms were in fact 'wholly dependent on stronger farms' if they wished to carry on farming (Kritsman 1925d, Part I, 50). While the sown area figures gave the impression of a decline in dependent farms unable to cultivate, they were actually obscuring signs of a growth of dependent farms, which were particularly vulnerable to exploitation by stronger farms, possessing scarce means of production which they leased out at extortionate rates. Clearly, the assumptions behind the use of sown area figures were highly dubious.

Originally, Kritsman conceded, sown area figures had been useful indicators of class differentiation, especially in pre-revolutionary times, in areas where large farms had grown up, employing regular wage labour and producing grain for the market. However, in the 1920s, when such large farms had mostly disappeared, and moreover in pre-revolutionary times in areas where extensive grain production for the market had not predominated, sown area was not a useful indicator. If it was more profitable in some areas to move from spring grain to winter wheat, maize, sunflowers, or flax, depending on local growing conditions and markets, farming would be intensified rather than expanded, and this development would not be reflected by sown area figures (Kritsman 1928a, 120–6).

Given the inadequacy of sown area figures, it was logical to consider whether ownership of working animals and farm stock would make better indicators of peasant wealth and differentiation. Since it was by comparison with these figures that sown area was shown to be an unreliable indicator, and since it was draught animals and stock that were the scarce means of production in the 1920s, it was debatable that they could replace sown area as adequate indirect indicators of class differentiation. Lenin, in his time, had used distribution of horses as a secondary indicator to sown area (Lenin 1899, 86–106, 114–24, 143–50), and some information on the distribution of both working animals and stock was already being collected in post-revolutionary Russia (TsSU 1927, 81–5). However, although grouping by animals and stock could indicate farms undergoing proletarianization because it measured the lack of the particular factors that caused the dependent position of weaker farms, it could not indicate which were potential capitalist farms as distinct from independent middle-peasant farms. In other words, without detailed information on relations between households, it was impossible to distinguish between households with sufficient means of production engaged in simple reproduction and those with sufficient or surplus means who were using them to exploit their weaker neighbours.

A further problem with the use of working animals and stock as indicators was that of extending analysis beyond any particular local set of conditions. The type of plough or of other implements used and the number and type of animals needed to pull them would vary according to such different factors as the types of soil, climate, and crop involved, and this would all make for great difficulties in generalizing from local studies, or conducting large-scale studies where working out the significance for class relations of various degrees of ownership of animals and stock in a wide variety of different local conditions would create very complicated problems (Kritsman 1928a, 127).[7]

Supporting Kritsman's critique of sown area figures and other measures of inequality as indicators of class differentiation, criticisms also arose in Party discussions concerning grain surpluses and their sources in different groups within the peasantry. As noted in Chapter 1, the figures on this issue released by the TsSU in 1925 gave rise to an intense debate within the Party. These figures suggested that 61 per cent of the grain surplus was produced by a stratum of rich peasants, comprising 12 per cent of all peasant households, and defined as those cultivating more than 6 desyatins of land. For some sections of the Party, and notably Kamenev, the figures suggested that class differentiation was already well advanced and that the Soviet state was in danger of suffering a *kulak* 'grain strike' against its policies.

The ensuing debate prompted a re-examination of the figures which suggested there were two main areas of confusion in the TsSU's approach to the question. First, there was a confusion between the estimate of a surplus in production provided by the TsSU with the amount of *marketable* surplus held by different groups. Although poor and even middle peasants had little or no grain to spare beyond their own consumption needs, they nevertheless required money for taxes or essential purchases and were therefore forced to sell grain.

Second, the grouping of peasant farms was ill conceived in that there was serious doubt that the TsSU had correctly delineated the stratum of rich peasants.[8] The basis for both criticisms was laid by the Commission of the Workers' and Peasants' Inspectorate (Rabkrin) under the leadership of Ya. A. Yakovlev.[9] Using the grouping of the TsSU, dividing the peasants into groups of poor, middle, and rich by their extent of sown area, Yakovlev and his colleagues showed that, although the poor did not produce a surplus over and above their needs, they nevertheless produced 21.7 per cent of the marketable grain, while the middle peasants produced 48.6 per cent and the rich peasants 29.7 per cent (Carr 1970, Vol. I, 333).[10]

Furthermore, Yakovlev and his group went beyond correcting a confusion of interpretation and questioned the whole basis of the grouping used by the TsSU. For Yakovlev, the problem was that Popov and Khryashcheva were equating sowing groups with classes even though it was clear from their own statements that they recognized such an equation to be invalid. Their approach was particularly misleading for discussions of the distribution of the marketable grain surplus because it obscured the significance of poor and middle peasants as sources of grain (Yakovlev 1925b, 35).

According to Yakovlev, in all regions where field cultivation was prevalent the TsSU used the following method of grouping farms. First, they included in the middle group those households whose sowing was close to the statistical average for that region. For example, in the Producer Zone the average was 3.4 desyatins and the middle group was made up of households sowing between 2 and 6 desyatins, while in the Ukraine, where the average was 5.4 desyatins, the middle group consisted of households sowing between 4 and 10 desyatins. Rich and poor groups were then identified, respectively, as containing households sowing above and below the range decided on for the middle group. The problem was, Yakovlev argued, that there was no basis for assuming that all the households in any such group would share common social characteristics just because they sowed similar areas of land (Yakovlev 1925b, 35–6).

In place of the TsSU approach, Yakovlev proposed to define class groups in terms of the criteria that Lenin had used in his theses on the agrarian question to the second congress of the Communist International (Lenin 1920b).[11] In these theses, Lenin explicitly defined class groups within the peasantry in terms of relations of exploitation. The middle group (the small peasants in a West European context) were largely self-sufficient, neither exploiting nor exploited; while the rich engaged in exploitation of their neighbours, mainly through the hire of labour, and the poor were those who were exploited through the necessity of having to sell their labour power.

Adopting Lenin's ideas, Yakovlev produced broader sets of criteria, relating to a wider range of relations of exploitation, as a means of allocating households into one group or another. Rich farms were those that systematically used hired labour, widely resorted to renting land (usually using hired labour for its cultivation), had sufficient means of production to make it worth hiring labour and renting land, possibly also had income from *promysly* of a capitalist business character, and, finally, produced a surplus from such relations to be turned into capital. In contrast, the poor peasant farms had insufficient means of production and a meagre income from agriculture which was not enough to meet their families' needs. Consequently they had to sell at least part of the labour power of the household. The middle peasants in this scheme were those displaying insufficient levels of either exploiting or exploited characteristics, but they would not necessarily be the same as those sowing land close to the average for the area (Yakovlev 1925b, 37–8). In this way Yakovlev suggested a possible alternative grouping based clearly on class criteria, although, somewhat confusingly, he continued to use terminology more suited to a stratification approach, calling his groups rich, middle, and poor, rather than capitalist, independent, and proletarian.

However, given the nature of the TsSU data available, it was impossible for Yakovlev to construct an alternative grouping, although there were sufficient data for him to show up some of the problems of the grouping based on sown area, and at least to suggest ways of modifying the TsSU grouping by using a series of indicators rather sown area alone. For example, it was possible to use data on the distribution of means of production between sowing groups, and of certain social relations such as renting land and hiring labour, as well as data on income from *promysly*. Judging from such data, Yakovlev thought, it could at least be shown that many households had been incorrectly classified in class terms using the TsSU approach. For example, taking the rich peasant group in the Consumer Region, 2.3 per cent of these were without horses, and 50.6 per cent had only one horse, while only 2.6 per cent employed seasonal hired labour. From such figures, Yakovlev argued that most of the rich group should in fact have been classified in the middle group (Yakovlev 1925b, 40–1).

As a means of criticizing the approach of the TsSU, the work of Yakovlev and his colleagues had a significant effect, ironically, in supporting arguments that the official figures underestimated the significance of the middle peasantry since most of the rich farms were not clearly capitalist. Tackling the question from a different point of view, Kritsman and his colleagues were later to cast doubt on the significance of an independent middle peasantry and to argue in general that antagonistic relations were more prevalent among the peasants. However, in 1925 the work of the Rabkrin commission had a similar effect to some of the early work of Kritsman in undermining the position of the TsSU statisticians.[12] The chief task for the critics now was to devise a better alternative.

The main alternative to the use of measures of inequality for class analysis suggested by Marxist theory was to use measures of the employment of wage labour. Such an approach had been attempted before the revolution in the studies by Baskin and Groman; but among researchers of the time these had generally been thought not to have been very successful, since they failed clearly to differentiate any significant employing group emerging within the peasantry. In the 1920s Baskin persisted with the approach he had developed before the revolution, replicating his 1913 study in the same area, but still, his results showed little clear sign of the emergence of capitalist farms (Baskin 1927a, 101–2). Two different possible conclusions seemed to follow. Either Baskin's results meant that there was little significant class differentiation taking place in the Soviet countryside, or, as Kritsman and his colleagues were to argue, employment of hired labour by itself was no more suitable an indicator of class differentiation than sown area, in the conditions of the countryside in the 1920s.

For Kritsman, the use of data on the hire of labour on peasant farms was undoubtedly a theoretically correct method in conditions of a more developed capitalism, but it could not be used in the conditions of the Soviet Union in the 1920s. There were a variety of reasons for this. First, there was the problem of inadequate data. During the early 1920s Soviet statistics were not interested in the question of the extent of hired labour in agriculture, and attempts to measure this systematically across the Soviet Union began only in the mid-1920s. In 1924, Narkomtrud set up an investigation to gather information, and this was followed up by a number of studies on aspects of the problem which were published in *Na Agrarnom Fronte* during 1925 and after (Antselovich 1925a, 1925b; Baturiniskii 1926; Baskin 1927b; Larin 1925a, 1925b; Shestakov 1925; Strumilin 1925).

However, in addition to the insufficiency of data, there was a second problem. Figures collected by different organizations did not agree, sometimes by considerable margins.[13] Figures were collected on different bases in different studies; for example, most studies collected information on hire for a given period (whether a season or a part of the year) and ignored the hire of workers by the day or of piece-workers. Other studies included the latter two categories but did not differentiate between them in their detailed figures. An example (possibly extreme) of how misleading the data could be was provided by Yakovlev in a study of a part of Kursk *guberniya*; there, if one took account only of seasonal hire, one would have a figure for 1922 that was less than 20 per cent of the equivalent figure for 1917, but if one also took hire by day and piece-work into account one would find these latter categories had more than doubled in the same period (Yakovlev 1923; quoted in Kritsman 1925b, Part 2, 20).

Third, the data that were collected could well be inaccurate because of deliberate attempts by peasants to hide the true situation. Until 1925 there were laws against most forms of the hire of labour, and this meant that peasants would try to hide any hiring arrangements they undertook, both from government officials and from researchers. Indeed, they would probably have made little distinction between these two types of literate urban professional. Furthermore, the hiding of hiring arrangements need not always require straightforward concealing of evidence. Certain relationships which objectively amounted to the expropriation of someone's labour power took place in other guises, such as fictional marriages of a peasant *khozyain* to a woman worker, the fictional adoption of young people in order to use them as workers, or bogus forms of co-operation or amalgamation of farms where one 'partner' provided all or most of the scarce means of production while the other's 'half' of the bargain was to provide the labour. Many of these 'hidden forms of hire of labour', as Kritsman called them, seemed non-exploitative to observers because they seemed traditional practices, part of the practices of the Russian peasant commune. The whole pattern of organization of the commune had tended to assume an association of households, and therefore unattached individuals or very small and weak households came under pressure from landlords and commune leaders to be incorporated into a viable household (Kritsman 1925d, Part IV, 42–3; Carr 1966, Vol. II, 250).

However, apart from the inadequacies of the statistics on the hire of labour, a further problem, and for Kritsman the main problem for research on class differentiation, was the question of whether direct hire of wage labour would in any case be the main form of exploitation for capital accumulation in its early stages. For some Russian writers of the 1920s the development of agrarian capitalism could be identified only in terms of the hire and sale of wage labour by the owners of capital. For them it was a clear-cut issue: either relations of hire and sale of labour power could be observed, and there was rural capitalism, or they could not be observed and there was no capitalism (Dubrovskii 1928, 133–4; Sukhanov 1927, 140). However, as Kritsman pointed out, such indicators would be observable only where capitalist development was already well under way; there was more of a problem when it came to observing its early stages. In a petty commodity economy, with peasant households as separate production units, the appropriation of the fruits of labour of some households would not necessarily be by the most direct method of hire of labour power. Although hire of labour was probably more common than Soviet statistics showed, and therefore was one way in which a surplus was being appropriated, for Kritsman, other forms of appropriation were probably more important at the current stage of development.

Although little direct evidence of such other forms of appropriation was available, Kritsman attempted to piece together some information through a review of various local studies which had been published in the early and mid-1920s. He examined these various studies, criticizing the ways in which their collection and presentation of data served to obscure the issue of whether class differences were developing and, where possible, using the information they contained to demonstrate the existence of relationships not brought out by the standard research.[14]

Although most of the information contained in the local studies was still presented to show the distribution of variables between strata such as groups defined by sown area, in some cases it was possible to reorganize some of the data to discover something about the signficance of levels of distribution of factors of production for the class relations of different farms. This could be done by working out

the relationship between the size of a peasant's own farm and the extent of his own means of production. Where the extent of his own means of production exceeds the size of his own farm, then as a rule, the means of production are used on others' farms—then we have before us farms with a concentration of means of production, that is, farms of a hidden capitalist type. Where, on the contrary, the size of the farm exceeds the extent of the owner's own means of production, there as a rule, others' means of production are used on the farm—then we have before us farms with a concentration of labour power, that is, farms of a hidden proletarian type. Where the size of the farm corresponds to the extent of [the peasant's] own means of production, there we have before us either farms of a petty bourgeois type, or of a clearly capitalist type (with the daily or seasonal hire of labourers), or finally of a clearly proletarian type of an insignificant size (a vegetable patch attached to a farmstead).

(Kritsman 1925d, Part II, 8)

Of the range of studies carried out, Kritsman found only three that were of much use for a class analysis along such lines. In these cases (*Litso* . . . 1925; Yakovlev 1923, 1925a) it was possible at least to discover the relationship between extent of sowing and ownership of working animals for each household, and, in the two studies by Yakovlev, also to relate sown area to ownership of farm stock and hiring of both horses and stock. As a result, households which by their sown area alone had seemed to belong in middle groups could be identified as heavily dependent because of a lack of working animals and stock which they were obliged to hire from their stronger neighbours (Kritsman 1925d, Part II). In this way, some more accurate judgement could be made to distinguish dependent households, potentially undergoing proletarianization, from more independent peasant households.

Furthermore, the information from Yakovlev's studies on the hire of means of production had produced a very interesting finding which Kritsman described as 'the democratization of capitalist exploitation'. By this he meant that it was not simply a case of a few very strong farms with a large surplus of means of production that were able to exploit their weaker neighbours, but it was also the case that small farms, which themselves had only sufficient amounts, or small surpluses of the means of production, also engaged in the exploitation of their neighbours. 'In the contemporary countryside we are in the initial stages of the process of class stratification,[15] where those carrying out capitalist exploitation are broadly not only the strong but also the smaller peasants possessing means of production' (Kritsman 1925d, Part II, 29). For Kritsman this meant that the conventional categories of rich, middle, and poor peasants were called into question and, in particular, the 'middle peasant' farm was clearly not characterized by independent farming, neither exploiting nor being exploited.

However, as Kritsman noted, the picture was still as imperfect one. There was a problem for example, with assessing households with no sowing and no working animals. They might well be proletarian households, that is, households surviving mainly by wage work but also cultivating a subsidiary vegetable plot; but some of them might be small rural artisans, traders, or businessmen who had given up cultivating all but a subsidiary plot in order to spend more time on a more lucrative non-agricultural enterprise. There was also a more general problem in accurately determining class boundaries between peasant households. While it was possible, using Yakovlev's figures, to identify as proletarian those households that were cultivating their land without owning any working animals or plough, this left unknown the number of households with some, but insufficient, means of production, who would also be in a dependent position on stronger neighbours. Such figures were also unable to distinguish between independent households who had sufficient means of production for their own subsistence and those with surplus means, which they could use for the exploitation of their neighbours. In this sense, although it provided less detailed information in general, the survey of the Don region (*Litso* . . . 1925) was more useful than Yakovlev's studies, because it provided details of local norms of the extent of means of production required to cultivate a given area of land, thus actually offering a means of measuring surplus, sufficiency, or insufficiency of means of production.[16]

In general, despite the fact that a small number of studies had produced some useful information, it was clear that most existing agrarian statistics were useless as a basis for a class analysis of the peasantry. Somehow a more adequate approach to the whole question of class differentiation had to be devised. The data Kritsman surveyed in 1925 enabled him to draw a number of critical and negative conclusions about the methodology of the study of class differentiation. It was at least clear now, he thought, how not to collect and organize data. On the other hand, at this stage he had no worked-out alternative to put in the place of the conventional approaches. It had been possible, in an unsystematic way, to gain insights into the nature of exploitation within the peasantry, but it had not been possible to explore these relations at all extensively or systematically, and it had not been possible, on such a basis, to identify what the boundaries were between different groups relative to each other in such relations of exploitation.

Basically, the problem with existing approaches was that they conceived the problem in terms of social stratification rather than social class in the Marxist sense of the term. They involved the use of indicators of inequality to place households on scales of privilege or deprivation. Yet this was really quite different from the question posed in the Marxist theory of the nature of the social relations of production. Interest here was focused on how wealth became capital and how some people expropriated the surplus product of the labour of others in order to accumulate capital. Classes in this view were therefore groups which had different positions in the processes of the production and expropriation of the surplus product. Marxist theory should therefore have required empirical research to find some way of isolating and observing the relationships and processes through which the surplus was expropriated, and a simple accounting of the distribution of various factors of production, singly or in combined groupings, could not in itself open up such relationships to observation.

Despite the difficulty of exposing capitalist relations of expropriation within the peasantry, the suspicion was for Kritsman that they existed and were probably growing under the conditions of the NEP. The evidence that could support such suspicions was not available in a direct form, but suggestions of it could be seen if attention was directed beyond the patterns of distribution of factors of production, to examine the interrelationships between the distribution of various means of production in the context of the relations and processes taking place on actual peasant farms.

For Kritsman, the partition of the land brought about by the revolution did not succeed in creating the conditions for the existence of a class of independent small farmers such as the peasants themselves, for the most part, had aspired to. As Kritsman put it, the partition had in fact been a retrograde step in the development of the forces of production in agriculture, and therefore marked 'a step backwards' after the initial major advance of the overthrow of the large landowning class. People who would have been better off objectively as wage labourers were forced to cultivate a plot without the necessary means of production. For Kritsman, 'the flourishing of this type of small-scale economy is simply an expression of the fact that these "small owners" have lost, for a time, the possibility of being proletarians' (Kritsman 1925d, Part I, 50).

Moreover, the theoretical possibility of a more radical solution to the problem of scarce means of production had been blocked by what Kritsman called 'the real petty bourgeoisie [*serednyaks*]'. These were the peasants who had adequate means of production to cultivate their own farms more or less independently, and who felt themselves to be threatened by demands from poorer peasants for schemes to share means of production between the farms of a locality, such as had been attempted during the period of 'war communism'. For Kritsman, the poorer peasants subscribed to a basically Utopian ideology according to which better-off peasants would share resources with their poorer neighbours in order to enable all peasants to farm as independent cultivators. The failure of the Bolshevik government to intervene with sufficient support for the committees of poor peasants, which had aspired to organize such a system of sharing, meant that the logic of the situation favoured the development of conditions where poor peasants were obliged to cultivate their farms without adequate stock. They were therefore forced into dependency on better-off peasants, who were able to exploit their neighbours' weakness, insisting on harsh terms for the lease of stock, and thus expropriating part of the surplus of the poor. Such expropriation between peasant farms could lead back to the re-establishment of capitalism in the Soviet countryside.

Thus, the conditions of the NEP were such that inequalities of distribution of the means of production could reasonably be supposed to favour the development of exploitative relations between peasant farms. For Kritsman this meant that 'the disparity between land and means of production [was] making for the inevitability of the class stratification of the peasantry from the moment of the severing of the dictatorship of the *bednyaks*.' In its complete form, this process of 'class stratification' could be recognized as 'a process of the separation of the worker from the means of production: the conversion, on the one hand, of the worker, the owner of his means of production, into the proletarian, the hired labourer; the conversion, on the other hand, of the means of production into capital' (Kritsman 1925d, Part I, 51–2).

However, this was a description of the end-point of the process, not of its early stages, and herein lay the problem of the class analysis of the peasantry. The first faint traces of the 'separation out' of agrarian bourgeois and proletarian classes had to be looked for within a class whose current class nature was petty bourgeois.

The initial point of this process is however the quantitative differences within the petty-bourgeoisie, and, more exactly, the differences in wealth. These differences in the degree of wealth of different strata of the petty bourgeoisie amount to a different relationship between the means of production and labour power in different petty-bourgeois enterprises (farms).

(Kritsman 1925d, Part I, 52).

Kritsman's point was that on many farms this relation between labour power and means of production was out of balance. On weak farms there would be labour power which could not be fully utilized because of insufficient means of production, while on strong farms there would be means of production which could not be fully utilized without hired labour because there was insufficient labour power available from members of the household. For this reason, 'the differences in capacity of farms inevitably become the initial point of a process of stratification of the peasantry, that is, the growth of class differences; and in its initial stages, this process became apparent precisely in the strengthening of differences in farm capacity' (Kritsman 1925d, Part I, 52–3).

It could, of course, have been argued that 'differences in capacity' were not 'inevitably' the starting point of the development of class differences, and that problems of supply of either means of production or labour power could have been overcome by means other than exploitative commerical relations between the strong households and the weak. Given the state's stress on co-operatives as a means of building socialism, it could be argued that more co-operative solutions to such problems of supply could have been found. However, since the NEP had reintroduced petty commodity relations as the predominant form in the countryside, and since 'traditional' co-operative relations had already been largely under-mined while state-supported new forms of co-operation remained undeveloped in practice, it seemed obvious to Kritsman that the main response to shortages in the factors of production would be determined by the laws of the market. Means of production would become capital, and peasant farmers would aim to 'capitalize' on their ownership of scarce resources; while the labour power of weak peasant households would become a commodity, whether in an open or a hidden form, thus having the combined effect of building on and exacerbating inequalities in peasant agriculture.

It followed, therefore, for Kritsman, that, given a petty commodity economy, the most common solution to inequalities in the distri-bution of the means of production would be the lease and hire of working animals and farm stock. In fact, these transactions, rather than the overt hire and sale of labour power, would be the main forms of the expropriation of surplus value in such conditions. What Kritsman seems to have been suggesting here was that surplus value was extracted from the formally self-employed labour of the peasant household by means of extortionate rates for the hire of scarce animals and farm stock.

Moreover, given the prevalence of peasant, as opposed to more commercial or proletarian, attitudes to labour, as well as the possibility that overtly commercial transactions would attract official attention (and much hire of labour or rent of land transactions would have been illegal, especially before 1925), many transactions took place in complex and concealed forms. For example, according to Kritsman, a widespread form of exploitation involved the hiring out of working animals and stock in such a way that exploiters appeared in the guise of workers, hiring themselves, their animals, and stock out to a hirer, to work on land belonging to the hirer, and exploited peasants appeared in the guise of employers who hired someone else to work their land rather than working on it themselves. Despite superficial appearances, however, because working animals and ploughs were in short supply in the Russian countryside following the ravages of war and civil war, it would have been the peasants doing the manual labour who were in fact exploiting the weakness of the peasants who had hired them because they had insufficient animals or stock to work the land themselves. In such a case, the peasants with their own team and plough would have received the larger share of the harvest, in some cases amounting to a very large proportion of it. In effect, argued Kritsman, the true nature of this relationship was the concealed renting of land by peasants with excess capacity of means of production relative to the land actually held by them. Given legal restrictions on the rent of land, this was the best way for such peasants to extend their operations in order to accumulate capital (Kritsman 1925d, Part IV, 42).

The facts that both 'owners' still worked on the land themselves, and that ownership of the various means of production were split between them, was for Kritsman a reflection of the early stage of capitalist development then prevalent in the Soviet countryside. He described the phenomena he was analysing as 'incomplete capitalist forms'. Nevertheless, he was in no doubt that the logic of the situation in abstract (if it were not for the context provided by Soviet state power) would lead to full capitalist development, and that it was therefore valid to interpret the forms of exploitation going on as already in essence capitalist, despite their 'incompleteness'.

The incompleteness . . . reflects here the initial stages in the development of the process. Therefore the terms 'capitalist' and 'proletarian' mean . . . not only capitalist and proletarian in their complete aspect, but also in their incomplete aspect—becoming capitalist or proletarian. Growth (or decline) in numbers and importance of these latter is no less a characteristic of the dynamics of stratification than growth in the numbers and importance of the fully-formed [types].

(Kritsman 1925d, Part IV, 41ff.)[17]

This was the most complex hidden form of capital accumulation. Others mentioned by Kritsman included fictional marriages in order to appropriate a widow's land or stock, and pseudo-co-operative arrangements involving seemingly the sharing of stock or returning of favours, which in fact concealed an inordinate share of the returns going to the stronger of the 'partners' (Kritsman 1925d, Part II, 6–8; Part IV, 42). Information about such transactions could be found in various monographs and articles about life in particular villages or rural areas (e.g. Yakovlev 1923; Morosanov and Yermolenko 1925), but data were not collected systematically on such matters by statistical agencies.[18]

However, it also had to be borne in mind that the situation Kritsman had described was not necessarily prevalent over the Soviet Union as a whole. On the basis of the local studies he had surveyed, he suggested that, in some *volosts* of south-eastern Russia and the Ukraine, the 'hidden forms of capitalist exploitation' he had described might involve up to three-quarters of all peasants, while in other regions they would be less widespread. In some regions, such as south-eastern Russia, Siberia, and the Central Agricultural Region which concentrated on cereal production, hidden capitalist exploitation would take place mainly through the hire of working animals. In other regions, such as the Ukraine and the Central Industrial Region, where there was a greater concentration on industrial crops and livestock farming, exploitation took place more through the hire of farm stock. In interpreting data on the industrial regions, Kritsman warned, it was necessary to distinguish grain production for a household's own use from the production of grain as a commodity which would be less common in such regions.[19]

Furthermore, it could be expected that the situation would change over time. Already there was some growth of capitalism in its more usual form, reflected in the open hiring of labour. Since the revolution, hire by the day had largely replaced seasonal hire, but Soviet statistics had failed to keep up with this change. (Of course, daily hire was not a deliberately concealed form of exploitation.) Moreover, along with more extensive renting of land as legal restrictions eased after 1925, it could be expected to increase as time went on (Kritsman 1925d, Part IV, 43).

Finally, Kritsman drew attention to the sometimes forgotten forms of rural capitalism whose main sphere of activity was outside agriculture. Alongside, and connected with, capitalist agriculture (which could be seen as a form of industrial capitalism where capital appeared as the owner of means applied to production), there were also rural forms of commercial and credit capital. The basis of each of these types lay in different aspects of the underdeveloped nature of peasant agriculture.

Credit capital, mainly in the form of money-lending, flourished as a result of the continuing insecurity of peasant farming and its generally low level of productivity. The peasants were never secure from the threat of natural or economic disaster, and there was often little likelihood of their building up reserves of food, seed, or money. In such conditions, resort to credit, often at usurious rates, was common.

Trading capital, on the other hand, flourished as a result of the geographical isolation of peasant farming. Given poor communications, large distances to markets, and the general lack of horses in the 1920s, the situation was ripe for middlemen to take over rural trade.

All three forms of rural capital were closely interrelated. Credit was required sometimes to start production, and often in order to make essential commodity purchases. Also, both trade and credit were factors forcing peasants out of subsistence production and into commodity production: 'the pressure of exploitation from the side of trade and loan capital, taking away a significant part of the farm produce from the peasants they exploit, drives the peasants into the clutches of industrial capital' (Kritsman 1925d, Part IV, 43–4).

Above all, Kritsman's early work on the class differentiation of the peasantry was a plan for further research. Really very little was known about the various relations within the peasantry which he had identified. For the next few years, in his own research as well as in his capaicty as director of research projects at the Agrarian Section of the Communist Academy and as editor of *Na Agrarnom Fronte*, Kritsman aimed to promote research on the questions he had outlined in an attempt to rectify both the lack of knowledge and the lack of analysis of the key relationships which he thought were shaping Soviet rural society.

Notes

1. Kritsman's career up until the mid-1920s had been more in the service of the Party and the Soviet state as an economist and writer than as an agrarian expert. He was born in 1890 and had joined the RSDLP as a young man in 1905. He spent some time abroad in exile before the revolution and became particularly interested in the organization of the German war economy during the First World War. On his return to Russia in 1918 he became a member of the Bolshevik Party and developed particular interests in planning and economic policy. He held various positions in the VSNKh and was a member of the Presidium of Gosplan. In the early 1920s he published various works on economic planning and the Soviet economy (Kritsman and Larin 1920a, 1920b; Kritsman 1921a, 1921c), becoming a strong supporter of the idea of a 'single economic plan' for the Soviet economy. For this, along with Larin and Milyutin, he attracted the criticisms of Lenin. With the introduction of the NEP Kritsman continued his support for planning, arguing unsuccessfully (alongside Larin, Trotsky, and Preobrazhenskii) against the weakening of planning organizations (Carr 1966, Vol. 2, 376–8).

   In the 1920s Kritsman moved away from economic policy to take up more academic and journalistic work. He became a member of the Presidium of the Communist Academy in 1923, and in the following years he joined the editorial boards of *Pravda*, *Problemy Ekonomiki*, and *Ekonomicheskaya Entsiklopediya* and *Bolshaya Sovetskaya Entsiklopediya*. He became a member of the board of the TsSU, as well as director of the Agrarian Section (later Agrarian Institute) of the Communist Academy and chief editor of *Na Agrarnom Fronte*.

   In addition to his writings on economic and agrarian issues, Kritsman was the author of a major study of the War Communism period (1925b), which to this day is widely recognized as one of the few major analyses of that period.

2. The most obvious example here was the tendency of the Organization and Production School to look at peasant economy in isolation from wider aspects of state and economy. For Kritsman's criticisms of these writers, see Section 2 below.

3. Among the former students of the Timiryazev Academy were Anisimov, Naumov, Sulkovskii, and Uzhanskii.

4. See pp. 56–7 above.

5. Further criticism of the work of the Organization and Production School were published by Marxist writers during the 1920s, including U. (Uzhanskii?) (1925) and Raevich (1926–8). The output of criticism was increased and its tone became more vitriolic in the late 1920s, as the

political climate changed and Chayanov and his colleagues came to be seen as enemies of the regime.

6. Solomon (1977) has judged the work of Kritsman and his colleagues as comparing poorly with the more comprehensive theory of the peasantry of Chayanov and his school. She has even gone so far as to portray the Agrarian Marxist research as 'exclusively empirical' (1977, 33). Part of the aim of this chapter is to refute this judgement by demonstrating the theoretical basis to the work of Kritsman and his colleagues. It is of course true that the Agrarian Marxists did not construct an elaborate theory of the peasantry as such. This was partly because such an exercise would have distracted from their main political priority of uncovering the true situation of the differentiation of the peasantry. However, it is also the case that for Marxist theory there can be no peasantry in general and therefore no general theory of the peasantry, but only of peasants in particular modes of production. For a discussion of this point see Ennew *et al.* (1977).

7. Despite his reservations, however, Kritsman did work on a project using ownership of working animals and stock as indicators of class differentiation. The study was set up by the Communist Academy to study the agrarian revolution in Russia from 1917 until the mid-1920s. Since the official figures for this period offered no alternative means of studying differentiation, inequality data were used.

The approach of the commission was to draw up fourteen different possible combinations of forms of ownership of working animals and stock and then to simplify these into six main types. (Kritsman 1928b, 99–111). Their final six groups were:

1. farms without working animals and stock;

2. farms without *either* working animals *or* stock;

3. farms with one head of working animals and basic stock;

4. farms with one head of working animals and advanced stock;

5. farms with two or more head of working animals but without advanced stock;

6. farms with two or more head of working animals and advanced stock.

Kritsman, although a member of the commission, remained sceptical about the usefulness of such an approach. He accepted that, like groupings based on the distribution of working animals alone, it could approximately distinguish between weak farms with insufficient means of production and stronger farms with sufficient means to carry out independent farming; 'but also it cannot, of course, draw boundaries with sufficient definiteness between petty-bourgeois middle peasants and peasant capitalists' (Kritsman 1928a, 127).

8. For further discussion, see Carr (1970, Vol. 1, 321, 329, 333); Grosskopf (1976, 139–42).

9. Other members included F. Tsyl'ko, A. Rybnikov, A. N. Chelintsev, A. Lositskii, M. Lifshifts, V. G. Groman, and S. Strumilin.

10. See also Yakovlev (1925c, 1926), where the figures were presented slightly differently using a classification into four groups.

11. Strictly speaking, these remarks of Lenin were aimed at capitalist countries rather than at the Soviet Union, and were not devised with empirical research in mind. However, they were clearly more useful for Yakovlev's argument than references to Lenin's pre-revolutionary work, where he had used sown area as his main indicator.

12. Further support for such criticisms came from inside the statistical profession in an article by V. S. Nemchinov, then head of the Urals *oblast* statistical bureau (Nemchinov 1926a). In addition to criticizing the indicators used and Khryashcheva's insistence that alternative direct indicators of exploitation were unmeasurable (see Chapter 2), Nemchinov also located the problem of the outlook of official Soviet statistics in its organizational structure. It was, he argued, much too centralized and hierarchical, with a division of labour in which the *raion*-level personnel carried out the immediate gathering of information, which was then processed, refined, and tabulated at *okrug* and *oblast* levels before going up to central state level where analysis was carried out to produce more general conclusions (Nemchinov 1926a, 35). Such an organizational structure was detrimental to good research, on the one hand, because the insights of local observers about life at local level could not be used either in constructing hypotheses or in analysing the results, and on the other hand because centrally based analyses were limited in the generalizations they could make and hypotheses they could test, because the data they received had already been processed, with consequent loss of some of the raw information, before they received it.

13. Kritsman undertook a comparison of figures from the TsSU and the Union of Agricultural and Forestry Workers (Vserabotzemles) showing the percentage of farms hiring workers in various regions of the Soviet Union. The biggest discrepancy was for the North Caucasus but the figures did not agree for any of the ten regions listed (Kritsman 1926a, 292).

14. Kritsman's review of the local studies was published in two versions, first as a serialized article in *Na Agrarnom Fronte* (Kritsman 1925d), and then in a longer revised edition in book form (Kritsman 1926b). This later version was then republished in Kritsman (1929c), and has recently been published in an edited form in English (Kritsman 1984).

The main works on which Kritsman drew were: Yakovlev (1923, 1924), Yancheskii (1924), Bolshakov (1925); Morosanov and Yermolenko (1925); Lezhnev-Finkovskii and Savchenko (1925); *Litso* . . . (1925); and *Krest'yanskoe* . . . (1923). Between them, these studies covered all the available information, taking in *volosts* in such different parts of the USSR as the Central Agricultural Region, the Volga Region, Ukraine, the Central Industrial Region, the North-West, the Urals, and Siberia. For criticisms of the *methods* employed in the local studies, see Kritsman (1925d, Part II, 3–4, 12–13; Part III, 23); Khryashcheva (1923).

15. Rather confusingly, for someone trying to break with the whole Russian tradition of seeing the peasants in terms of social strata defined simply by inequalities rather than the social relations associated with them, Kritsman used the term that was standard in Soviet research of the time, *rassloenie*, which means, literally, 'division into layers or strata' (*sloi* = 'stratum'). In some ways it might seem better to have used *differentsiatsiya*, that is, 'differentiation'. Presumably this was not used because of its association with rival approaches, notably that of Chayanov and his colleagues, for whom the term implied a number of different processes of differentiation, of which only one minor process would tend to the creation of new social classes within the peasantry (see pp. 54–5 above).

16. In determining what number of working animals were sufficient or surplus to the requirements of any given farm, the research team had established a norm that the maximum land area per head of working animal was 4 desyatins.

17. It is noteworthy that, in discussing such hidden forms of exploitation, Kritsman explicitly understood the relationship as involving the appropriation of surplus value. 'Whether the "hired" peasant works on the farm of the hirer does not change the essence of the matter. In these relations, capitalist appropriation of surplus value is not created by the labour of the "hired worker" with his horse and stock, but by the labour of the "hiring boss" ' (Kritsman 1925d, Part IV, 42). In this, therefore, Kritsman was following Lenin in arguing that, although labour power had not necessarily fully taken on the commodity form, nevertheless the prevailing relations should be construed as an early stage or incomplete form of relations which were capitalist, as opposed to belonging to some pre-capitalist structure (for Lenin, see pp. 16–17 above).

18. While information on renting of land and hire of means of production as well as hire of labour were produced by the TsSU, they were usually presented as aggregates for each group defined by sown area and therefore could not be used as a means to classify households into class groups themselves. Moreover, there were grave doubts that the statistics did not reflect the extent of all relations of exploitation and

that they were insensitive to the complex phenomenal forms in which such relations appeared in the Russian countryside.

19. A problem with much previous research had been the failure to note this distinction, thus using data on the extent of sowing of subsistence crops as evidence of a lack of differentiation when in fact it should not have been expected that stronger households would wish to expand their operations in such crops (Kritsman 1925d, Part IV, 42, 45).

4

The Empirical Research of Kritsman and his School: The First Stage

After 1925, a series of research projects was carried out, each of them building on the findings and methods of earlier Russian rural research, but also seeking to adapt and transform those approaches to conform with the new guidelines suggested by Kritsman. Most of the projects involved initiating new research, focusing on different local areas in different parts of the Russian countryside, and making use of household surveys and, in some cases, budget surveys. All of these projects were carried out in areas outside the traditional heartland of Russian agriculture. Two were located in Moscow *guberniya*, while others were carried out in the 'borderlands' of European Russia: in the Urals, Samara, and Saratov. In addition, there were some projects which attempted to analyse existing data from surveys of different parts of the Soviet Union.

As a whole, the projects were part of a search by Kritsman and his colleagues to find the most appropriate approach to the study of the class character of the Russian peasantry. Although Kritsman's initial work had offered an ingenious means of analysing the existing imperfect data, it was not clear what approach should be adopted for new research which could provide more appropriate data. Simply relating the size of a farm to the extent of its means of production enabled tentative conclusions about whether a surplus of means of production might indicate a household able to exploit its neighbours, or whether a lack of means of production might indicate a household likely to be exploited by others, but there was no certainty that such outcomes actually took place. What was required was clearer evidence of actual processes of exploitation, which, according to Kritsman, would be most likely to occur, in the conditions of the NEP, through transactions involving scarce means of production. The implication, therefore, was that evidence of the extent of such relations should be used as indicators of the class tendencies within households, in conjunction with evidence of the hire and sale of labour. This was the solution to be adopted in different ways in the various research projects that followed.

Each project contained a different combination of approaches and methods of research and contributed its own innovations. All the projects involved some attempt to characterize and classify households in terms of the extent and nature of their involvement in relations of exploitation with other households. However, in most cases such an approach was not seen as sufficient by itself, and was usually used in conjunction with a second classification based on a measure of the economic strength of households.

There were also variations in the methods used to collect information. Some projects, aiming at a relatively broad coverage, sought ways of acquiring information through household surveys based on a list of questions to each household's head, while others combined this with more detailed recording by researchers of the accounts of a smaller sample of household budgets.

The various methods and approaches will be discussed in the next two chapters in relation to each project. This chapter will discuss the relation between Kritsman's initial ideas and the approaches actually adopted in the first two projects in the Urals and Moscow province (Volokolamsk), as well as a third study, in the Middle Volga region, influenced strongly by Kritsman's ideas. Chapter 5 then examines some slightly later projects which, like their predecessors, sought to explore Kritsman's ideas in practice, but which also explored a number of new variations and innovations of various kinds.

1   The Research of V. S. Nemchinov

The first attempt at a new research approach came from V. S. Nemchinov in a study of 835 household budgets in the steppe area of Troitskii *okrug* in the Urals. According to Nemchinov, the aim of his survey was to

make clear the entrepreneurial and dependent elements in the peasant economy. With this aim the census questionnaire must contain questions to clarify whose [labour] power, stock, animals, and seed the farm is run with, and also questions about the use of its own labour power, animals, stock, and land on the farms of others. In such a way, at the centre of our attention must be the relations of production in the countryside, that is, relations connected with the land, circulating capital (seed and fodder), and fixed capital (stock and cattle) in agriculture. In order to clarify the capitalist elements in the countryside, it is necessary to approach the peasant farm as an agricultural enterprise.

(Nemchinov 1926b, 47)

Having gathered such information, Nemchinov drew up the scheme shown in Table 4.1 as a means of identifying the different tendencies within households resulting from their transactions in different factors of production. He took four basic types of factor and cross-classified them with information concerning who owned them and on whose farm they were used.[1] Depending on the nature and scarcity of any particular factor of production, its use on a peasant's own farm or on the farm of another peasant would signify a particular set of relations with a particular position of strength or weakness in each case. The different positions of strength could be described as: (1) entrepreneurship, where the surplus value went to the given farm through hiring other's labour, leasing out animals and stock to others, or renting the land of others, thus expanding farming at the expense of peasants unable to farm their land; (2) dependence, where the surplus value was removed from the given farm through leasing out land to others because of the inability of the household to farm it themselves, selling household labour power

Table 4.1.

Conditions and Means of Production in Peasant Agriculture

	Means of production on a peasant's own farm		Peasant's own means of production on another's farm
	Other's	Own	
1. Land	Entrepreneurial	Independent	Dependent
2. Fixed capital (animals, stock, farm buildings)	Dependent	Independent	Entrepreneurial
3. Circulating capital (seed, fodder, manure)	Dependent	Independent	Entrepreneurial
4. Labour power	Entrepreneurial	Independent	Dependent

Source: Nemchinov (1926b, 48).

to others, or hiring means of production from others because it would be impossible to farm their own land without them; (3) independence, where a peasant's own labour and means of production were fully and adequately employed on their own land, and therefore none of the above relations were entered into with other farms and surplus value was neither taken nor given up. The aim was to measure the extent of relations of each type in a household's farming in order to determine its overall character.[2]

Having decided on the data to be collected, and the indicators to be used, further problems then had to be resolved in measuring the extent and direction of a household's involvement in relations of exploitation. Not all transactions would be conducted for cash, and even those that were would not have been recorded in detail. Less precise information on the length of time of a transaction had therefore to be used, and a method had to be devised for assessing its significance in relation to other transactions. The particular solution adopted by Nemchinov was to give each factor a money value based on knowledge of local values and prices. This involved a series of judgements about the quality and value of various factors, and assumptions that transactions were in fact conducted at locally prevailing rates.

On the above basis, Nemchinov's research therefore required details of the prevailing local prices of labour power, working cattle, farm implements, fodder, and seed, and the local rates for their hire or sale where appropriate. Land, although in Soviet conditions it did not have a selling price, had to be accounted for in terms of its rental value locally. A number of problems had to be resolved in carrying out such valuations. For example, for fodder and seed, seasonal prices had to be taken into account; for working animals and stock, amortization rates were preferred to the money rate of hire. This made it necessary to ensure that the correct value was attributed given the time of year of a transaction or the stage in the life of the capital involved. As far as labour power was concerned, it was necessary to distinguish between seasonal hire, hire by the day, and piece-rates, as well as the age and sex of the household member hired, if a correct valuation was to be made. Similarly, the age and type of working animals had to be taken into account (Nemchinov 1926b, 51–3).

Drawing on information collected by the local statistical bureau, Nemchinov attempted to established the values he would use for his analysis (Nemchinov 1926b, 53–5). Then, by reference to the significance in class terms of the different inter-household relations (as shown in Table 4.1), he was able to measure the degree to which different households were tending to exploit, or be exploited by, others. He offered two examples: a mainly exploiting farm, displaying entrepreneurial tendencies, and a mainly exploited farm, showing dependent tendencies.

In order to calculate the class tendencies exhibited by each household, it was then possible to add up the values of all transactions showing signs of entrepreneurship, all those showing signs of dependence, and all those indicating independent farming. Building on Kritsman's idea that analysis should focus on the relation between a household's own land and its own resources, Nemchinov then proposed that a household's class tendency could be determined by calculating the extent of its entrepreneurial or dependent tendencies as a percentage of its independent elements, that is, as a percentage of the value of its own means of production employed on its own farm.

To take the example of Table 4.2, the sum of entrepreneurial elements in farm A was $(27.25 + 351.00 + 11.0) = $ R389.25. The sum of its independent elements was R1046.08 and there were no dependent elements. The class character of the household, as revealed in its relations, could therefore be calculated by taking the entrepreneurial elements as a percentage of the independent elements, which worked out as 37.2 per cent entrepreneurial. For farm B, there were no entrepreneurial elements. The sum of the dependent elements was $(20.99 + 8.24 + 17.99 + 266.67) = $ R313.89, and the sum of the independent elements was R247.88. The character of this farm could be calculated by taking the dependent elements as a percentage of the independent elements, in this case 123.63 per cent dependent.[3] Where elements of both entrepreneurship and dependence coexisted within the same household, each would be calculated as a percentage of the independent elements and the balance taken to determine the household's class character (Nemchinov 1926b, 55–6).

In this way, the character of a household could be determined from the relations of exploitation in which it was involved. By itself, however, this would not reveal how far such relations were actually bringing about changes in the organization of a farm to the point where it was becoming clearly capitalist or proletarian. Some further

Table 4.2.
Evaluation of Farms (roubles)

	Factors of production on own farm*		Peasant's own means of production on someone else's farm*	Totals
	Belonging to someone else	Belonging to own farm		
A Farm N. A. G-dov				
Arable land and hay fields	(e) 27.25	(i) 76.84	(d) —	104.09
Stock and animals	(d) —	(i) 104.58	(e) 11.0	115.58
Seed and fodder	(d) —	(i) 499.66	(e) —	499.66
Labour power	(e) 351.00	(i) 365.00	(d) —	716.00
Total	378.25	1046.08	11.0	1435.33
B Farm N. P. B-noi				
Arable land and hay fields	(e) —	(i) 23.88	(d) 17.99	41.87
Stock and animals	(d) 20.99	(i) 0.38	(e) —	21.37
Seed and fodder	(d) 8.24	(i) 10.29	(e) —	18.53
Labour power	(e) —	(i) 213.33	(d) 266.67	480.00
Total	29.23	247.88	284.66	561.77

*(e) = entrepreneurial; (d) = dependent; (i) = independent.
Source: Nemchinov (1926b, 55).

measure was required, Nemchinov thought, to identify the capacity of a farm to consolidate an entrepreneurial tendency, or its lack of capacity to overcome dependence and avoid proletarianization. He suggested that a useful measure for this purpose was expenditure on constant capital, which would include the total amount expended by a household on production, excluding labour power. This would be useful because it would measure a household's expenditure on those factors of production which (as Nemchinov and Kritsman had argued) were the main resources for exploitation in the Soviet countryside. For entrepreneurial households, it could distinguish those with resources to build on the surplus they were appropriating from those whose relations were predominantly entrepreneurial at the time of the survey but did not have sufficient strength of resources to be likely to consolidate their position and become capitalist farms. Similarly, for dependent households it could distinguish those with a weak resource base which were undergoing proletarianization from those that were mainly dependent at a given time but had sufficient resources to prevent full proletariarization.[4]

The results of Nemchinov's study are shown in Tables 4.3 and 4.4. First, Table 4.3 shows the distribution of households into different groups according to their degree of dependence or entrepreneurship. Table 4.4 then shows a cross-classification of these groups with Nemchinov's classification by economic capacity.

Table 4.3.
Distribution of Households by Degree of Dependence
or Entrepreneurship

Type of farm	Numbers	%
More than 50% dependent	81	9.7
15–50% dependent	109	13.1
2.5–15% dependent	81	9.7
2.5% dependent–2.5% entrepreneurial	442	52.9
2.5–15% entrepreneurial	101	12.1
15–30% entrepreneurial	15	1.8
More than 30% entrepreneurial	6	0.7
Total	835	100

Source: Nemchinov (1926b, 57).

Table 4.4.
Distribution of Households by Economic Capacity

| Entrepreneurial and dependent elements | Annual expenditure on constant capital per farm (roubles) | | | | | |
| | Poor | | | Middle | Well-to-do | |
	up to 100	100–200	200–500	500–700	more than 700	
More than 50% dependent	67	9	5	—	—	
15–50% dependent	36	53	20	—	—	
2.5–15% dependent	16	34	27	3	1	
2.5% dependent—2.5% entrepreneur	40	88	233	49	32	
2.5–15% entrepreneur	—	3	18	29	51	
More than 15% entrepreneur	—	—	7	6	8	
Total	159	187	310	87	92	

Source: Nemchinov (1926b, 61).

Combining the two classifications enabled a tentative conclusion; Nemchinov suggested that various groups within the peasantry could be distinguished with discernable class characteristics. First, there were 8 households that were both 'well-to-do' and more than 15 per cent entrepreneurial in their relations. These Nemchinov distinguished as *kulak* or petty-capitalist farms (comprising 0.96 per cent of his sample). At the other end of the scale, there were 165 households that were classified both as poor and as more than 15 per cent dependent. These were proletarian households. The remainder, Nemchinov thought, should be classified as independent producers, with further subdivisions into poor, middle, or well-to-do (Nemchinov 1926b, 58–61).

2   Kritsman's Response to Nemchinov's Research

In general, Nemchinov's approach attracted a great deal of attention and was influential on the work of other researchers. However, it was not accepted as a fully adequate solution to the problems of conducting research on peasant class relations. For Kritsman, despite a generally positive reaction, Nemchinov's conceptual basis, using classifications of 'entrepreneurial', 'dependent', and 'independent', was not sufficiently rigorous and his method of calculating class tendencies was misleading. Kritsman preferred to classify households into groups more explicitly defined in class terms as 'capitalist', 'petty-bourgeois', and 'proletarian', each of which should be determined more directly by the different relations in each type between their labour power and their means of production. Whereas capitalist farms would own means of production which would be worked on exclusively by the labour of others, petty-bourgeois households would work on their own means of production with their own labour, and proletarian households would work only on others' means of production. Any household could be classified according to which type it most closely resembled (Kritsman 1926–7, Part 1, 8–9).

Responding to the stimulus of Nemchinov's work, Kritsman went on to develop his own ideas further, both in terms of a more detailed conceptualization of the peasantry and in terms of more adequate ways of identifying and measuring their class characteristics. His conceptualization of the peasantry proceeded from the idea of a pure type of independent household, in which there would be a full correspondence between their own labour power and their own means of production on their own farm. In practice, however, as households were moving away from true independence, there would increasingly be a lack of correspondence between their own labour power and means of production. In the context of small commodity production, this would mean either that a household's means of production were increasingly turned into capital, or that its labour power was becoming a commodity to be sold.

Kritsman's analysis involved breaking down peasant agriculture into six basic elements: own farm, other's farm, own means of production, other's means of production, own labour power, and other's labour power. There could be no general theory of how these six elements were interrelated because this would vary according to the complexities of different forms of transitional society. The precise form of interrelation of elements could therefore be established for each case only by empirical research. Such research would involve, on the one hand, calculating the extent to which different households were made up of different combinations of elements and which predominated in the total complex of their relations, and on the other hand taking into account the general context in which peasant farming was conducted and working out the social character of the different possible combinations of elements. Each of these aspects of Kritsman's thinking will be discussed in turn.

Kritsman's method of calculating the class tendencies of households

In order to calculate the extent of a household's class tendency, Kritsman argued that, instead of calculating values for transactions in each type of factor separately, as Nemchinov had done, it was preferable to calculate the relation between labour and means of production more directly. In the context of the NEP, thought Kritsman, land was not significant as a commodity and labour power was significant only to the extent that means of production were available to work with. Land and labour power should not, therefore, be treated as independent variables on a par with basic and circulating capital. It was only to the extent that a household's own land and labour power were used in conjunction with their own means of production that independent farming was really possible. The most suitable way of calculating class tendencies, therefore, was to examine the relationship between labour and means of production. Kritsman demonstrated his proposed method using the same two examples that Nemchinov had used. The exact details of the approach would vary according to whether the household showed higher values of what Nemchinov had called dependence or entrepreneurship.

For *household A*, which according to Nemchinov's calculations was 37.2 per cent entrepreneurial, Kritsman proceeded as follows:

1. Calculate the relation between the household's own labour power and all labour power employed by the household:

$$\frac{R365}{(R365 + R351)} = 51\%.$$

2. Calculate the relation of the household's own means of production used on its own farm to all means of production belonging to the household:

$$\frac{R604.24}{(R604.24 + R11.0)} = 98.2\%.$$

3. Multiply the two figures obtained above to obtain the percentage of the household's own means of production used in conjunction with its own labour power:

51% of 98.2% = 50.1%.

Thus, for household A, its own labour power was employed on only 50.1 per cent of its own means of production; in other words, 50.1 per cent of the household's operations could be described as independent petty-bourgeois. The remaining 49.9 per cent of the household's means of production was used in conjunction with labour hired from others, so the household was *49.9% petty-capitalist.*[5]

For *household B*, which according to Nemchinov was 126.63 per cent dependent, Kritsman used the following approach:

1. Calculate the relation between the household's own labour power used on its own farm and all of the household's labour wherever it was employed:

$$\frac{R213.37}{(R213.37 + R266.67)} = 44.4\%.$$

2. Calculate the relation between the household's means of production employed on its own farm and the total of all means of production used on its farm:

$$\frac{R10.67}{(R10.67 + R29.23)} = 26.7\%.$$

3. Multiply these two figures to obtain the proportion of the household's own labour power employed on its own means of production:

44.4% of 26.7% = 11.9%.

Thus, for household B, its own labour power used in conjunction with its own means of production accounted for only 11.9 per cent of all the household's activities. It was therefore 11.9 per cent independent. The remaining 88.1 per cent of its labour power was used on other's means of production, so the household was *88.1 per cent proletarian* (Kritsman 1926–7, Part 1, 9–10).[6]

Thus, rather than calculating the exploited or exploiting aspects of a household's operations as a proportion of its independent operations, a procedure that could produce the rather awkward result of a household that was more than 100 per cent dependent as in the case of household B above, Kritsman offered a calculation of the different elements as a percentage of the total operations of a household.

However, despite his criticisms and revisions, Kritsman's overall view of Nemchinov's work was highly positive; indeed, he recognized it as showing the lines on which further research should be conducted. Furthermore, Nemchinov's particular attempt to characterize households prompted Kritsman to develop further his own ideas on the social character of households and the different combinations of elements that constituted them.

The identification of different combinations of elements

With possibly obsessive thoroughness, Kritsman went on to enumerate every hypothetically possible combination of elements. Some of these were clearly impossible in practice because they would not have allowed for any farming to be carried out. Among these, for example, was a combination of 'own labour only' with 'no labour on own farm'. In all, Kritsman listed sixty-four combinations, although only the thirty-nine that were actually possible are given below (Kritsman 1926–7, Part II, 13–14; Part III, 3–11); their numbers refer to those assigned to them in Kritsman's listing:

(2) only own means of production on other's farm (a capitalist type);

(5) only own labour on other's farm (a proletarian type);

(9) own means of production and own labour power on own farm (a petty-bourgeois type);

(11) own means of production and other's labour power on own farm (a capitalist type);

(14) own means of production and own labour power on other's farm (a mixed type, its overall character depending on the quantitive relations between element: if sale of labour is the predominant factor it would be proletarian; if hiring out of means of production is predominant it would be capitalist; if neither were predominant it would be petty-bourgeois—e.g., as in the case of a craftsman working to order with the customer's materials);

(16) own labour power and other's means of production on own farm (a proletarian type although still taking the form of petty-bourgeois independent farming);

(18) other's labour power and other's means of production on own farm (a capitalist type, using hired means of production, or a feudal landlord);

(23) own labour power and own means of production on own farm, own means of production on other's farm (depending on the quantitative relations, a petty-bourgeois small farmer partly using means of production in a capitalist way, or a capitalist family still cultivating their own farm themselves);

(25) own means of production on own and other's farm, other's labour power on own farm (a capitalist type);

(26) own labour power and own and other's means of production on own farm (either a petty-bourgeois small farm with some dependence on hiring means of production, or small farms in a co-operative);

(28) own and other's means of production and other's labour power on own farm (either a capitalist type, hiring some means of production, or a feudal landlord owning some means of production);

(29) own labour power and own means of production on own farm,

own labour power and other's farm (either a petty-bourgeois type selling some of the household's labour power, or a proletarian type cultivating its own allotment with its own means of production);

(30) own and other's labour power and own means of production on own farm (a petty-bourgeois farm also hiring workers);

(31) own means of production and other's labour power on own farm, own labour power on other's farm (either a capitalist farm selling the labour of a member of the household, or a proletarian farm living mainly by wages but hiring someone to cultivate its own allotment);

(32) own labour power and other's means of production on own farm, own means of production on other's farm (a petty-bourgeois farm becoming capitalist, hiring out own means of production for a profit and hiring other's means to maintain own farm);

(34) other's labour and other's means of production on own farm, own means of production on other's farm (a capitalist type);

(38) own labour power and other's means of production on own farm, own labour power on other's farm (a proletarian type);

(39) own and other's labour power and other's means of production on own farm (either a proletarian type obliged to hire another peasant and his stock in order to cultivate his own land, or a capitalist type hiring means of production);

(40) other's labour power and means of production on own farm, own labour power on other's farm (a small capitalist type, as in case (18), but selling the labour of a family member as well);

(42) own labour power, own and other's means of production on own farm, own means of production on other's farm (either a capitalist or a proletarian type depending on the quantitative relations);

(44) other's labour power, own and other's means of production on own farm, own means of production on other's farm (a capitalist type);

(45) own labour power and own means of production on own and other's farms (either a feudal peasant or, depending on the quantitative relations, a mainly petty-bourgeois or a mainly capitalist type);

(46) own and other's labour power and own means of production on own farm, own means of production on other's farm (a capitalist type);

(47) other's labour power and own means of production on own farm, own labour power and own means of production on other's farm (either a capitalist or a proletarian farm);

(48) own labour power, own and other's means of production on own farm, own labour power on other's farm (a proletarian type);

(49) own and other's labour power, own and other's means of production on own farm (a proletarian, petty-bourgeois, or capitalist type depending on the quantitative relations);

(50) other's labour power, own and other's means of production on own farm, own labour power on other's farm (either a capitalist or a proletarian type);

(51) own and other's labour power and own means of production on own farm, own labour power on other's farm (either a capitalist or a proletarian type);

(52) own labour power and other's means of production on own farm, own labour power and own means of production on other's farm (a proletarian type);

(53) own and other's labour power and other's means of production on own farm, own means of production on other's farm (a capitalist type);

(53) other's labour power and other's means of production on own farm, own labour power and means of production on other's farm (either a capitalist farm or a craftsman hiring labour and stock to cultivate his own allotment);

(56) own and other's labour power and other's means of production on own farm, own labour power on other's farm (either a capitalist or a proletarian type);

(57) own labour power, own and other's means of production on own farm, own labour power and means of production on other's farm (a feudal peasant, petty-bourgeois, or capitalist type);

(58) own and other's labour power, own and other's means of production on own farm, own labour power on other's farm (either a capitalist or a proletarian type);

(59) own and other's labour power and own means of production on own farm, own labour power and means of production on other's farm (either a capitalist or a proletarian type);

(60) other's labour power, own and other's means of production on own farm, own labour power and means of production on other's farm (either a capitalist type or a craftsman hiring labour and stock to cultivate his own land);

(61) own and other's labour power, own and other's means of production on own farm, own labour power on other's farm (mainly a capitalist type);

(62) own and other's labour power and other's means of production on own farm, own labour power and means of production on other's farm (either a capitalist or an independent craftsman type);

(63) own and other's labour power, own and other's means of production on own farm, own labour power and own means of production on other's farm (either a capitalist, petty bourgeois, or proletarian type).

The above list clearly shows the complexity of peasant farming in a commodity economy and indicates how difficult it would be to judge the class character of farms simply from appearances or from one or more descriptive indicators of inequality. Even with an approach attempting to observe directly the different social relations of a farm, in many cases more than one interpretation was possible of the class character of the combination of relations observed. For Kritsman and his colleagues, this showed the absolute necessity of quantifying the various relations rather than using only a typological analysis, as Khryashcheva had suggested. Without quantification, the same combination of relationships might just as easily have been a form of proletarian farm or capitalist farm.

In specifying some of the above types, moreover, Kritsman also allowed for the possibility that their class character might not conform to any one of the three types appropriate to conditions of a commodity economy developing into capitalism; for example, he suggested that some types could have been feudal peasants, feudal landlords, or peasants in co-operatives. As noted above, in outlining the general framework within which the class differentiation of the peasantry was taking place, Kritsman discussed Soviet society in terms of a range of different structures, each of which could give rise to different sets of class relations. Although he was concerned mainly with the varieties of capitalist relations which were developing, the other possible relations also had to be kept in mind. Several different relations could be abstracted from peasant society, each of which could be seen as the starting point of a particular pattern of social development.

Appearing as a confusion of embryonic forms of different economic structures and various classes, peasant agriculture is distinctive not for its simplicity but its exceptional complexity. From the point of view of every separate line of development, peasant agriculture appears as the starting point of this development and therefore its most simple form. But at the same time, it contains within itself possibilities of various lines of development, and in this lies its complexity, which is the object of our discussion.

(Kritsman 1926–7, Part III, 4)

Apart from capitalist development, Kritsman had earlier discussed other possible tendencies in Soviet society, including the survival of feudal relations, the development of socialism, and the development of state capitalism based, in agriculture, on co-operative forms of organization. In studying peasant agriculture in complex detail, albeit with the main aim of identifying aspects of capitalist development within it, it was necessary to be able to recognize elements of other 'lines of development', at least so as not to confuse them with signs of proletarian, petty-bourgeois, or capitalist farming.

A major practical problem emerged, however, in Kritsman's approach when it came to distinguishing signs of other 'lines of development' in that, by opposing 'own' factors to 'other's' factors, whether it was farm, labour power, or means of production, 'other's' was never clearly specified. 'It is a negative meaning, coherent only in its opposition to own labour power, own means of production, and own farm, and capable of hiding within itself various meanings (for example, "other's farm" can be other individually owned farms or a socialised farm).' (Kritsman 1926–7, Part II, 9). This problem related to distinguishing both feudal elements and elements of socialized agriculture. The problem in relation to feudalism will be discussed first.

In their developed form, feudal agrarian relations would have directly involved the compulsion of peasants by a lord to carry out certain services and give up a certain part of their produce. Labour for the lord would be obligatory and not part of any contract. This situation was supported by law. However, with the juridical abolition of feudalism in Russia, a number of aspects of feudal relations had remained. This had been revealed in the pre-revolutionary period by the various obstacles met by peasants in giving up farming in the communal village. Also, certain forms of feudal exploitation persisted after the emancipation, and even into the 1920s. These included labour rent (*otrabotochnaya renta*), whereby a period of labour was carried out unpaid in return for the use of land or stock, and bonded hire of labour (*kabal'nyi naem*), whereby labour was forcibly required of someone rather than its hire being the subject of an agreed contract.

The problem in the 1920s, as in the years before the revolution, was that feudal and commodity relations coexisted and had become interwoven in complex ways. On the one hand, feudal relations were gradually undergoing a transition to commodity relations so that they took the form of exchange relations, which sometimes, nevertheless, concealed an element of compulsion. On the other hand, given the political climate in all except the middle years of the 1920s, it was probably expedient for commercially oriented peasants to conceal renting land or hiring labour behind the façade of more traditional relationships. For such reasons it was likely that research would not always be able to distinguish accurately between commodity relations and transitional relations based on more direct compulsion. However, given the juridical abolition of feudalism and the growing strength of a commodity economy, except perhaps for parts of Soviet Central Asia, there could hardly be a feudal line of development in Soviet society, and so 'feudal' exploitation, or exploitation based on compulsion, would lead not to the consolidation of the positions of lord and serf, but rather to capital accumulation and proletarianization.

For this reason, the achievement of a clear identification and separation of semi-feudal relations from straightforward commodity relations was probably never likely to be a major priority. This was just as well, given the limits of Kritsman's approach. In the absence of complete audits of farms in money terms, which would hardly have been possible, researchers could not have known what the actual terms of transactions were between peasant farms. Kritsman's methodology only allowed the observation of the transfer of factors of production between farms, and estimated the direction and rate of profit on such transfers by taking prevailing local prices and conditions into account and assuming they applied to all the transactions observed. The problem with this approach was that it was therefore impossible to know whether a transfer of factors involved compulsion or was a 'freely' engaged commodity transaction. (Similarly, it was impossible to know whether the transfer reflected genuine selfless help or co-operation between farms, or whether for some other reason the prevailing price was not actually charged, which again would undermine assumptions that the transaction represented the expropriation of a known amount of surplus in a known direction.)

Kritsman did not extend his discussion of feudal relations or the problems of identifying them any further. As shown above, he merely noted that certain combinations of elements in the structure of farms could be interpreted in different ways, including seeing them as signs of the persistence of feudal relations. No doubt, for European Russia, where most of the research on peasant differentiation was conducted, the problem was not of great importance, but if Kritsman and his colleagues had eventually been able to extend their analysis to Soviet Central Asia, or if modern scholars wished to adapt Kritsman's methodology for peasant societies where forms of coercive relations between households still exist, then the question of the identification of feudal relations would need to be given much closer attention.[7]

Of more immediate practical importance was the problem of distinguishing elements of socialized agriculture from proletarianization as part of capitalist relations. As Kritsman put it,

farms with a surplus of their own means of production in the conditions of a commodity economy are inevitably to some extent capitalist in that the surplus part of their means of production is used with the help of someone else's labour power on their own or someone else's farm and cannot be used otherwise. As opposed to this, farms with a surplus of their own labour power . . . can be not only to some extent proletarian, in the sense that the surplus part of their labour power is used on the means of production of other individually owned farms . . . and are consequently parts of a capitalist economy, but they can also be proletarian in the sense that they supply the workers of the socialist economy.

(Kritsman 1926–7, Part II, 9)

If the household's members were employed on a state farm, or even on their own farm with means of production belonging to the state, or as employees of agricultural co-operatives, or as members of agricultural co-operatives, then these elements of their productive activity would be part of the initial development of a socialist agriculture. Such households would still be displaying proletarian tendencies, but with a very different significance for their class character than if they were employed by other peasant commodity producers.[8] Kritsman suggested the use of four subgroups to his main class groups so that the employment of household labour outside its own farm could be distinguished as either (1) on state means of production, (2) on co-operative means of production, (3) on other's privately owned means of production, and (4) in work of a mixed character including employment by co-operatives of non-members (Kritsman 1926–7, Part II, 10).

Presumably, as in the case of identifying feudal tendencies, membership of such subgroupings could be determined only by direct observation extra to the categories of the main scheme of analysis. In the case of socialized forms of agriculture, however, this would probably have been easier than for feudalism, since it would not be an officially disapproved form of activity and there would be no need for peasants to hide what they were doing from researchers. On the other hand, there would have been a problem in distinguishing pretended forms of co-operation which acted as a façade for the expansion of *kulak* employers.

Finally, Kritsman turned his attention to a further qualification to his research scheme. This was concerned with the problem of how to account for non-productive activities on peasant farms. This included both work outside material production and means of achieving an income without work. As with productive labour, its character could be capitalist, petty-bourgeois, or proletarian.

Kritsman's suggested method of identifying income from unproductive labour was to take the gross income of a farm (i.e. the value of its gross turnover minus the value of its material costs of production) and calculate what proportion of it arose from capitalist, petty-bourgeois, or proletarian activities. Capitalist non-productive income would include income from trade, from giving credit, and from investment. Under the category of petty-bourgeois would come income from hiring out services or professional employment of some kind. Proletarian non-productive income would derive from employment in service occupations for the state, co-operatives, or private individuals. Kritsman also outlined a fourth category of 'indeterminate' class nature, which included income from pensions, begging, and selling one's belongings.

Having determined the amount of non-productive income and its proportion of total revenue, and the proportions of different class types of non-productive income, the overall character of households could be calculated. In rare cases where all of a household's revenue was from non-productive activity, its class character would simply be the result of the balance between the different class elements of non-productive income. For most households, however, if they had income from non-productive employment, it would form only a part of their total income, most of which would be derived from material production. For such households, Kritsman proposed the following procedure.

He took as his example a household whose income was 80 per cent from material production and 20 per cent from non-productive activity. On the productive side, the farm was 75 per cent petty-bourgeois and 25 per cent capitalist. Taking into account that this constituted only 80 per cent of the household's activities, in terms of the overall class character of the household, these figures would become 60 per cent petty-bourgeois and 20 per cent capitalist. If the non-productive income of the household broke down, for example, into 50 per cent capitalist, 30 per cent petty-bourgeois and 20 per cent indeterminate, in terms of the overall character these figures would be reduced to 10, 6, and 4 per cent, respectively. The overall class character would therefore be 66 per cent petty bourgeois, 30 per cent capitalist, and 4 per cent indeterminate (Kritsman 1926–7, Part II, 11–13).

It is not clear from Kritsman's rather sketchy discussion of this issue how the figures for gross income and the proportions of it from different sources were to be measured, but presumably it would have required detailed accounting of household budgets of a kind not required by the rest of his methodology. Here Kritsman was requiring detailed figures of turnover, expenditure, and income from different sources of a kind which peasants would not have kept as a matter of course. By contrast, the information required for the main part of his analysis was to have been acquired by asking peasants about the amount of various factors involved in transactions and the duration of the transaction. Values were then attributed to these *post hoc*. Although the methods of budget research necessary for Kritsman's purposes in regard to non-productive labour had been developed, notably by Chayanov and his colleagues, it must be doubtful that they could have been applied to a large sample, or even the 5–10 per cent which Nemchinov had suggested for surveys based on his work.

Kritsman's thoughts on the details of his research approach, especially in relation to the more peripheral aspects of his main question, were clearly rather tentative. Probably they represent the limits of his thinking in advance of actually attempting detailed fieldwork, when problems would have been confronted concretely and more precise solutions found. The main contribution of the articles of Kritsman and Nemchinov discussed above was, on the basis of the knowledge then available, to put forward a general characterization of the class nature of the Soviet peasantry and its likely trend, and to devise the framework of a research strategy for more clearly identifying and measuring such characteristics and their trends. In this, they made some very significant innovations in the whole approach to the study of peasant class differentiation.

Moreover, Nemchinov's own contribution to these innovations was absolutely crucial. Before his work, Kritsman had not been able to go much beyond Lenin's best work on differentiation, based on Postnikov. In this, data on inequalities in the distribution of factors had been related to judgements about levels of their sufficiency or insufficiency, and it was then assumed that, 'as a rule', problems concerning the excess or lack were resolved by entering into unequal relations (as exploiter or exploited) with other households. This was, of course, still indirect evidence that the appropriation of a surplus was actually taking place. It was partly on the basis of Nemchinov's research, however, that Kritsman was able to refine his own ideas on the most suitable approaches and concepts for the research he advocated. These ideas were reflected most directly in the next main piece of empirical research, that of Ya. Anisimov, I. Vermenichev, and K. Naumov.

3   The Volokolamsk Research

The research of Anisimov and his colleagues was carried out in the flax-growing region of Volokolamsk, Moscow *guberniya*, in 1925. Information was collected from a general household survey and, more especially, from sixty household budgets, adopting a system of double-entry bookkeeping to organize the budget information. The

Volokolamsk project was of particular interest because it drew directly on the two different traditions of Russian agrarian research. On the one hand, its choice of methods drew on the ideas of Chayanov, under whom the authors of the research had studied at the Timiryazev Academy. Since the project was one of a series of budget studies carried out by Chayanov's group at the Scientific Research Institute of Agricultural Economics, Chayanov in fact actively co-operated in the work, taking an overall supervisory role. On the other hand, the team based themselves closely on Kritsman's ideas in the organization and analysis of their data, adopting his proposed method of calculating the class tendencies of household in preference to Nemchinov's approach.

In choosing Voloklamsk for their research, the team were no doubt working on the principle that, if class differentiation was not occurring there, it was unlikely to be very pronounced anywhere in the Soviet Union at that time. By contemporary Russian standards, Volokolamsk *uezd* was highly commercialized, with a relatively intensive system of production. Fields had mostly been consolidated instead of the more usual pattern of households cultivating different strips in different parts of the village territory, and most households were operating a system of crop rotation. Furthermore, it was not uncommon to find relatively advanced farm machinery such as metal harrows or seed drills, especially on the better-off farms. Flax production had been developed in the area at the end of the nineteenth century, and flax had become the main commodity crop of the peasants in this area (Anisimov *et al.* 1927, 13–14).

The aim of the survey was to gather information on a range of topics of interest for the study of peasant class relations and different types of production organization in different groups within the peasantry. The information required for such purposes could be obtained only by a combination of household and budget survey approaches. First of all, the research team carried out a household survey of 648 peasant households in twelve villages in Volokolamsk *uezd*. In addition to the usual questions asked in such surveys (on land use, farm stock and buildings, membership of the household, employment outside the household farm, and the hire of seasonal labour), the Volokolamsk survey included questions on the sale of produce and of livestock, hire and lease of stock, hire of day labourers, and participation in co-operation. Off-farm employment was further subdivided into wage labour (agricultural and non-agricultural), independent trades, and ownership of enterprises involved in hiring labour.

On the basis of the results of the household survey, a smaller sample of sixty households was chosen for a more detailed analysis of household budgets. The various transactions of the chosen households over the course of a year were recorded and organized according to a double-entry accounting system in order to show the balance of income and outgoings. Further information was gathered about participation in co-operatives, credit relations, techniques and organization of crop cultivation, animal breeding, and especially flax cultivation. In all, the research yielded fifty-two complete budgets in 1925, and (for reasons unstated) eight additional budgets were added to these from the 1911 research of Chayanov. The detailed information was collected both for the purpose of studying peasant class relations and for the study of the production characteristics of different groups, although the second part of their analysis was never published (Anisimov *et al.* 1927, 15–16). (The researchers discussed their research methods in more detail than any of the other Agrarian Movement projects but only a brief outline has been included here. For further discussion, see Cox 1983a, 339–56).

As far as the analysis of class relations was concerned, the researchers aimed to use the detailed accounts they had collected to approach more directly the question of the relation of farm size to the extent of labour and means of production used on it. In order to calculate the specific relations involved in this, which Kritsman had identified, seven variables had first to be worked out for each household, as follows:

1. *The value of all means of production belonging to a household.* This included both fixed and circulating capital used both in agriculture and in other production such as crafts. This value was represented by *a*.

2. *The value of the household's own means of production leased out to other households.* This was represented by *b*.

3. *The value of other's means of production employed on a household's own farm.* This included both animals and farm stock which had been hired by the household, and circulating capital such as seed or cash which had been borrowed by the household. This was represented by *c*.

4. *The value of all the labour power of a household,* including labour provided by its own members for its own agricultural, craft, or trading activities, as well as labour hired and sold by it. This was, represented by *d*.

5. *The value of the household's own labour power employed in its own farm or other activities.* This was represented by *e*.

6. *The value of the labour power hired by a household from outside for work on its own farm or other activities.* This was represented by *f*.

7. *The value of the labour power sold by a household to others.* This was represented by *g*.

The relation between the different elements of a household's operations could then be calculated along the lines proposed by Kritsman in his criticisms of Nemchinov. For a predominantly exploited farm where sale of labour and hiring in of stock predominated, a calculation was made of the relation of a household's own means of production used in its own production to all means of production used by it, represented by xp, according to the formula

$$xp = \frac{a - c}{a} \quad \text{or} \quad \frac{a - (c - b)}{a}.$$

Second, for the same type of households, the relation of their own labour power used on their own farm to all of their labour was represented by yp where

$$yp = \frac{e}{d} \quad \text{or} \quad \frac{e}{e + (g - f)}.$$

The result of these two calculations could be expressed as percentages and multiplied to give the total percentage of independent elements (own labour used on own means of production), as Kritsman had done in his re-working of Nemchinov's figures. Subtracting this figure from 100 would give the percentage degree to which a household was proletarian.

For predominantly exploiting households, the relation of the household's own means of production used on its own farm to all of its means of production, represented by xk, was calculated according to the formula

$$xk = \frac{a}{a + b} \quad \text{or} \quad \frac{a}{a + (b - c)}.$$

The relation of the household's own labour power used on its own farm or business to all labour power used by it was represented by yk where

$$yk = \frac{e}{d} \quad \text{or} \quad \frac{e}{e + (f - g)}.$$

Again, the two results could be expressed as percentages and then multiplied to give the percentage of independent elements. When subtracted from 100, the result showed the extent of capitalist development within the household (Anisimov *et al.* 1927, 37–8).

On the basis of their calculations, the researchers classified their sample into groups as shown in Table 4.5. It is not clear why the researchers chose their particular cut-off points between groups, and

Table 4.5.

The Class Composition of the Volokolamsk Sample

Class	Description	Indicator	No. of households in sample
I	Proletarian households with a small plot of land	50.1% and more proletarian	5
II	Semi-proletarian households, carrying out their own farming but with elements of proletarianization	20.1–50% proletarian	6
III	Small commodity producing households which could develop in either class direction	0–20% proletarian	21
IV	Semi-capitalist households, carrying out their own farming with elements of capitalism	0–20% capitalist	22
V	Capitalist (predominantly small capitalist) households	20.1% and more capitalist	6

Source: Anisimov *et al.* (1927, 39)

Table 4.6.

Value of Means of Production and Labour Power on Average per Household per Group (roubles)

	Groups				
	I	II	III	IV	V
Total value of all means of production in the budget year	245.63	532.74	652.57	1003.17	1635.07
Value of own means of production on own farm	190.95	459.14	626.57	953.59	1547.50
Value of others' means of production on own farm	54.68	73.60	26.0	—	—
Value of own means of production on others's farm	—	—	—	49.54	87.57
Total value of labour power in the budget year	567.59	462.11	630.18	835.01	1818.41
Value of own labour power on own farm	253.11	375.53	615.81	826.46	1398.55
Value of hired labour on own farm	—	—	—	26.55	419.86
Value of own labour power sold	314.58	86.58	15.06	—	—

Source: Anisimov *et al.* (1927, 39)

it must be assumed that their judgement here was in fact somewhat arbitrary. However, they argued that it did provide a meaningful classification of households, offering evidence of clear differences between their chosen groups as shown in Table 4.6. It can be seen that, in terms of total value of means of production, the proletarian group was clearly the poorest, that each higher group was better off than the one below it, and that the capitalist group was the best off. Furthermore, the more capitalist groups were clearly distinct from the more proletarian groups in that they leased out means of production but did not hire any, and bought labour but did not sell any, while the more proletarian groups hired means of production but did not lease any out, and sold labour but did not buy any.

On the basis of these results, the researchers felt able to conclude that their approach had been a satisfactory one in revealing the developing class structure of the peasantry in their sample (Anisimov *et al.* 1927, 41). Kritsman also seemed well pleased, and he did not produce any detailed criticisms of it. However, although the approach used in the Volokolamsk study seems to have been the closest attempt to put Kritsman's ideas into practice, most of the later projects did not follow it in many important aspects, and produced approaches closer to the practice of Nemchinov.

The only other survey to follow the basic design used in Volokolamsk was one produced for another project organized in association with the Chayanov group's Institute, and directed by G. A. Studenskii. Although he was not a member of the group working with Kritsman at the Communist Academy, and had earlier carried out research of differentiation using stratification approaches (Studenskii, 1926), Studenskii became interested in the use of the Agrarian Marxist approach in research, and used it in a study of the Middle Volga region. On the basis of detailed budget information from several villages in Samara *guberniya*, he reproduced the same kind of analysis of data and the same methods of calculating the class characteristics of households as Anisimov and his colleagues had used, and, like the Volokolamsk researchers, proclaimed the approach to have produced very satisfactory results (Studenskii 1929, 19).

In a sample that included households farming under four different systems of farm organization—the three-field system, mixed cultivation, the long-fallow system, and suburban cultivation—Studenskii and his team then determined the class structure of their sample. Here, however, they departed from the details of the scheme used in Volokolamsk, including a middle group with no clear class tendency in either direction (although this group was still subdivided into those showing slight proletarian or slight capitalist tendencies), and using different percentage scores of exploiting or exploited tendencies as the dividing lines between their groups. The criteria for Studenskii's grouping, along with percentages of each group in the sample as a whole, is shown in Table 4.7.

Despite the fact that the researchers concerned in the Volokolamsk and Volga studies expressed general satisfaction with their

Table 4.7.
Class Composition and Production Organization in Studenskii's Sample

Social types	Characteristics	Extent and character of exploitation relations	Nos. of each type in:				
			3-field farms	Mixed farms	Long fallow farms	Suburban farms	Total sample
I	Proletarian	> 20%	10	9	6	10	35
II	Independent Commodity Producers	20% proletarian– 20% capitalist	20	20	23	18	81
Sub-divided into:							
(II$_2$)	(Dependent)	(0–20% proletarian)	(8)	(9)	(14)	(9)	(40)
(II$_2$)	(Upward-moving)	(0–20% capitalist)	(12)	(11)	(9)	(9)	(41)
III	Capitalist	> 20% capitalist	6	7	7	8	28

Source: Studenskii (1929, 20)

results, there were two problems in particular with their work. First is the question of how adequately the results of such research can be used to delineate actual classes in the peasantry. The Volokolamsk researchers clearly thought that evidence of tendencies within a household to exploit others or to be exploited by others signified the evolution of such households gradually into classes of capitalists or proletarians. Moreover, it seemed to be assumed that, if households had overall tendencies to exploit or be exploited by their neighbours, this was a sufficient cause of the development of those households into one or other fully-fledged class type. It was implied that the process of class formation was a one-way process and was not to be significantly modified by other factors. This view contrasts with that of Nemchinov, who, as noted above, held that analysis of the relations of exploitation of households had to be supplemented by measures of their economic strength in order to be translated into the identification of a class structure.

The second problem, arising specifically out of the Volokolamsk research, is the question of how to treat the middle range of households having only slight, or mixed, elements of capitalist and proletarian tendencies. In the Volokolamsk research, these households were placed in a group described as either capitalist or proletarian according to their dominant tendency, however weak. The researchers argued that this was justified, since nearly all members of any potential middle group showed signs of dependence or entrepreneurship and could not therefore be regarded as truly independent peasant farmers. Again, this was in contrast to the work of Nemchinov and other earlier Russian writers, who regarded households in the middle of their scale as not showing clear enough tendencies to be classified as definitely developing in a particular class direction. It is interesting to note that the slightly later, but otherwise similar, research of Studenskii did not follow the Volokolamsk research on this issue.

Both of the above problems will be discussed further in Chapter 5 in relation to the attempted solutions to them of all the different projects of the Agrarian Marxists. The studies by Nemchinov on the one hand, and Anisimov and his colleagues on the other, raised between them most of the range of questions that empirical research on class differentiation would need to resolve. However, they did involve very intensive and complex methods in order to give results based on only rather small samples. As well as pursuing further some of the problems raised by the first set of projects, therefore, the later projects also sought to devise simpler approaches, or to extend their analysis to larger, more representative samples. These projects are discussed in Chapter 5.

Notes

1. It should be stressed, of course, that Nemchinov's scheme was drawn up strictly for the conditions of Russia in the 1920s. In other peasant societies, or in other periods, land or labour might be scarcer in relation to means of production, and therefore more important as determinants of a household's class position. If an approach of the kind proposed by Nemchinov were to be adapted for research elsewhere, the most appropriate indicators would have to be determined from prior empirical enquiry into the society under study. This is precisely what Kritsman and Nemchinov had done in deciding on their chosen indicators on the basis of knowledge of local conditions derived from local statistical bureaux and monographic studies of local areas.

2. More of a problem for classification than agricultural activity were trading and industrial activities. Nemchinov's solution for trade, and for industrial enterprises of peasant households such as mills or dairies, was to treat them as entrepreneurial and add the value of the household's means of production employed in them to the entrepreneurial elements. However, there were exceptions to this. For craft production where the peasant household worked on raw material belonging to someone else, the labour involved was seen as labour on someone else's enterprise and classified as dependent. The classification of the raw materials used in such cases depended on the extent of credit received by the household from the buyer of the craft product. Where the level of credit was high they were classified as other's means of production in the peasant's own enterprise, that is, as an aspect of dependence; but where the household was less dependent on such credit, they were classified as 'own' means in 'own' enterprise, that is, as an aspect of independent production (Nemchinov 1926b, 50).

3. Nemchinov mistakenly gives this figures as 123.3 per cent (1926b, 56). It should be stressed that what he was working out was not receipts or profits: instead, he was attempting to put a money value on the factors of production which, given prevailing conditions, should have provided a *basis* variously for extracting a surplus, giving up part of a surplus, or maintaining independent production. Actual performance in achieving a profit, sustaining a loss, or maintaining independence could not be directly measured.

4. It should be noted that Solomon is incorrect in stating that the grouping in terms of prosperity of farms was based on a measure of income (1977,

97). As noted above, Nemchinov's indicator was expenditure on constant capital. She is also rather tendentious in the footnote to her discussion of Nemchinov's approach in attributing to him the motives of academic entrepreneur rather than serious researcher. She suggests that his motives for combining his two groupings, instead of simply using one based on class characteristics, were part of 'a clever strategy for an innovator not to try to pre-empt the entire field but to claim superiority on the basis of expertise in a more limited area' (1977, 247 n. 22). She produces no evidence that Nemchinov was motivated by any such concerns.

5. The figures in Kritsman's text were incorrect and the corrected figures are given here. Kritsman mistakenly took the total value of the household's own means of production on their own farm to be R504.24 instead of R604.24. The value of all the household's means of production on 'own' farm was 97.9 per cent of all of 'own' means of production. As a result, Kritsman calculated a figure of 50.1 per cent for independent elements and therefore of 49.9 per cent of entrepreneurial elements.

6. Kritsman calculated the percentages as 44.5 and 26.8 per cent, but multiplying them still produces a figure of 11.9 per cent.

7. Kritsman was conforming to standard Bolshevik and Soviet usage of the term 'feudal' to describe pre-capitalist non-commodity relations. He was not drawn into the debates in the 1920s in the Soviet Union on whether the Asiatic Mode of Production was a valid concept in relation to the Russian Empire or parts of the contemporary Soviet Union. For a discussion of this debate, see Sawer (1978).

8. With hindsight, an alternative interpretation is possible which would see such households becoming dependent on a newly emerging class which would eventually become a ruling class on the basis of its control over socialized means of production. This, of course, did not form part of Kritsman's sources of ideas in the mid-1920s.

5

Further Developments in Empirical Research

While the later research projects in the series followed Anisimov and his colleagues in using Kritsman's more explicit use of class terminology instead of Nemchinov's categories of 'entrepreneurial' and 'dependent' households, they differed from the Volokolamsk research in three important respects which were in fact closer to Nemchinov's practice. First, they incorporated a measure of the economic capacity of households along with their main classification based on exploitation indices; second, they used evidence of transactions in labour, and in some cases in land, as separate indicators of exploitation relations; and third, they included a group of 'middle peasants' without clear class tendencies among the groups in their classifications.

In other respects, however, the later projects departed from the practice of both earlier studies, some of them adopting simpler survey methods which did not involve the collection of such detailed budget information, and using simpler means of identifying exploitation between households. Also, instead of attempting to attribute money values to transactions, some studies experimented with a 'points systems' to make different measures of transactions commensurable. Finally, still other studies, reflecting growing political demands for information on the rural class structure on a national scale, attempted to devise methods to apply Agrarian Marxist class analysis methods to mass data.

1 The Samara and Moscow Studies

Both of these studies were carried out in 1927 on the basis of household surveys, and using approaches to the analysis of their data which drew in significant respects on Nemchinov's model rather than that of the Volokolamsk study. The research in Samara *guberniya* was carried out by three researchers, I. Vermenichev, who had been part of the Volokolamsk team, A. Gaister, and G. Raevich. They collected data on 710 households in Aksakov *volost'* in the spring of 1927. Along similar lines was the research of K. Naumov, who was formerly in the Volokolamsk team, along with D. Shardin, who surveyed 776 households in two *uezds* in Moscow *guberniya*, taking 340 from Mozhaiskii *uezd* and 436 from Volokolamsk *uezd*.

In some ways, however, both studies departed from Nemchinov's practice. For example, they started by dividing their samples into households whose income came predominantly from agriculture and those whose income was mainly non-agricultural. Also, the range and description of their chosen indicators was different. For agricultural households, both studies used the hire and sale of labour, the hire and leasing out of animals and stock, and the rent and lease of land. Unlike Nemchinov, they did not make use of data on transactions in seed, fodder, or manure. Nor did they record all cases of the use of one household's factors of production on the farm of another household, but instead used information directly on transactions of hire, lease, or sale. For the mainly non-agricultural households, in the Samara study classification was based on the type of occupation or business the household was involved in, and the degree to which this entailed buying or selling labour, or hiring or leasing out means of production. In the Moscow study, non-agricultural households were classified by the level of qualification (and therefore, it was assumed, of income) of each worker's job, along with the same indicators of transactions in agricultural as described above for any subsidiary agricultural production (Vermenichev *et al.* 1928, 43, 137–8; Naumov and Shardin 1928, 28, 32).

A further innovation adopted by both studies was the use of a 'points system' to make their different indicators of exploitation commensurable instead of expressing them in money equivalents. The details of the scheme adopted in the Samara research are shown on page 131 (Vermenichev *et al.* 1928, 43).

In determining the number of points to allocate for transactions involving the hire of labour, the researchers reasoned that most labour was hired in the busy period from spring to autumn and that 90 days would roughly cover the whole of this period. Therefore, a household hiring a worker for a period of 90 days or more was effectively hiring a worker constantly for its crop-growing season and therefore could be considered as entrepreneurial in relation to employing wage labour in order to carry out its production and would be awarded +5 points. On the other hand, employment of

Hire of labour power		*Sale of labour power*	
Up to 10 days per annum	+1	Up to 10 days per annum	−1
11–50 days p.a.	+3	11–30 days p.a.	−3
51–90 days p.a.	+4	31–50 days p.a.	−4
More than 90 days p.a.	+5	More than 50 days p.a.	−5

Hire of cattle or stock
Hiring simple stock only, or no more than 2 items of advanced equipment   −1
Hiring working cattle and 3 or more items of advanced equipment   −2

Leasing out cattle or stock
Income of up to R10	+1
Income of up to R11–R50	+2
Income of more than R50	+3

Leasing out of land
Up to 30% of own arable land   −1
More than 30% of own arable land   −2

Rent of land
Up to 2 desyatins	+1
More than 2 desyatins	+2

labour for up to 10 days would not have placed a household in an entrepreneurial position and therefore should be allotted only +1 point, indicating an independent small producer. Between these two extremes, other households would then be allocated either +3 or +4 points depending on the extent to which they employed labour.

In allocating points for the sale of labour, the researchers decided that a household with proletarian characteristics would be one selling between 31 and 50 person-days of labour power. This, they argued, reflected the situation in the Russian countryside where the redistribution of land had created many very poor households trying to cultivate their own plots, as opposed to *batrak* households living entirely by the sale of labour power. For such households, each unit of labour power sold was more significant as a loss for their own farming than it was as a gain to the household that bought it; therefore, it was argued that a household selling between 31 and 50 days of labour was showing signs of serious weakness and a clear dependence on selling labour to survive.

Having decided their range of figures indicating proletarianization, the researchers then decided that the sale of up to 10 days of labour did not represent any significant level of dependence and therefore that households selling such amounts could be considered independent small producers. This then left an intermediate group of households selling between 11 and 30 days of labour who were considered strong enough to be small producers, but with elements of dependence. Again, however, the authors offered no explanation of exactly why the cut-off points of 10 and 30 days should have been chosen (Vermenichev *et al.* 1928, 40, xi).

Further problems were encountered in devising a system of points for leasing out and hiring stock and animals. It was thought in this case that measuring transactions in terms of the number of days of lease or hire could be very misleading because it would not take into account the degree of complexity of the stock used, or the age and strength of the animals involved. Moreover, there were distinctions to be made concerning whether different items of live or dead stock were necessary simply to carry out farming, or whether they were desirable as means to greater productivity and profit. For example, such a distinction could be made between the hire of a horse or wooden plough and the hire of more advanced machinery. It was assumed that an evaluation of the relative values of necessary and desirable items would be reflected in the price of their hire. The researchers decided, therefore, to measure the leasing out of cattle and stock in terms of cash (or estimated cash equivalent) income per annum from leasing out, as shown on p. 131 above. For the hire of animals and stock, presumably because of a lack of other data, the researchers opted for a different approach again, allocating points according to the character of the items hired as shown above. Similarly, no reasons were offered in the text for the chosen measures of land rented or leased out.

Having decided how to allocate points for different transactions, the sum of them could then be found in a similar way to Nemchinov's procedure using monetary values. All points bearing a positive sign would be added together to represent capitalist tendencies, while all negative points would be added together to represent proletarian tendencies. The size and sign of the balance would indicate the overall class character of a household. For example, if a household hired labour for less than 10 days in a year (+1 point) but also leased out cattle and stock to the value of R50 (+3 points), and rented 2 desyatins of land (+1 point), then the sum of these would indicate a semi-capitalist farm with +5 points. If, however, in addition to the above, the household also sold labour for up to 10 days (−1 point) and hired certain items of stock (−1 point), then the sum of its tendencies would be +3 points, indicating a small producer household with some entrepreneurial tendencies. A range of different permutations was possible using this scheme, amounting to a total of 85 in all (Vermenichev *et al.* 1928, 42–3, ix–x). On the basis of the sum of points calculated for each household, Vermenichev and his colleagues classified the sample into groups as shown in Table 5.1.

Table 5.1.
Class Tendencies of the Samara Sample

Class group		Points	% of sample
I	The agricultural proletariat living mainly by the sale of their labour power	−5 or less	10.3
II	Small producers with signs of dependence on others, managing to farm only by also selling some labour power or by hiring working cattle or farm stock	−4 to −2	22.4
III	Independent or neutral small producers, mainly with their own labour power and with only limited involvement in hiring or selling labour, or renting or leasing stock	−1 to +1	40.4
IV	Small producers with some entrepreneurial activity, hiring some wage labour or leasing out some stock	+2 to +4	18.9
V	Semi-capitalist or small capitalist farmers, farming by means of large amounts of wage labour	+5 or more	8.2

Source: Vermenichev *et al.* (1928, 40–4)

The next step, following Nemchinov, was then to combine the above classification with one based on economic strength in order to determine more concretely the likely emerging classes in the Samara countryside. However, whereas Nemchinov had used annual expenditure on constant capital, Vermenichev and his colleagues opted for total value of all basic means of production (excluding the land owned by a household). Their preference for this indicator was based on their belief that it was a good measure of all the main aspects of a household's farming, including its expenditure of labour power and its use of land (Vermenichev *et al.* 1928, 45–6).[1]

On the basis of their chosen indicator, the researchers obtained four groups as shown in Table 5.2. By cross-classifying the two groupings, they discovered the distribution shown in Table 5.3. On the basis of this cross-classification, the class structure of the sample was determined. Group V was split into classes of small capitalists and semi-capitalists, while group I was split into proletarians and semi-proletarians. Table 5.4 shows the final classifications of the 679 agricultural households in the sample.[2]

Table 5.2.

The Stratification of the Samara Sample

Group	Value of means of production	% of sample
(a)	up to R250	32.0
(b)	R251–R500	31.4
(c)	R501–R1000	27.0
(d)	more than R1000	9.6

For the most part, the problems of measuring exploitation and determining the class character of households were approached in a similar way in the Moscow research of Naumov and Shardin. They also used measures of relations of exploitation along with a measure of economic strength; but the novelty of their scheme was that, instead of keeping the two measures separate, as bases for two different schemes of classification which were then cross-classified, they integrated the two into a combined system, making use of a points system not only to make different measures of transactions commensurable, but also to make these commensurable with a measure of economic strength (Naumov and Shardin 1928, 23). The details of their scheme are shown in Table 5.5. In order to account for various, possibly contradictory, characteristics of households, points totals were taken as indicators of membership of classes, as shown in Table 5.6.

While Kritsman did not publish comments on the research of Naumov and Shardin, he did record his views on the Samara research, and therefore, given the similarity in approach between the two studies on many points, his comments can to some extent be read as applying to both. While being generally positive about the

Table 5.3.

Cross-Classification of Class Groups and Strata

Groups by value of means of production	Class groups (%)				
	I Proletarians	II Dep. small producers	III Indep. small producers	IV Entrepr. small producers	V Semi-capitalists
(a) up to R250	81.4	54.6	26.7	3.1	—
(b) R251–R500	12.9	35.5	39.2	31.4	5.4
(c) R501–R1000	5.7	7.9	30.8	45.2	44.6
(d) more than R1000	—	2.9	3.3	20.3	50.0

Source: Vermenichev *et al.* (1928, 46)

Table 5.4.

The Class Structure of the Samara Sample

Class	% of sample
Proletarian	1.4
Semi-proletarian	8.5
Small dependent	21.4
Small independent (neutral)	38.5
Small independent (entrepreneurial elements)	18.0
Semi-capitalist	7.9
Small-capitalist	3.9

Source: Vermenichev *et al.* (1928, 138)

results of Vermenichev and his colleagues, he made three points of criticism of their approach. First, he suggested that it was unnecessary to separate 'agricultural' and 'non-agricultural' households for analysis. There did not seem to be any clear reason why a points system could not be worked out to make the varying activities of each kind commensurable (as Nemchinov had done using monetary values in his research). Second, in line with his criticism of Nemchinov, Kritsman raised objections to the use of rent and lease of land as a significant indicator of exploitation.

Third, and perhaps most important, he had critical comments concerning the use of the points system which in Samara, he thought, had produced a grouping which was generally 'cumbersome and lacking in clarity'. The way the points had been allocated for transactions in labour seemed to incorporate a bias towards finding a suspiciously large group of middle peasants. For example, very extensive hiring of labour, of a few hundred person-days per annum, would receive +5 points, while a much smaller extent of selling labour, of 55 person-days, would be sufficient to balance this with a score of −5 points. The result was that a household that was hiring much more labour than it sold, and on balance was therefore clearly an exploiting household, in fact received a score of 0 for its transactions in labour, indicating an independent 'middle-peasant' household. The solution suggested by Kritsman was to take the balance of hire and sale of labour measured in days before allocating points.[3]

Furthermore, with regard to the use of a points system, there seemed to be no clear rationale behind the way points were allocated. It was not clear, and the researchers gave no explanation, why the various indicators received the particular points scores allocated to them. For example, no explanation was offered by the Samara researchers of why hiring labour for up to 10 days was

Table 5.5.

The Scheme of Classification in the Moscow Survey

Class	Indicators	Points
Labour power		
I	Selling more than 1.5 months of labour power	−6
II	Selling 0.35–1.5 months of labour power	−4
	Selling up to 0.35 months of labour power	−2
III	Hiring up to 0.35 months of labour power	+2
IV	Hiring 0.35–1.5 months of labour power	+4
V	Hiring more than 1.5 months of labour power	+6
Farm stock		
I	Hiring more than 50% of stock used	−3
II	Hiring 30–50% of stock used	−2
	Hiring up to 30% of stock used	−1
III	Leasing out stock for receipts of up to R8	+1
IV	Leasing out stock for receipts of R8–R15	+2
V	Leasing out stock for receipts of more than R15	+3
Land		
I	Leasing out land for receipts of more than R18	−1.5
II	Leasing out land for receipts of R5–R18	−1.0
	Leasing out land for receipts of up to R5	−0.5
III	Renting land for payments of up to R5	+0.5
IV	Renting land for payments of R5–R18	+1.0
V	Renting land for payment of more than R18	+1.5
Value of means of production		
I	up to R400	−6
II	R400–R600	−4
	R600–R700	−2
III	R700–R800	0
	R800–R900	+2
IV	R900–R1200	+4
V	more than R1200	+6

Source: Naumov and Shardin (1928, 28)

Table 5.6.

Class Structure of the Moscow Sample

Class	Description	Points	% of mainly agricultural households in the sample
I	Proletarian	−11 and below	7.04
II	Semi-proletarian	−6 to −10.5	10.42
III	Middle-peasant (with signs of dependence)	−5.5 to +5.5	53.54
IV	Middle-peasant (with signs of exploiting)	+6 to +10.5	20.28
V	Small capitalist	+11 and above	8.72

Source: Naumov and Shardin (1928, 29–31)

exploitative to the same degree as leasing out R10 worth of stock, or renting 2 desyatins of land (Kritsman 1928d, x–xi). To a large extent, the same problems can also be raised in relation to the work of Naumov and Shardin, where, again, no detailed explanation of their reasoning was offered. However, on the particular issue of the points allocated for hire and sale of labour, Naumov and Shardin would seem to have found a more balanced allocation.

2 The Research of Sulkovskii and Gaister

All of the studies discussed so far involved trying out a chosen set of methods in the study of particular localities. In the last few years of the 1920s, however, more attention was given to translating some of the methodological innovations into the analysis of larger-scale census data. One way of attempting this was by extrapolation from a small number of intensively studied peasant budgets to a larger sample from which the budgets had been selected on a representative basis. For the larger sample the less detailed methods of a general household survey were used.

Two studies used this approach. One, by A. I Gaister, used existing budget and household survey data collected by the TsSU for different regions, while the other, directed by M. Sulkovskii, drew on a smaller-scale study of localities in Saratov *guberniya*.

Sulkovskii's study was based on a survey carried out in 1927 by a team headed by Sulkovskii together with A. A. Kuplenskii and E. A. Rudakova.[4] Like the research of Anisimov and his colleagues and Studenskii, the Saratov study was part of the series of projects undertaken by the Scientific Research Institute of Agricultural Economics; and also, like its precedessors, it combined adaptations of budget research methods developed at the Institute by Chayanov and his colleagues with the basic definition of the problems of studying class differentiation as outlined by Kritsman.

A total of 71 budgets[5] were collected in four different parts of Saratov *guberniya*: Vol'skii *raion*, Bazarno-Karabulakskii *podraion*, Petrovskii *raion*, and Serdobskii *raion*. The four areas were chosen to reflect different levels of involvement in commodity production, with different concentrations on the main local cash crop of sunflowers. Information collected by means of the budgets included the hire and sale of labour power, the hire and lease of cattle and stock, the rent of land, commodity exchanges for cash, credit relations, and the uses of household income. For his scheme of class analysis, Sulkovskii based his approach on the main points of Kritsman's ideas, arguing that the key variables were the different relations of means of production to labour power, and that the chief indicators for classifying households should be drawn from evidence of transactions between households involving means of production, labour power, and land. On the basis of this, by now familiar, approach, Sulkovskii derived three main classes: I, proletarian (18 households); II, *serednyak* petty-bourgeois (42 households); and III, capitalist (11 households). Class II were then further subdivided into (a) households with elements of proletarianization (4 households); (b) simple households (27 households); and (c) households with capitalist elements (11 households) (Kuplenskii *et al.* 1930, 58–74; Sulkovskii 1930, 6–8; Bokarev 1981, 52).

Sulkovskii's next step was then to cross-classify his grouping in terms of relations of exploitation with a grouping based on the value of each household's means of production, taking into account agricultural and non-agricultural implements and stock, buildings, and working and productive animals. This is shown in Table 5.7. He also produced the average value of means of production for each 'class group' in each region (Table 5.8).

On the basis of these figures, Sulkovskii argued that there was a close correspondence between the two ways of classifying his sample in that membership of a particular 'class group' tended to

Table 5.7.
Stratification of Households by their Economic Strength

Class groups	Groups based on value of means of production					
	up to R200	R200– R400	R400– R600	R600– R800	R800– R1000	more than R1000
I	17	1	—	—	—	—
II (a)	2	2	—	—	—	—
II (b)	1	9	8	6	2	1
II (c)	—	—	1	4	2	4
III	—	—	—	1	1	9

Source: Sulkovskii (1930, 11)

Table 5.8.
The Distribution of Means of Production Between Class Groups

Class groups	Average value of means of production per farm (roubles)			
	Vol'skii	B.-Karabulakskii	Petrovskii	Serdobskii
I	98.91	93.93	92.59	162.64
II (a)	163.47	234.84	—	216.83
II (b)	522.41	540.33	467.96	703.66
II (c)	879.51	—	751.04	969.17
III	1313.60	2193.49	1765.62	2444.09

Source: Sulkovskii (1930, 11)

correspond to membership of a group sharing similar values of means of production at similar points on each scale. Although such a correspondence was in fact much clearer for the top and bottom groups on each scale than for those in the middle, he nevertheless concluded that a given value of means of production could be used as an indicator of a household's class position. It was therefore possible, he thought, to extrapolate from his budget sample to a larger sample of 1,025, based on a household survey of the same regions. For this purpose, class I, proletarian households, would be indicated by values of means of production of up to R200; class II, middle peasants, would be in the range R200R–R1000; and class III, capitalist households, would be those with more than R1000 value of means of production. It was then possible to classify the households in the larger sample, as shown in Table 5.9.

A similar approach involving extrapolation from budget data was used by Gaister in an analysis of the 1,242 peasant household budgets which had been collected by the TsSU for 1925–6, comprising information from the North Caucasus, the steppe and forest-steppe regions of the Ukraine, Novosibirsk *okrug*, Smolensk *gubemiya*, and, uniquely in Agrarian Marxist research, some data from the Central Black Earth zone, from Tambov *gubemiya*. Since the budgets had not originally been collected for the purposes of class analysis by the Agrarian Marxists, Gaister did not have an open choice of indicators for classifying households, having to construct a scheme of classification from the data available to him. However, as far as possible, he adapted the information available to the requirements of the same basic approach as had been used in other Agrarian Marxist studies.[6]

For a classification in terms of main relations of exploitation, Gaister devised the following scheme.

A   *Proletarian and semi-proletarian households*
   I   Proletarian households, selling labour for more than 50 days
   II   Semi-proletarian households (*bednyak*), selling labour for 20–50 days, or hiring animals for more than 20 days, or hiring stock for more than 10 days

B   *Independent producers (Seredynak)*
   III   *Serednyak* households, selling or hiring labour for up to 20 days, or hiring or leasing out cattle for up to 20 days, or hiring or leasing out stock for up to 10 days
   IV   Entrepreneurial households, hiring labour for 20–50 days, or leasing out cattle for more than 20 days, or leasing out stock for more than 10 days, or renting more than 2 desyatins of arable land or more than 5 desyatins of meadow

C   *Small capitalist farms*
   V   Semi-capitalist and small capitalist (*kulak*) farms, hiring labour for more than 50 days

The problem for Gaister in devising such a scheme was that, unlike the various local studies, he did not have specific information

Table 5.9.
Classification of the Larger Household Sample

		Region								
		Vol'skii		B.-Karabulakskii		Petrovskii		Serdobskii		Totals	
Class	Value of means of production	No.	%	No.	%	No.	%	No.	%	No.	%
I	up to R200	69	34.2	30	36.6	96	28.0	134	33.6	329	32.0
II	R200–R400	64	63.8	17	56.1	113	66.8	92	59.9	286	62.7
	R400–R600	44		20		73		79		216	
	R600–R800	10		9		24		41		84	
	R800–R1000	10		—		19		27		56	
III	over R1000	4	2.0	6	7.3	18	5.2	26	6.5	54	5.3

Source: Sulkovskii (1930, 11)

on local rates and prices which would have enabled him to make some kind of informed judgement about the significance of various transactions between households. Instead, he had to fall back on his second classification in terms of the economic strength of households, to give some guidance on where to draw the line between various extents of hire, sale, lease, or rent of different factors.

The particular scheme adopted by Gaister for his classification of economic strength was based on the total value of a household's means of production. His scheme produced five groups as follows:

1. households with means of production worth up to R200;
2. households with means of production worth R201–R500;
3. households with means of production worth R501–R800;
4. households with means of production worth R801–R1400;
5. households with means of production worth more than R1400.

Gaister's suggestion, on which he based the justification of his approach, was that households in the strata described above shared not only similar economic positions, but also similar social characteristics. While in poorer households wage labour was an important source of income, in middle and well-off households independent farm income was more important; and, with the greater wealth of households, income from leasing out means of production increased. The main problem with such an approach, however, was that, although there may have been some correspondence in membership of groups on the different scales generally, there would have been a lot of exceptions at the level of particular households, and a very confused picture in the middle levels of the five scales.[7]

There were also more basic problems with the idea of allowing a classification on the basis of the value of means of production to determine the delineation of groups in terms of class characteristics. First, the reasons for drawing the lines between groups at the chosen level of value of means of production was in itself highly arbitrary,[8] and second, however reliable and consistent in itself, it still would have meant that position on a scale of stratification was being used as the basic determinant in the delineation of groups in terms of class characteristics. Thus, ultimately, Gaister's approach, in attempting to extend Agrarian Marxist methods to the use of mass data, in fact marked a step back from the specific feature which had made the Agrarian Marxist approach original (Gaister 1927b, 24–7; 1928a, 105–6).

However, having worked out his scheme of classification, Gaister's next step was to extend the analysis to the whole population of the regions he had studied in terms of budget surveys. He did this, in a manner similar to Sulkovskii as described above, by extrapolating from budget data to the data of the dynamic household survey for 1925 collected by the TsSU. This gave a total coverage of 21 million households. Gaister recognized that such an exercise was not without problems, but nevertheless he offered it as a useful attempt at an approximate outline of the Soviet rural class structure. His final classification of the household survey data is shown in Table 5.10.[9]

Table 5.10.

The Rural Class Structure of the USSR and Selected Regions

		Percentage distribution of class types			
Class types		USSR	Ukraine	N. Caucasus	Urals oblast
I	Proletarian	7.3	16.5	19.3	10.8
II	Semi-proletarian	18.5	21.7	16.8	11.9
III	*Serednyak*	59.6	45.8	40.3	52.6
IV	Entrepreneurial	11.0	10.3	18.3	15.4
V	Semi- and small capitalist	3.6	5.2	5.3	9.3

Source: Gaister (1927b, 28; 1928a, Ch. 8); Lewin (1968, 48)

While Gaister's work was recognized by his fellow researchers at the time as an interesting attempt to extend the Agrarian Marxist approach to the analysis of mass data, it also attracted a number of criticisms. First, it was argued that, for all Gaister's imaginative attempts to process the TsSU data to make it suitable for Marxist class analysis, the way the data had been collected and organized into categories by TsSU statisticians produced a bias towards the middle peasants. This was reflected both in the households chosen to be researched and in the way data was tabulated, so that, for example, figures on the hire of workers (a sign of proletarianization in the conditions of the NEP) were amalgamated with figures for the hire of workers with scarce stock (where, in the condition of NEP, the 'worker' would in fact be in the exploiting position) (Kristman 1928c, 317–32; Naumov 1928a, 208).

Second, it was argued that, while Gaister was attempting to offer an approximate picture of the rural class structure of the Soviet Union as a whole, his chosen regions were not sufficiently representative and displayed a bias towards areas of more extensive agriculture and high levels of commodity production (Popov 1928, 306). Third, problems were raised concerning Gaister's method of extrapolation. To be effective, it was suggested, it would be necessary to have very clear-cut types of peasant household so that extrapolation was clearly from a small number of one type to larger numbers of the same type; but in the conditions of the 1920s the character of the Russian peasantry was too mixed and contradictory for this to be likely.[10] The approach was further undermined by the lack of sufficiently close correspondence between the two different groupings used (Popov 1928, 306; Kritsman 1928c, 355). Finally, it was suggested that Gaister's choice of indicator of clearly capitalist and proletarian households was inadequate. Fifty days' hire of labour was not enough in itself to make a household clearly capitalist, nor was fifty days' sale of labour enough to necessarily make a household proletarian (Naumov 1928, 209).

Despite the many criticisms of Gaister's work, it nevertheless represented an interesting first attempt to go beyond studies of local areas and analyse mass data while still retaining a basis in the detailed information on exploitation provided by budget studies. However, given the problems of achieving sufficient correspondence between budget and household samples to make extrapolation between them successful, as well as the lack of sufficient detail in the budgets to construct a classification based on exploitation, which was independent of the classification based on economic capacity, it was by no means certain that the analysis of mass data was best achieved by using existing TsSU budgets. An alternative approach was also explored, therefore, using national survey data from household surveys only.

3 Analysis of Census and Household Survey Data

There were two main attempts at the analysis of existing census and general household survey data conducted by people associated with the Agrarian Marxist group, one headed by Nemchinov and the other by a commission chaired by Kritsman. The first approach, adopted by Nemchinov, for analysis of the 1927 TsSU dynamic survey, proposed a classification based on total value of the means of production in conjunction with a combination table which, reflecting the limitations of the TsSU statistics, was largely made up of qualitative indicators of exploitation.

The grouping based on value of means of production placed households in groups as follows:

1. without means of production;
2. with means of production of a total value between R1 and R200;
3. with means of production of a total value between R201 and R400;
4. with means of production of a total value between R401 and R800;
5. with means of production of a total value between R801 and R1600;
6. with means of production of a total value of more than R1600.

The same bands of values were to be used for all regions, and the main criterion for deciding on the particular cut-off points between them was that the richest and poorest households at the top and bottom of each group should not have means of production worth more than double their counterparts in the group below (Nemchinov 1928a, 112).

In order to categorize households in terms of relations of exploitation, the following grouping was adopted. For mainly agricultural households, classification was based on the hire and sale of labour and the hire and lease of means of production. For households whose income was mainly non-agricultural, the type and class character of their main activity was used. As far as actual measurement of exploitation in agriculture was concerned; while this was not possible given the data for transactions in means of production, it was possible for the hire and sale of labour. Hire of labour could be measured in number of days of hire, and although this was not possible for the sale of labour, it was possible to distinguish between households where sale of labour was the chief source of income, where it was the primary source of money income, or where only a little was sold.

The cross-classification of the two scales, and the resulting class categories obtained by Nemchinov is shown in Table 5.11. When used in the analysis of the 1927 dynamic household survey, a class composition for the USSR as a whole was obtained; this is given in Table 5.12.

The analysis of the dynamic survey provided the most comprehensive and detailed attempt there had been to analyse the class structure of the Soviet countryside, as opposed to its stratification in terms of groups defined by sown area. Figures were also provided, as a result of the same analysis, giving the class structure of each republic and of each economic zone. In addition, tables were produced showing the interrelation between the two schemes of classification by value of means of production and indicators of exploitation for each republic, as well as for the Soviet Union as a whole (TsSU 1929, 89–155). However, despite its wealth of detail, it must be suggested that various problems in the way the scheme of analysis was constructed may have undermined the reliability of its results.

First, although it did contain some element of measurement of exploitation, the final results were still strongly influenced by the main indirect indicator of class, the total value of means of production. Moreover, the intervals chosen for the grouping based on means of production seemed to be the result of a mechanical and rather arbitrary approach. The researchers allocated households to groups with the aim of maintaining clear dividing lines in terms of the figures, which meant that the grouping did not necessarily reflect a social division in terms of relations of exploitation between households. Finally, because of the weakness of the element of measurement of exploitation, it would also have been difficult to weigh up the relative significance of involvement in different relations in a household with complex or contradictory tendencies.[11]

Lastly, in this section one further attempt at the analysis of mass data should be mentioned. This was the result of a commission set up by the VSNKh in 1927 to determine the class structure of the Soviet population as a whole on the basis of the information produced by the 1926 national census. Among the members of the commission were Kritsman, Strumilin, and Larin. On the basis of a narrower range of information than was to be available from the 1927 dynamic census, they produced the classification shown in Table 5.13.[12]

While the advantage of these figures was that they were derived from the census, which had a wider base than the dynamic survey, the poorer quality of detailed information on which they were based made them of more dubious value. *Bednyaks* were defined entirely on the basis of traditional indirect indicators of class, that is, in terms of

Table 5.11.
Nemchinov's Scheme of Analysis of Dynamic Survey Data

Households	Value of means of production*					
	None	R1–R200	R201–R400	R401–R800	R801–R1600	more than R1600
1. Sale of labour the chief source of income	Prolet.	Prolet.	Semi-prolet.	Prolet.	—	—
2. Sale of labour the primary source of money income.	Prolet.	Semi-prolet.	Semi-prolet.	Semi-prolet.	—	—
3. Selling a little labour power	Prolet.	Semi-prolet.	Simple commod. prod.	SCP	SCP	SCP
4. Not hiring labour, and						
(a) hiring means of production	Semi-prolet.	SCP	SCP	SCP	SCP	SCP
(b) using own means of production	Semi-prolet.	SCP	SCP	SCP	SCP	SCP Small capital.
(c) leasing out means of production	—	SCP	SCP	SCP	SCP	
5. Hiring of labour for up to 50 days, and						
(a) hiring means of production	Semi-prolet.	SCP	SCP	SCP	SCP	SCP

(b) using own means of production	—	SCP	SCP	SCP	SCP
(c) leasing out means of production	—	SCP	SCP	SCP	Small capital.
6. Hiring labour for 51–75 days	—	SCP	SCP	SCP	Small capital.
7. Hiring labour for 76–150 days	—	SCP	SCP	Small capital.	Small capital.
8. Hiring labour for more than 150 days	—	SCP	SCP	Small capital.	Small capital.

*Prolet. = proletarian; Semi-prol. = semi-proletarian; SCP = simple commodity producers; Small capital. = small capitalist

Source: Nemchinov (1928a, 117–18)

Table 5.12.
The Class Composition of the Soviet Countryside
(from Nemchinov's analysis of the 1927 dynamic survey)

Groups	No. of farms thousands	% of each sector	% of total	Population thousands	% of each sector	% of total
Total	25,037	—	100.0	123,541	—	100.0
*Non-agricultural sector**	2,053	100.0	8.2	8,648	100.0	7.0
Prolet.	661	32.2	2.7	2,266	26.2	1.8
Semi-prol.	727	35.4	2.9	2,715	31.4	2.2
SCP	587	28.6	2.3	3,174	36.7	2.6
Small capital.	78	3.8	0.3	493	5.7	0.4
Agricultural sector	22,984	100.0	91.8	114,893	100.0	93.0
Collective farms	164	0.7	0.7	708	0.6	0.6
Proletariat in the socialist sector	526	2.3	2.1	1,592	1.4	1.3
Private sector	22,294	97.0	89.0	112,593	98.0	91.1
*of which:**						
Prolet.	1,841	8.0	7.3	7,255	6.3	5.9
Semi-prol.	4,643	20.2	18.5	18,383	16.0	14.9
SCP	14,914	64.9	59.6	81,096	70.6	65.6
Small capital.	896	3.9	3.6	5,859	5.1	4.7

*Abbreviations as for Table 5.11.
Source: TsSU (1929, 88)

Table 5.13.
Class Structure of the Soviet Agricultural Population
(based on the 1926 national census)

Class	Indicators	No. of people
Proletariat		4,713,000
Workers	Wage workers	4,374,000
Employees	Salaried workers	339,000
Peasants		108,010,000
Bednyaks	*either* (a) households without working animals and sowing up to 4 desyatins, along with 50% of those sowing 4–6 desyatins, *or* (b) households with 1 head of working cattle and sowing up to 1 desyatin	21,106,000
Serednyaks	Households without indicators of either *bednyak* or entrepreneurial status	81,045,000
Entrepreneurs	*either* (a) households with a total annual value of means of production of more than R1600, and employing hired labour for more than 50 days per year, *or* (b) households with a total value of means of production of R800–R1600, and employing labour for more than 75 days per year, *or* (c) households with a total value of means of production of R400–R800, and employing labour for more than 150 days per year.	5,859,000

Source: TsSU (1929, 42–3, 940)

sown area and ownership of working animals. Moreover, the highly arbitrary nature of the figures is shown by the adding of what must have been a guess of 50 per cent of the 4–6 desyatin group to the group sowing up to 4 desyatins to make up the *bednyak* category. Entrepreneurial households, on the other hand, were at least defined in terms of value indicators, and of evidence of the hire of labour, which were indicators more likely to be regarded as meaningful by Kritsman and his colleagues. However, information regarded as more important by Kritsman—on transactions in the means of production—were not available. Moreover, there was no way of knowing how many households also experienced exploitation, to be weighed against the apparent signs of entrepreneurship. Weakest of all was the category of *serednyak*, which was merely a residual category with no positive indicators of its own at all. It is not surprising in the circumstances that Kritsman tacitly accepted the bland labels of *bednyak*, *serednyak*, and entrepreneur instead of his usual insistence on class categories, because, clearly, the groups identified by the commission's analysis could not count as social classes in the way Kritsman and his colleagues understood the term.

4 Assessments and Criticisms

As can be seen from the discussion above, in the space of only five years, from 1925 to 1929, Kritsman and his colleagues produced research which, for a relatively small group of principal researchers, was impressive both in its volume and in its degree of sophistication.[13] They carried out five detailed local studies (including Nemchinov's Urals project), published full analyses of the findings of two of them (Samara and Saratov), and produced partial results of the others. They also devised new methods for the analysis of existing mass data, and in one case (that of Gaister), produced a full account of the results obtained. In the five years of their research, moreover, they effected a radical reorientation in the criteria for collecting and processing Soviet agrarian statistics as well as initiating a number of theoretical innovations in the study of the Soviet peasantry.

However, despite the impact their research had on the field of Soviet agrarian research at the time, the work of the Agrarian Marxists remained largely unfinished. Each of their projects was basically experimental, trying out new ideas or new combinations of existing ideas in the study of peasant differentiation. The various solutions proposed by the researchers to problems of both the collection and the analysis of data were only provisional, and by the time the research was brought to an end no finally agreed research approach had been decided upon. The various approaches adopted were probably debated both within the group and in discussion with other researchers.

The irony, therefore, is that, in attempting to evaluate the methodology of the Kritsman group's research, there is little detailed contemporary criticism to draw on. Nor is there any great amount of discussion of problems of research methods in the writings of the Kritsman school themselves. The most detailed account of their methods of study was provided by Anisimov and his colleagues in their report on the Volokolamsk study, but it is not always clear from this what problems of method the researchers faced or how precisely they resolved them. It is necessary, therefore, to raise some questions about what the likely problems of method were and how significant they might be for the production of reliable analysis by means of the approach developed by Kritsman and his colleagues. In most cases, because the researchers have not left any published record of their discussions of such problems, they can only be raised as questions. It is impossible to know how far such problems affected the results of the research. It is suggested that the questions below are the main issues about which it would be useful to know more in order to evaluate the results of the research of the Kritsman school, and which it would be necessary to give serious attention to in any modern replication of the work.

Questions concerning the survey research methods

The research methods adopted by Kritsman and his colleagues were primarily those of survey research which had originally been developed by the *zemstvo* statisticians. In the course of their work, they experimented with various applications of both mass household survey approaches and detailed sample survey budget studies. Most of the projects aimed in some way to combine a sample budget survey with a wider household survey, but by the end of the 1920s it was still not clear whether an acceptable approach could be found using household surveys alone, or, if not, exactly what the relationship between the two types of survey should be, and what kinds of issue each was most suited to studying.

For the purposes of classifying households into class groups, most of the work used a sample budget survey in order to examine in detail the transactions which were to provide the indicators of class differentiation; and then, in the cases of Gaister's and Sulkovskii's work, these results were extrapolated on to the data of a mass household survey. This was one way of using the methods that, for example, were pioneered in Volokolamsk, which were exclusively based on budget survey data, and of making them useful for a classification of all households in a given area. Presumably, however, there was an argument from some of the researchers that the use of budget survey methods was too costly (in time or labour). This at least might have been the reason for the experimental work of Naumov and Shardin (1928), or Nemchinov's attempt to analyse the dynamic survey data, both of which tried to develop a class analysis without using budget surveys. However, as noted above, neither the attempts to use household survey data only (Nemchinov 1927a, Naumov and Shardin 1928) nor the attempts to extrapolate from budget sample survey data on to household survey data (Gaister 1928a, Sulkovskii 1930) were entirely satisfactory in providing a detailed analysis of the kind called for by Kritsman.

If the goals of the Kritsman group's approach had been incorporated into the programme of TsSU agrarian research, some way of resolving the problem of choice of techniques would have had to be found. Presumably the ideal solution would have been mass budget surveys, but this would hardly have been practicable. Therefore the research of Naumov and Shardin would have had to be evaluated and compared with the approaches involving extrapolation from budget survey data. Most likely, there would have been further attempts to work out more effective bases for extrapolation from budget data. Depending on the success of these, it might then have been possible to construct a systematic research programme linking regular budget surveys of chosen samples to represent a wide range of economic and ecological conditions and regional variations within the dynamic household census.

Whatever the final research programme might have looked like, not only would it have needed to yield data enabling the classification of households into groups defined in terms of class tendencies, but, if such a class analysis was to be put to any practical purpose, it would also have needed to provide data for an analysis of the production relations and organization of farms in different class groups. For this, quite detailed budget survey data would have been essential. Given this consideration, it seems likely that a programme linking budget and household surveys would have been preferred to one concentrating on a household survey only.

The reliability of the data

Apart from problems of which type of survey method to use, there were also problems concerning the reliability of the information they produced. Problems in this category relate both to the question of whether, on the whole, the peasants proved to be trustworthy respondents, and to the question of whether their knowledge or memories were adequate to answer the questions posed them. On the question of trust, there was probably a significant problem in whether the peasants would have been prepared to divulge information about their income and wealth to urban intellectual outsiders who, moreover, would have been associated in peasants' minds with officialdom. Better-off peasants in particular would have been extremely wary of giving information to outsiders which could have led to their being categorized as *kulaks* or *zazhitochnye*, thus earning official suspicion in the mid-1920s, and outright hostile treatment at the end of the decade. Furthermore, for all peasants, any seemingly official enquiries about their income would have provoked the suspicion that the outsiders were working on behalf of tax authorities. In general, such problems may well have resulted in an underestimation of the growth of entrepreneurial households.[14]

On the other hand, another source of possible bias may have laid too much stress on the evidence from better-off households. This would have arisen from the excessive complexity of some of the questionnaire forms used, especially for the more detailed budget surveys, and especially where a researcher left forms with peasants to complete rather than guiding them personally through the forms. While one procedure involved questioning peasants only at the end of the agricultural year, which gave rise to problems of the peasant being able to remember various transactions and production activities adequately, an alternative approach, especially in budget surveys, was to ask peasants to keep regular records during the course of the agricultural year. This latter approach in particular, relying on certain minimum standards of literacy, was likely to find a better response rate among the more literate peasants, who in most cases tended to be among the more wealthy.

A further problem concerned the locations chosen for the various research projects. All the specially designed local surveys of the group were carried out in regions other than the Central Agricultural Zone of European Russia. The group chose to study either rural areas in Moscow *guberniya* (Anisimov *et al.* 1927; Naumov and Shardin 1928) or the 'borderlands' of European Russia in the Urals, Samara, and Saratov, (Nemchinov 1926b, Vermenichev *et al.* 1928,

Sulkovskii 1930). Only Gaister's more wide-ranging study included data from the Central Agricultural Region (Tambov *guberniya*), although in the case of his study the information from the TsSU budget surveys was much less comprehensive than that collected in the specially designed surveys of the Kritsman group. Although more local and detailed budget surveys were carried out in the same period, these did not use direct class indicators of the type advocated by Kritsman (Studenskii 1926, 1927; Chayanov 1929b).

It might be argued that the effect of locating their research outside the Central Agricultural Region was to overemphasize areas of greater availability of land where capitalist farming based on more extensive agriculture could more easily develop. From the point of view of the desirability of investigating the interrelation between class and production organization in all types of farming, such an argument is well-founded, although it must always be remembered that the research available was brought to an end long before it was finished. However, there are grounds for questioning whether concentration on either metropolitan, highly commoditized, areas or on borderlands actually slanted the research towards areas where capitalist development would be more likely. Kritsman, for example, in his review of existing studies in 1925, talked about capitalism emerging even more clearly on the basis of shortages in means of production in areas of intensive farming than in areas of extensive farming.

Finally, in considering possible bias, the question of the adequacy of information available on general economic conditions should be raised. An important category of information, on the basis of which an analysis of households' social characteristics was made, was local levels of prices and rates of hire of various factors of production. For the most part, the researchers relied on local statistical bureaux to provide these, which raises problems about the extent to which officials (even where locally based) would have been privy to the real rates of exchange between peasants—or, indeed, whether there were always generally prevailing values to be discovered. The Agrarian Marxists' research assumed that generalized commodity production prevailed among the peasants of European Russia to the extent that stable local or regional market price systems did exist and in most cases would have provided the basis for transactions between households. This was, however, an assumption, and no detailed study was conducted by Kritsman and his colleagues to verify it.

While there were statistics to show that all groups of peasant were heavily involved in commodity production and commodity transactions in means of production (e.g. Lositskii 1927, 13; Vermenichev 1928b, 138), such information did not extend to a consideration of how far general price levels prevailed. While it is very likely that there were generalized price systems in European Russia, and especially in the more heavily commoditized areas where most of the Agrarian Marxist studies were carried out, this might not have been true for all areas of the Soviet Union; and this would have given rise to problems when extending the research to provide a picture of the agrarian class structure of the country as a whole.

Problems of measuring exploitation

A discussion of the problems of establishing accurate prices leads in turn to the question of whether use of data on prices was in fact necessary for the purposes of research on peasant class relations. Clearly, the extent to which various Agrarian Marxist researchers were prepared to experiment with approaches that involved doing without detailed budgets, or, in the case of Nemchinov, without measures of the extent of inter-household transactions at all, implied that there was at least some sympathy for developing an approach which was not based on details of prices or monetary rates.

Indeed, if Marx's methods were to be followed to the letter, then value should have been measured in units of generalized labour time. Moreover, to some extent, the indicators chosen in some research projects were measured in units of time, especially in days of work. However, in a petty-commodity economy, where, as Kritsman was arguing, exploitation took place primarily through transactions in means of production, even though these were the relations through which he suggested a surplus was expropriated, the concept of generalized labour time may well have been very problematic. Perhaps for this reason, therefore, it seemed acceptable to adopt the alternative of using information of prevailing prices, which, in terms of the labour theory of value, was necessarily only an approximate measure of the degree to which a surplus was expropriated. It is, however, surprising that none of the group seemed to consider it worthwhile to discuss the interrelation of value and price in terms of their research, especially given that this has been a prominent theme in discussions of Marxist economists.

However, given that indicators expressed in terms of prices in a sense reflected value only indirectly, and, furthermore, that it was difficult to discover exact information on price levels anyway, the use of a points system, as used in the Samara study, to represent the approximate values involved in various transactions was, no doubt, more appropriate. It was probably no less approximate than attempts at putting money values to all transactions, and was certainly less arduous to apply in research. In order to prevent the points allocation being arbitrary, some idea of prevailing price levels would still be necessary in order to make the same points score represent roughly the same value lost or appropriated, but it would avoid the necessity of ascribing a money equivalent to every factor of production involved.

The adoption of a points system on the basis of more careful groundwork than that adopted in Samara or Moscow would probably be sufficient for research aimed at the grouping of households into class groups. However, more detailed information, expressed in monetary values, would probably be required for in-depth studies of the relations and organization of production, which was, after all, one of the main aims of the Kritsman group. With regard to the organization of production, involving a study of the relative values of investment and returns in different sectors of peasant farming, it is worth noting that even Chayanov and his colleagues were moving over to the use of precise monetary value expressions, and they, much more than the Marxists, would have had strong theoretical reasons to be wary of assuming the validity of expressing the processes of peasant farming in money values.

The schemes of analysis

In addition to the problems involved in carrying out the fieldwork, in collecting information, and in deciding how to measure it, there were further problems concerning how precisely indicators of class tendencies should be defined, and how they should be interrelated in a scheme of analysis.

Two particular differences of approach emerged on such questions in the various research projects. First, there was a clear difference in definition of indicators of exploitation between, on the one hand, the approaches of both Nemchinov's Urals research and the Volokolamsk study (and Studenskii's work in the middle Volga, which followed the Volokolamsk model) and, on the other hand, the Samara and Saratov studies and Naumov and Shardin's work on Moscow *guberniya*. The former gathered evidence of the extent to which factors of production from one household were used on the farm of another, and in what proportion to the factors belonging to the other household. Despite differences in the way they sought to determine the interrelation between 'own' and 'other's' factors, the same general idea was shared by Nemchinov, Kritsman, and the Volokolamsk researchers. The latter group, however, adopted the alternative approach of gathering information specifically on transactions between households, and in particular on the hire and sale of labour, rent and lease of stock, and rent and lease of land. This no doubt made the gathering of information simpler than it had been in the former approach, but an implication of this revision, unexplored in the published accounts of the research, was that there was no longer any way of assessing the relative weight of independent elements compared with either its exploiting or exploited aspects. While one household could be compared with another in terms of, for example, the number of points it gained from transactions at its neighbours' expense, there was no way of knowing how big a share of the total farming operations the exploiting elements consisted of. It would have been possible for households with equal points, reflecting the same amount of exploiting activities, to have differed from each other in the impact such exploitation made on their overall organization if the exploiting aspects coincided in one case with very little independent self-sufficient farming, and in the other case with a large amount of independent operations. It is difficult to know the consequences of the different approaches, but it seems quite possible that the same household could have been classified in a different class group according to the research approach adopted.

Second, there was a difference in approach between Anisimov and his colleagues, who allocated households into class groups purely on the basis of indicators of exploitation, and the other studies, which in addition incorporated a classification based on economic capacity. As noted above, this was seen in each case as a secondary classification to modify the results of the one based on exploitation indicators (except in the case of the analyses of mass data). To some extent it is possible to see the usefulness of such a second form of classification, perhaps as an alternative to a scheme which specifically incorporated a measure of the degree of a household's independent farming. On the other hand, it meant the extension of an element of a stratification approach, of ranking households in an order according to the extent of their possession of certain values, and this had been precisely the kind of approach, using indirect indicators, which Kritsman had argued against. In this context, it is interesting to note that the project in which Kritsman's influence was strongest, in Volokolamsk, was one example of a project not using a classification based on the extent of a household's income or ownership of means of production.

The problems of determining intervals between groups

A further problem for all forms of classification, whether by sown area, value of means of production, or indicators of exploitation, was that of establishing the most appropriate intervals at which the range of cases, from richest to poorest, or from most capitalist to most proletarian, would be broken in order to delineate different groups or classes. Given the lack, in most cases, of any detailed discussion in published research reports of the criteria by which groups were delineated, the suspicion must be that the lines of demarcation were drawn somewhat arbitrarily. Such a suspicion is reinforced by the tendencies for intervals to occur, for example, at convenient round numbers in percentage scales. Slightly more sophisticated was, for example, Nemchinov's stipulation, in his analysis of the dynamic survey, that the top or bottom cases of one group should have a score of at least double the corresponding case in the group below. This at least demonstrated an attempt to establish clear gaps between groups. Rather more sophisticated attempts to establish statistically significant intervals were made by Studenskii (1929), and more recently by Obozhda (1977).

However, whatever level of sophistication is introduced into such exercises, basic problems would seem to remain. First, there will always be households each side of a line which will share more characteristics with each other than with a household at the opposite end of their respective groups. Second, statistical neatness does not necessarily conform to social reality, and therefore the widest gap, statistically speaking, between households will not necessarily represent the best dividing line between one social class and another.

The conceptualization of capitalism and of class

Perhaps most basic of all the issues relating to the work of the Agrarian Marxists were the concepts of class and of capitalism. Following in the tradition of Marx and Lenin, their ideas were influenced by certain fundamental assumptions: first, that with the growth of small commodity production the development of capitalism in agriculture was necessarily under way, and second, that the end-point of such a process would be the formation of clear-cut classes of an agrarian bourgeoisie and a proletariat. As noted above, in Kritsman's hands the use of such a theory was open-ended. Following Lenin, Kritsman thought that Soviet post-revolutionary society was made up of a complex of different structures and that the future shape of the Soviet countryside would depend on which combination of structures became predominant. Furthermore, the existence of Soviet state power ensured the possibility of policies to counteract the inherent trends in small commodity production for capitalist relations to become fully developed.

Nevertheless, despite the degree of flexibility in Agrarian Marxist thinking, the research was framed in a context of basic assumptions which expected the emergence of capitalism out of a peasantry where small commodity production had increasingly taken hold. Even if they expected and hoped for a different, socialist, outcome to the development of peasant agriculture, their method consisted of abstracting the question of class differentiation from the complexity of processes taking place within the peasantry in order to analyse it more clearly, and, following what they saw as the logic of such differentiation, to identify the full development of capitalism. This meant, first, that their questions were phrased in ways which tended to see the expropriation of one household's surplus by another as capitalist exploitation, and, second, either that the preponderance of exploiting activities in a household was a sign that it was developing into a fully capitalist enterprise, or that a preponderance of exploited elements was a sign that a household was undergoing full proletarianization.

Such assumptions did not take the form of dogmatic predictions; but since they helped shape the research by defining what the researchers expected to be most likely (at least in abstraction from a complex situation which also included intervention by the Soviet state), the problem arises as to whether the Agrarian Marxist conceptualization of differentiation allowed sufficiently for alternative outcomes to that of complete capitalist development. First, on the question of whether the extraction of a household's surplus was necessarily capitalist exploitation, as noted above, Kritsman in fact enumerated a whole range of possible class meanings of different combinations of 'own' and 'others' means of production, labour, and land, which covered most possibilities from feudal survivals to new socialist relations. Furthermore, as will be discussed below in Chapter 7, the Agrarian Marxists began to turn their attention to empirical research on socialized agriculture in the last years of 1920s. However, it was not clear from these discussions how, in empirical research on class differentiation, exchanges as part of feudal relations, or socialist co-operative relations, were to be distinguished from the transactions of a commodity economy in transition to capitalism. The Agrarian Marxists had been criticized for this failing by Chayanov, who, given his perspective, worked on the assumption that transactions of a potentially capitalist type would figure only as a minor part of the relations between Russian peasant households (Chayanov 1929a, 321).

There was some awareness on the part of the Agrarian Marxists that such a criticism had to be answered. Raevich, for example, expressed the need for developing some method of establishing the meaning of different inter-household relations in their specific social contexts (Raevich 1928, 106). Part of the solution lay, no doubt, in maintaining a close link between survey research and ethnographic study. Although published accounts of the various surveys rarely mentioned such a link, it was not entirely absent. In fact, Kritsman's original formulation of the problem and his choice of key indices had been informed by ethnographic work, such as the studies by Bolshakov (1924) and Yakovlev (1923, 1924). The Kritsman group also would have remained in regular touch with later examples of such work through their editorial duties in *Na Agrarnom Fronte*, in which such studies were occasionally featured or reviewed.

Nevertheless, however 'sensitized' the survey research became as a result of its links with ethnographic work, the problem still remained that, at the level of the individual household, there was no entirely satisfactory means of determining the social meaning of a relationship. While direct observation of specific transactions such as the hire, lease, or sale of factors of production would seem, by definition, to rule out non-commercial exchanges, it would not necessarily have been very easy in practice to find out if an exchange was carried out on commercial terms, as part of traditional political obligations, or as part of some co-operative or neighbourly offer of assistance. No doubt these problems can be overstated, but in the case of transitional forms of social organization there may have been quite complex patterns of coexistence of different types of relations between households; and, in the absence of details of how far the researchers understood the social context and the subjective meanings involved, it cannot be certain that their judgements were always reliable.

Second, apart from the question of recognizing capitalism as distinct from other forms of social organization, there was also the problem of recognizing classes. More specifically, it involved the question of whether a predominantly exploiting or exploited character necessarily signified that a household was becoming clearly capitalist or clearly proletarian. Again, on this point Kritsman's discussions of the issue displayed a flexible approach. He explicitly took Gaister (1928a) to task, for example, for seeming to claim too categorically that his method had identified a clearly capitalist class in the countryside. The Agrarian Marxist approach, Kritsman insisted, could only indicate tendencies towards class formation within the generally 'petty-bourgeois mass' of the peasantry (Kritsman 1928c, 342). The problem still lay, however, in deciding when such tendencies could be construed to have culminated in the clear formation of a capitalist farm.

The implication in Kritsman's own work, and in the Volokolamsk research, seemed to be that, when the proportion of entrepreneurial or exploiting elements in a household's activities had gone beyond a certain point, then a household could be regarded as capitalist. For Nemchinov, and in many of the other projects which followed his lead on this point, a combination of a certain level of exploiting elements with a certain minimum capacity measured by income or total value of means of production were necessary. What both approaches seem to have lacked, however, was any means of establishing the extent to which a household was *accumulating* capital.

In this they were by no means exceptional in the context of research on peasant differentiation. Earlier or contemporary Russian approaches were equally silent on this point, as have been most more recent studies in other parts of the world. In one important respect, however, the work of the Agrarian Marxists showed greater clarity and originality than other studies or schools of thought. In practice, although not fully self-consciously, Kritsman and his colleagues were beginning to develop an approach which put more stress on relations than on concrete, fully formed classes in their understanding of the differentiation issue. Whereas other approaches operated with concepts of clearly formed classes which were largely homogeneous and had clearly discernable class characteristics and interests, Kritsman's view of the peasants was more in terms of fluid relations of complex and contradictory characters which permeated each household, so that during the transitional period it was not usually clear which class characteristics would become predominant. Implicit, although not developed by Kritsman, was even the possibility that some households might never take on a clear class character, but might remain as part of an internally contradictory 'petty-bourgeois mass'.

However, despite the originality of their conceptualization of the class character of the peasants, these ideas were never fully developed by the Agrarian Marxists. Nor did they ever fully confront the questions of identifying and measuring capitalist accumulation, or of deciding on indicators of a fully developed capitalist farm. In the end, the work remained unfinished. Indeed, it was suddenly cut off before the group had time to consolidate it, or take stock of the results of their initial experimental projects. How the thinking of the Agrarian Marxists would have developed is impossible to say. However, despite the various unresolved problems discussed in this section, their work remains an interesting source of ideas on methods and methodologies for the study of peasant class relations, and a powerful stimulus for further thinking. Moreover, despite problems with their methods and the data it produced, the studies of Kritsman and his colleagues offered a great deal of useful information and interesting insights into aspects of Russian peasant society which were not revealed by other approaches and sources of information. In the next chapter it is to these findings of the Agrarian Marxist research, tentative and incomplete as it was, that discussion turns.

Notes

1. In order to arrive at a figure for the total value of a household's means of

production, the researchers took the sum of the value of farm buildings, farm and transport stock, and all animals and poultry. However, there must be some doubt about the reliability of their figures because of the way they obtained them. Their method was simply to ask each householder to estimate the value of their own means of production. The researchers spent little time trying to justify this approach in the text, merely commenting that there were differences of opinion on the best way to evaluate means of production.

2. No explanation is given in Vermenichev *et al.* (1928) for why the figures add up to only 99.6 per cent.

3. Since both Kritsman and the Samara researchers agreed that days of labour hired were not exactly equivalent to days of labour sold in terms of the significance for exploitation, presumably Kritsman would have retained some kind of weighting in his calculation.

4. Two books were published on the basis of this study: A. Kuplenskii *et al.* (1930), which included a methodological introduction, followed by tables showing the complete research data, and Sulkovskii (1930), containing detailed discussion and analysis of the data. The following discussion is based mainly on Sulkovskii (1930).

5. An earlier article, reporting a preliminary stage of the research, reported on 72 budgets (Sulkovskii 1928b), but the final reports (Kuplenskii *et al.* (1930), and Sulkovskii (1930)) discuss only 71.

6. The project, of which Gaister's book was the main product, was set up at the Communist Academy in 1926 under the sponsorship of Rabkrin, and under the direction of a committee led by Kritsman and including Gaister, Vermenichev, Raevich, and Nemchinov. The project as a whole was to be concerned with various aspects of the peasantry and their farming, and with the process of transition to socialist agriculture. Topics for study, apart from the question of class differentiation, included the organization and techniques of peasant farming, agricultural co-operatives, state farms, and agriculture in relation to internal and international trade. Reports of the project were published under the general editorship of Yakovlev in 1928. Analysis of data on peasant differentiation was carried out by Gaister along with S. G. Uzhanskii, I. D. Lopatin, P. P. Pleshkov, and I. D. Belikevich. It seems, however, that the study was never fully completed, and Yakovlev was obliged to draw on the work of Gaister alone in the report of the project (Yakovlev 1928, v, 22). Gaister published his analysis in a number of places, initially in article form (Gaister 1927a, 1927b) and as part of Gosplan's Control Figures for 1927–8, and then in book form (Gaister 1928a).

7. For Gaister's justification that such a clear relation between the two classifications existed, see his table (1927b). However, even if this is accepted, there must remain doubts that such a relation would normally hold, and therefore the technique used here might not be

generally more suitable for research of a similar type.

8. Some very interesting recent work by modern Soviet scholars has attempted to devise more adequate methods for determining the dividing lines between strata using the budget studies of the 1920s; See, e.g., Bokarev (1981, 115–26); Obozhda (1977, 25–36). For all its sophistication, however, such approaches do not overcome the second problem referred to in the text above, that of Gaister's giving priority to a stratification grouping in order to determine the dividing lines between class groups.

9. Although the figures for the Ukraine total only 99.5 per cent, no explanation for this is given in Gaister's text.

10. For the same reasons, Sulkovskii's use of extrapolation may have been equally problematic, although, since both the smaller and larger samples were drawn from a more narrowly defined area, there would have been more chance of an adequate correspondence between the samples. Because Sulkovskii's work was not published until 1930, shortly before the work of the Agrarian Marxists was terminated, no published criticism of his work from fellow researchers was available.

11. Nemchinov had earlier proposed an alternative scheme along similar lines which, while more comprehensive in the range of indicators it used, in fact relied exclusively on qualitative indicators for its characterization of the relations of peasant farms. This qualitative grouping would then have been used in conjunction with the same grouping in terms of value of means of production as described above (Nemchinov 1927a, 80; Cox 1983a, 419–22).

12. For a report on the findings of the commission, see Larin (1928, 27), where he gives rather different figures from those above. I have assumed that the figures given in Table 5.13, which were published later than Larin's work in the official handbook of the TsSU are more likely to be accurate. For further background to the commission and its works, see Carr (1976, 443–9).

13. In addition to the studies described above, there was at least one other attempt to use a version of the Agrarian Marxist approach in empirical research. This was carried out by V. Kavraiskii and I. Nusinov in Siberia (1927, 1929). While not actually part of the Kritsman school, these two authors attracted the attention of Kritsman and his colleagues who gave their work critical approval (Kritsman 1928a; Libkind 1928; see also Orlov 1929). It seems that the work focused on southern Siberia, drawing on household and dynamic survey data, using a combination of indicators including sale of labour and lease of stock alongside 'natural' indicators. Unfortunately, I have not been able to trace copies of either work of these two authors.

14. Such a judgement is confirmed, for example, by an in-depth study of cluster samples of households in the Ukraine which suggested that the

data produced by a 1927 survey of households led to an underestimation of the emergence of a small capitalist group. For discussion of this point see Davies (1980, 26).

6

The Social Character of the Peasantry:
The Findings of the Agrarian Marxists' Research

1 The Comparison between Official Statistics and the Agrarian Marxists' Findings

To appreciate the different perspective offered on Russian peasant society by the Agrarian Marxist research, it is useful to compare their findings with the conventionally accepted picture provided by official spokesmen, statisticians, and researchers up to the mid–1920s. The drawing of such comparisons was also important for the Agrarian Marxists at the time because, by demonstrating inconsistencies between the picture of differentiation produced by sown area figures and their own approach, they were able to reinforce the doubts about the TsSU figures which the critiques of Kritsman and the Rabkrin commission had raised.

First, using data for the Soviet Union as a whole, discrepancies could be seen between sown area groupings and those based on total value of means of production; these are shown in Table 6.1. A similar lack of congruence can be seen in comparisons at local level with classifications based on relations of exploitation. These are illustrated, for example, from Nemchinov's Urals study in Table 6.2 and from the Samara study in Table 6.3, where in both cases a classification based on relations of exploitation is compared with groupings based on sown area and an ownership of working animals. In each example, the degree of congruence between groups defined by 'natural indicators' and groups defined by value indicators or by balance of relations of exploitation was rather weak.[1] If the arguments (outlined in Chapters 4 and 5 above) for the superiority of exploitation or value indices over natural indices were accepted, which increasingly they were, then the above comparisons seemed conclusive proof of the inadequacy of sown area or even ownership of animals as indicators of class tendencies.

However, as noted in the chapters above, the main purpose of much of the work of the Agrarian Marxists was not only to develop

Table 6.1.
Classification of Farms Based on Sown Area and Value of Means of Production

Groups defined by total value of means of production	Percentage distribution of farms by sown area									
	0–0.09 ha	0.1–1.19 ha	1.20–2.29 ha	2.30–3.38 ha	3.39–4.47 ha	4.48–6.66 ha	6.67–8.84 ha	8.85–11.03 ha	11.04–17.59 ha	17.60+ ha
I Without means of production	46.4	28.8	14.5	6.1	2.3	1.4	0.4	0.1	0.0	0.0
II Up to R100	21.4	33.3	23.0	12.1	5.6	3.6	0.7	0.2	0.1	0.0
III R101–R200	8.2	23.8	28.4	19.0	10.3	7.7	1.8	0.5	0.3	0.0
IV R201–R400	3.1	11.7	22.1	22.4	16.0	16.3	5.6	1.8	0.9	0.1
V R401–R800	1.5	6.1	13.1	18.6	17.3	22.7	11.1	5.1	3.9	0.6
VI R801–R1600	1.5	4.7	7.0	11.0	12.8	22.0	14.8	9.3	12.4	4.5
VII more than R1600	5.3	8.2	7.0	7.0	6.5	13.5	11.0	8.6	15.5	17.4

Source: TsSU (1929, 128)

Table 6.2.
Classifications of Farms based on Relations of Exploitation, Compared with Groupings based on Sown Area and Ownership of Working Animals: The Urals

Grouping by natural indicators	Grouping by dependent and entrepreneurial elements (no. of households)							
	Dependent households		Independent households			Entrepreneurial households		
	more than 50%	15–50%	15–2.5% depend.	2.5% depend.–2.5% entr.	2.5–15% entr.	15–30% entr.	more than 30% entr.	Totals
Total no. of households	81	109	81	442	101	15	6	835
Sown area (desyatins)								
not sowing	24	6	3	15	—	—	—	48
0.1–2	45	52	28	63	2	—	—	190
2.1–4	6	47	33	117	5	—	1	209
4.1–6	6	3	10	104	6	1	1	131
6.1–10	—	1	6	94	30	6	1	138
10.1–16	—	—	1	37	35	7	—	80
16.1–25	—	—	—	10	14	1	3	28
more than 25	—	—	—	2	9	—	—	11
Working animals								
None	71	61	25	59	—	—	—	216
1	9	44	41	171	10	1	—	276
2	1	4	12	118	14	9	3	161
3	—	—	2	55	24	2	2	85
4–7	—	—	1	39	53	3	1	97

Table 6.3.

Classification of Farms based on Relations of Exploitation, Compared with Groupings based on Sown Area and Ownership of Working Animals: Samara

Grouping by natural indicators	Grouping by class characteristics (% distribution)				
	I Proletarians	II Dependent small producers	III Independent small producers	IV Entrepreneurial small producers	V Small capitalists
Sown area (desyatins)					
not sowing	1.4	—	0.4	—	—
0–1	17.7	9.7	1.1	—	—
1.01–2	24.2	23.1	16.9	6.2	12.5
2.01–4	37.1	38.2	41.2	24.2	17.8
4.01–6	14.2	21.7	27.2	28.1	12.5
6.01–8	2.7	5.2	7.0	18.7	21.4
8.01–10	2.7	1.3	3.3	14.2	21.4
10.01–16	—	0.6	2.9	7.2	7.2
16.01–25	—	—	0.4	0.8	7.2
more than 25	—	—	—	—	—
Working animals					
None	44.3	22.4	6.2	—	—
1	48.6	61.2	50.2	32.0	5.3
2	7.1	15.1	41.0	59.4	66.0
3 and more	—	1.3	2.6	8.6	28.7

Source: Vermenichev *et al.* (1928, 47)

critiques of existing ideas and methods, but also to carry out experimental research projects to test alternative approaches. By 1930 their work was far from finished, and they had not published any analysis of the rural class structure which they regarded themselves as definitive. The question therefore arises of how far the Agrarian Marxist research offers information on the Soviet countryside and what was happening in it.

2   Research Findings on the Extent and Nature of Class Differentiation

Eventually, the main aim of the Agrarian Marxist research would have been to establish the extent of class differentiation in the Soviet peasantry. Unfortunately, the results of their studies up to 1930 fell far short of achieving such an aim. For the purposes of trying out new methods and approaches, their surveys had no need to be based on fully representative samples and, indeed, since the main aim was to find the best means of identifying specifically proletarian and capitalist characteristics, it made sense to weight the sample in favour of households which might be expected to display such characteristics. This probably explains both the range of sizes and, in some cases, the large size of both capitalist and proletarian groups identified by different studies. For capitalist farms the figures in the various local studies ranged from 'kulaks' comprising 0.96 per cent in Nemchinov's Urals study to 'capitalists' comprising 15.49 per cent of Sulkovskii's Saratov sample. Households identified as 'proletarian' ranged from 1.4 per cent of the Samara sample to 25.35 per cent of the Saratov sample. None of these figures should be taken as, nor were they claimed to be, reflections of the actual proportions of such classes in the localities studied. Nor can the figures for different areas be compared with each other, because of the different methods and definitions used in their calculation.

Also problematic were the results of the analyses of mass data, which did entail some greater claims to representativeness. For the USSR as a whole, Nemchinov's analysis of the 1927 dynamic surveys suggested that 3.7 per cent of all agricultural households were 'small capitalist', while the commission studying the 1926 national census suggested that 5.2 per cent of the agricultural population was 'entrepreneurial'. Gaister's study of TsSU budget data classified 3.6 per cent of households in all the regions he studied

as 'semi- and small capitalist', a figure which rose to 5.2 per cent for
the Ukraine, 5.3 per cent for the North Caucasus, and 9.3 per cent
for the Urals. On the other hand, Nemchinov's figures had 8.0 per
cent of Soviet agricultural households as 'proletarian', while the
census figures showed 3.88 per cent of the agricultural population to
be 'wage-workers', and Gaister gave a figure of 7.3 per cent
'proletarian' for all regions studied. This rose to 10.8 per cent in the
Urals, 16.5 per cent in the Ukraine, and 19.3 per cent in the North
Caucasus.

Clearly, there were problems with these figures. Although they
were based on wider and more representative coverage of larger
populations, as attempts at class analysis according to Kritsman's
criteria they were based on less detailed information and less
appropriate sets of indicators than the local studies. Also, their
different methods and definitions made cross-reference or comparison between them very difficult.

The nature of the research meant that, by 1930, when it was
abruptly brought to an end, the Agrarian Marxists had not been
able to offer any detailed or coherent view of the Soviet rural class
structure to put in the place of the earlier view based on sown area
figures. As far as their work had gone, it was not possible to assess
accurately the size of different classes, or to judge whether there had
been a growth of the middle peasantry, as Khryashcheva had
suggested. Because of the short time span of the Agrarian Marxists'
research, none of their studies was followed up in order to measure
any changes in class membership over a given period of time.

However, despite these problems and limitations, the research did
reveal much of interest on the issue of class differentiation. Although
they could not show the extent of differentiation, all the studies were
able to establish the fact that, according to the definitions and
measures they used, groups of proletarian and capitalist households
had emerged. Moreover, for each of the class groups they had
identified, most studies went on to demonstrate how different groups
displayed different characteristics which distinguished them from
other groups. In other words, membership of the class groups
delineated by the research was found to correlate with other
characteristics, and this was seen as further evidence of the reality of
the class differentiation process.

The main focus of interest in all the studies was to show the
relation between class membership and various economic character-

istics, which would be relevant for changes in the way production was organized in peasant farms of different types. The published reports of most of the studies offered only a limited discussion of this kind, but nevertheless the relation was evident. Nemchinov, for example, in his Urals study, showed that there was a tendency for the value of constant capital to be higher per unit of labour power, the more entrepreneurial the character of a farm. This can be seen from Table 6.4.[2]

Table 6.4.

Constant Capital per Unit Labour Power on Farms of Different Social Character: Urals

Grouping by social character	Percentage of farms where for R1 of labour power there was constant capital to the value of:					
	0–10 kopeks	11–20 kopeks	21–30 kopeks	31–50 kopeks	51–100 kopeks	100+ kopeks
More than 50% dependent	33.33	28.40	19.75	12.35	6.17	—
15–50% dep.	4.59	15.60	15.60	37.61	28.85	2.75
2.5–15% dep.	1.23	11.11	9.88	37.04	30.87	9.87
2.5% dep.– 2.5% entr.	1.36	1.58	4.75	18.33	40.72	33.26
2.5–15% entr.	—	—	—	0.99	22.77	76.24
More than 15% entrepreneurial	—	—	—	—	23.81	76.19

Source: Nemchinov (1926b, 60)

Somewhat similar information was offered for Volokolamsk by Anisimov and his colleagues, but in their case they took the total value of all means of production and showed how this increased in moving from proletarian to capitalist ends of their continuum. They also showed how different class groups were distinguished by the extent to which 'own' and 'others' ' factors of production of various kinds were distributed. (These figures are shown in Table 4.6 above.)

A rather larger range of information was provided by Studenskii in his study of the middle Volga region, which replicated the research approach of the Volokolamsk study. As noted, in Chapter 4, this study also contained an added dimension in that it sought to examine the relationship between class and economic variables in the context of different types of agriculture. Within this framework Studenskii first investigated the value of means of production on peasant farms of different emerging class types. He offered figures both for basic means of production (cattle, machinery and implements, and farm buildings) and for all means of production per household. The distributions per class group are shown in Table 6.5. For all types of cultivation except long fallow, the figures showed the clear separation of the group with proletarian tendencies from the other groups with lower total value both of basic and of all means of production, per farm and per hectare. (Studenskii unfortunately offered no explanation for the variation displayed by the long fallow figures.) The group with capitalist tendencies also seemed to be clearly separate judging by figures per farm, but the figures per hectare seemed to show a much more confused picture, with no clear distinction between the capitalist group and the better-off sections of the middle 'independent' group; and in some cases the middle group even had a higher value per hectare. This seemed to imply that the capitalist group, according to Studenskii's classification, was in fact less capital-intensive than the middle group. To non-Marxist opponents this would no doubt have suggested that there was in fact no emerging capitalist group. To more sympathetic critics it may have suggested that there were problems in Studenskii's classificatory scheme. Studenskii however preferred to postpone judgement, merely commenting that more information would be required on precisely how the households in this capitalist group used their means of production (Studenskii 1929, 22). Presumably the implication here was that a lower value per hectare may have reflected a more efficient use of means of production among the emerging capitalist group.

A similar interpretation could be offered for further figures provided by Studenskii on annual expenditure on labour and means of production. The figures per farm again showed the clear emergence of three separate class groups, but the figures per hectare produced a more confused picture which could be interpreted as showing higher but less economical expenditure by poor and middle groups than for the emerging capitalist group. Other figures,

Table 6.5

The value of Means of Production on Farms of Different Class and Types of Production Organization

Social types of households	Three-field		Mixed		Long fallow		Suburban	
	Basic means of production	All means of production	Basic means of production	All means of production	Basic means of production	All means of production	Basic means of production	All means of production
Average value per household in each class group of means of production (roubles)								
With proletarian tendencies	202.21	354.80	206.75	294.25	565.28	1000.70	392.06	607.81
Independent commodity producers	894.51	1286.31	733.54	1052.38	964.65	1404.90	948.27	1380.41
of which:								
(1) with dependent tendencies	678.05	995.68	580.24	807.45	545.49	952.08	818.79	1217.64
(2) with upward tendencies	1038.81	1480.06	849.87	1161.87	1616.24	2107.20	1077.82	1543.18
With capitalist tendencies	1190.29	1690.14	998.46	1257.67	1560.98	2057.20	1734.86	2196.80
Average value of means of production per hectare of land used in each class group (roubles)								
Proletarian tendencies	27.58	48.40	33.18	47.23	31.56	55.81	35.90	55.66
Independent commodity producers	62.59	90.01	64.97	93.21	35.99	52.42	62.50	90.99
of which:								
(1) with dependent tendencies	51.72	75.94	68.66	97.83	27.26	47.58	70.64	105.06
(2) with upward tendencies	68.29	97.30	62.67	86.68	43.23	56.37	57.51	82.34
Capitalist tendencies	53.54	80.97	44.27	55.77	57.36	75.57	77.98	98.11

Source: Studenskii (1920, 22)

moreover, seemed to confirm for Studenskii the distinct character of the three class groups he had delineated. Figures on gross farm revenue from agriculture, on grain surpluses, and on personal consumption showed, with very few exceptions, that the group with proletarian tendencies and the group with capitalist tendencies were both distinct from the middle 'independent' group. Finally, from figures on family size, which did not show any overall consistent increase from proletarian to capitalist, it could be argued that the picture of differentiation obtained from the figures could not be adequately explained as demographic differentiation (Studenskii 1929, 24–5).

A more detailed analysis of their findings, along with a wider range of information, was provided by Vermenichev and his colleagues in their study of Samara *guberniya*, in an area neighbouring the one discussed by Studenskii. Again, with a few exceptions, they were able to show a general picture of clear distinctions between the class groups they had identified in terms of a series of different characteristics. As can be seen from Table 6.6, the more capitalist-inclined groups were more likely to hire labour, rent land, and lease out stock and working animals than the more proletarian-inclined groups, while the latter were more likely to sell labour, lease out land, and hire cattle and stock than the former. Furthermore, the more capitalist or less proletarian a farm, the more land it sowed, the more cattle it owned, and the higher was its total value of means of production. There was also a steady increase in family size through the range from proletarian through to more capitalist. Table 6.6 represents the most detailed analysis provided by the Samara researchers for the final class groups (i.e. those arrived at by using indicators based on exploitation relations in conjunction with an indicator of economic strength). However, more detailed analysis was provided in relation to the groups delineated in terms of relations of exploitation only.

Table 6.7, referring to the five groups based on exploitation relations, offers more detail especially on the nature and extent of transactions in labour and land. While it confirmed the general picture provided in Table 6.6 by showing clear differences between households that were mainly exploited and those that were mainly exploiting, it also revealed interesting differences between adjacent exploited groups (I and II) and exploiting groups (IV and V). For instance, while group V clearly hired much more seasonal labour

Table 6.6.

Classes Within the Peasantry and their Characteristics: Samara

Class	Percentage of total	Ave. family size	Ave. value of agricultural means of production	Ave. no. of head of cattle	Ave. sowing (des-yatins)	Percentage of households					
						selling labour	hiring labour	leasing out land	renting land	hiring stock and cattle	leasing out stock and cattle
Proletarian	1.4	4.6	62.4	0.2	1.18	100	0	100	0	80.0	0
Semi-proletarian	8.5	4.9	179.7	0.7	2.82	100	6.7	66.7	1.7	86.7	15.0
Small dependent	21.4	4.9	262.1	0.9	3.20	44.7	7.9	11.0	2.0	84.0	13.8
Small independent (neutral)	38.5	5.2	436.1	1.4	4.07	7.3	29.7	11.0	16.5	84.9	48.0
Small independent (entrepreneurial elements)	18.0	5.9	698.1	1.7	5.87	3.1	65.6	6.3	50.8	67.0	83.7
Semi-capitalist	7.9	6.8	1248.5	2.4	10.57	5.4	94.6	5.4	77.0	42.8	94.6
Small-capitalist	3.9	7.5	1809.8	2.8	14.72	1.2	96.5	3.0	82.1	28.6	96.4

Source: Vermenichev *et al.* (1928, 138)

Table 6.7.

Class Groups and their Characteristics: Samara

Class group	Percentage of farms in the sample	Percentage of each class group									
		hiring workers		selling labour		renting land:		leasing out land:		hiring stock or animals	leasing out stock or animals
		daily	seasonally	daily	seasonally	up to 2 des-yatins	more than 2 des-yatins	up to 30% of arable	more than 30% of arable		
I	10.3	4.3	—	31.4	68.6	1.4	—	30.0	42.9	85.7	12.9
II	22.4	7.9	—	41.5	2.6	2.0	—	26.3	9.9	94.7	13.8
III	40.4	29.7	0.7	7.4	—	14.3	1.1	7.0	3.3	84.9	48.0
IV	18.9	54.0	10.9	3.1	—	38.3	12.5	6.3	—	67.1	83.6
V	8.2	26.8	67.9	5.4	—	37.5	39.5	3.6	1.8	42.8	94.6

Source: Vermenichev *et al.* (1928, 44)

than group IV, they hired much less labour by the day. This, it could be suggested, showed a difference in patterns of hiring between slightly entrepreneurial peasant farms hiring labour as and when required, by the day, and more consistently entrepreneurial farms, taking on the characteristics more of small capitalist farming and hiring workers for a whole season. Similarly a distinction could be made between group I, more than two-thirds of which sold labour on seasonal terms, and group II, who sold labour mostly on daily terms. Whereas group II could be seen as dependent peasant farms, needing to sell their labour occasionally, group I showed clearer tendencies of proletarianization in that they had to sell labour for a whole season instead of employing it at least partially on their own farm.

A similar pattern could be seen in relation to land. Group IV had the largest proportion of members renting up to 2 desyatins, while group V had the largest proportion renting more than 2 desyatins, suggesting a distinction between emerging capitalist farms, attempting a significant extension of their cultivation, and entrepreneurial farms, renting a little extra to employ their surplus of means of production. As far as leasing out land was concerned, however, group I had the largest share of their members both leasing up to and over 30 per cent of their arable land.

Further support for the picture of emerging class differences could be seen, to some extent, in the pattern of landholding in the different groups. Although the majority in all groups continued to hold communal land, a higher proportion of farms in groups III–V, and especially group V, had consolidated lands separate from the village on the *otrub* model. There was also a higher proportion of group V among members of *artels* involved in some form of co-operation. The figures are shown in Table 6.8.

More capitalist-oriented groups also tended to have more land at their disposal for cultivation, and to make more extensive use of it. As can be seen from Table 6.9, a higher proportion of their own arable land was actually sown by upper-class groups than by lower-class groups. This was explained partly by the fact that more upper-class households had consolidated lands (rather than the small strips with narrow margins between them to allow access, which decreased the area of land actually sown in the *obshchina* system), and partly by the fact that the upper groups rented more land, and in doing so rented only the amount of land they wished to sow and not the fallow that accompanied it.

Table 6.8.

Class Groups and Landholding: Samara

| Class group | Forms of landholding | | | | | | | | | |
| | Obshchina | | Otrub | | Khutor | | Membership of an artel' | |
	% farms	% land	% farms	% land	% farms	% land	% farms	% land
I	94.3	91.3	4.3	7.6	—	—	1.4	1.1
II	92.1	89.8	5.3	8.2	—	—	2.6	1.1
III	88.2	81.7	5.5	10.2	1.5	2.6	4.8	5.6
IV	85.9	82.2	7.0	9.7	1.6	2.9	5.5	5.2
V	71.4	58.2	12.5	11.4	—	—	16.1	30.4
Average	87.8	80.0	6.2	9.8	0.9	1.6	5.0	8.6

Source: Vermenichev *et al.* (1928, 127)

Table 6.9.

Class Groups and Land Use: Samara

Class group	Sowing per farm (desyatins)	Percentage of all arable land
I	2.72	58.4
II	3.20	61.5
III	4.07	66.1
IV	5.87	72.5
V	10.57	81.0

Source: Vermenichev *et al.* (1928, 127)

When it came to the pattern of crops sown however, the differences between groups were not nearly so marked. Table 6.10 shows some differences between groups, notably that upper groups allotted more of their sowing to oats and grasses, and, in the case of group V, also to sunflowers, and sowed less rye. However, the limited extent of these differences did not show any clear emergence of a distinctive capitalist organization of production or orientation to the market in terms of crop choice. Vermenichev and his colleagues explained this by reference to the continuing prevalence of communal landholding, even in group V. Significant changes would

Table 6.10.

Sowing of Each Crop as a Percentage of the Total Sowing of Each Group

Class groups*	Rye	Wheat	Oats	Millet	Other grains	Potatoes	Sunflowers	Flax/hemp	Grasses	Others
I	33.7	46.1	3.7	4.2	—	4.1	5.1	1.6	—	1.5
II	36.1	43.7	5.5	3.9	0.5	3.2	5.5	1.0	—	0.6
III	35.1	44.8	6.8	3.2	0.1	3.2	4.6	1.3	0.03	0.8
IV	35.8	41.6	8.2	2.4	0.3	2.4	4.6	1.5	0.5	2.7
V	26.8	45.8	10.2	2.5	0.1	2.0	6.1	0.8	4.6	1.1
V (a)	20.7	35.0	14.1	2.4	—	1.8	9.1	—	12.3	—

*The figures for Groups III and V (a) are not quite complete, each falling slightly short of 100%.

Source: Vermenichev *et al.* (1928, 128)

be possible in terms of peasant household production only if fields were consolidated and were not subject to reallocation by the commune. Only then would peasants be able to respond to market opportunities, if they had the resources, by cultivating the crops they chose, and in the quantities they chose. Within the *obshchina*, although a household could extend cultivation by renting extra land, there was little incentive to make improvements because both rented land and allotment land were subject to communal rules governing the choice and rotation of crops. Although some changes were possible, for example by using improved seeds and fertilizer, new crops, different patterns of weeding, and improved machinery, if such changes were introduced on some strips while the neighbouring strips continued to be farmed by old methods, the extent and efficacy of the changes was likely to be limited.

The researchers attempted to provide support for their argument by referring to the information contained in the bottom row of Table 6.10 (group V(a)) on the sowing of the 14 households (25 per cent) of the semi-capitalist group V which had split off from the commune. The cultivation of these farms showed greater differences from the general pattern than did the cultivation of group V as a whole, signifying the more extensive changes in production organization of farms beginning to develop as capitalist enterprises rather than simply expanding their sowing or building up surpluses of means of production for leasing out.

In contrast to the data on crops, the figures for the ownership of animals and stock showed clear differences between the groups. As is shown in Table 6.11, not only did the upper groups own more horses than their weaker neighbours (and some of their weaker neighbours, including 44.3 per cent of group I, owned none at all), but the more entrepreneurial a farm, the more likely it was to have younger horses and more valuable horses. Such farms also owned greater quantities and higher values of farm stock, the differences here being much wider than for horses. Taking into account the greater ownership of animals and stock among the upper groups and the high proportions of farms without key means of production in the lower groups, the scope for exploitation between households can clearly be seen.

A further area in which differences between groups could be discerned was their main sources of cash income. While the sale of grain was an important source of income for all groups, it was

Table 6.11.

Class Groups and the Distribution of Stock: Samara

	Class groups				
	I	II	III	IV	V
Ave. no of working horses per farm	0.63	0.95	1.4	1.78	2.39
Young horses as % of all horses	18.2	17.4	22.0	26.3	28.4
Foals as % of all horses	6.8	7.6	10.5	9.2	10.5
Ave. value of a working horse (roubles)	97.7	118.1	123.4	138.3	170.0
% of farms without machinery or implements	62.8	36.2	13.9	—	—
% without ploughing equipment	77.1	55.9	28.9	8.6	7.1
% without advanced equipment	87.1	80.2	48.0	14.1	3.6
% without farm buildings	32.7	11.4	6.3	—	—
Ave. value of equipment per farm (roubles)	54.9	71.5	119.7	187.7	368.5

Source: Vermenichev *et al.* (1928, 131–2)

especially so for the middle groups. Rye was much less significant for groups IV and V. The sale of animal products was more important in groups III–V than for the lower groups, and the sale of wood was important for group V. The sale of agricultural labour was important only for the lower groups, and mainly for group I. Among non-agricultural activities, the groups also conformed to their class tendencies. While group I's off-farm activities mainly involved wage work, groups II–IV were mainly involved in independent trades and crafts, and group V operated small businesses (Vermenichev *et al.* 1928, 134–5).

The researchers also collected information on some other areas: family composition, literacy, and education. Families tended to be slightly bigger in upper groups than in lower ones and, perhaps of particular significance, were much more likely to be without male workers in the lower groups, possibly reflecting the effects of the war. Households in the middle of the range tended to have slightly more male workers than households in extreme groups, but female workers were more numerous in lower-class households. In the semi-capitalist group V there was a slightly lower proportion of both male and female workers than in groups beneath them. Such tendencies may well have been accounted for by the possibility that more family members did not work on the farm in the higher groups. The figures are shown in Table 6.12.

Families in more capitalist-oriented groups were also a little more likely to include literate members and students. The percentage of literate men ranged from 19.8 per cent in group I to 25.7 per cent in group V (figures for women, for some reason, appear not to have been collected). The percentage of students, of both sexes, in each class group ranged from 4.4 per cent in group I to 7.3 per cent in group V (Vermenichev *et al.* 1928, 134).

At the time of its publication in 1928, the Samara study was the first detailed study of a rural locality to be published using the new methods and concepts of the Agrarian Marxists. As such, whatever problems there were with its methods and approach, it marks one of the high points in their work. It was surpassed in the detail and complexity of its findings by only one other study, that of Saratov, by Sulkovskii and his colleagues, published in 1930. While similarly

Table 6.12.
Class Groups and Family Composition: Samara

Class group	No. in family	Workers on family farm per 100 pop.		Percentage of households without male workers
		Male	Female	
I	4.8	19.5	31.0	25.7
II	4.9	23.1	27.3	11.2
III	5.2	21.5	25.5	6.6
IV	5.9	23.2	22.4	4.7
V	6.8	19.9	21.0	1.8
Average		22.2	25.3	8.8

Source: Vermenichev *et al.* (1928, 125)

containing a wide range information on the production characteristics of different class groups, the Saratov study also incorporated a
feature of Studenskii's work by comparing class groups in different
types of agricultural production; however, in its wealth of published
detail, Sulkovskii's work went well beyond Studenskii's tentative
findings.

As noted in Chapter 5 above, Sulkovskii's study involved a sample
drawn from villages in three *raions*, comprising a cross-section of
different levels of development of commodity production and
specialization in sunflower production. Taking figures from the
sample as a whole, clear distinctions between groups were apparent
in a number of aspects of their production organization. First, it was
clear that, with a few exceptions in the relative positions of adjacent
groups in the scale, the higher the class group, the greater its share
of means of production. This is shown in Table 6.13, which also
shows the percentage which each category of means of production
comprised out of the total in each class group, thus showing in which
kinds of means there was greatest investment.

Second, clear differences between class groups could be seen in
terms of the extent of cultivation. This is shown in Table 6.14.
Furthermore, the class groups could also be distinguished by the
different average size of family of the households within them. This
is shown in Table 6.15.

In these two tables a clear distinction can be seen between groups
I and III, and in nearly all cases there is a steady increase in values
moving along the range from group I to group III. For Sulkovskii
and his colleagues this led to the conclusion that class differentiation
was indeed taking place in the Saratov countryside. However, given
the figures on family size in Table 6.15, there might seem to be some
support for an alternative neo-Populist interpretation in terms of
demographic differentiation. In order to argue against this,
Sulkovskii produced the information given in Table 6.16 on the ratio
of consumer units to labour units on average per household in each
class group and each *raion*.

The general lack of large or consistent differences in these ratios
between class groups seemed effectively to refute the idea that an
increase in the weight of labour units in a household could account
for the higher scores of the upper groups on various scales of
distribution. This was further supported by the figures on land use
per worker, which showed that, even if it was larger families who

Table 6.13.
Class Groups and the Distribution of Means of Production: Saratov

Class groups	Animals Value	%	Birds Value	%	Bees Value	%	Buildings Value	%	Implements Value	%	Stock Value	%	Cash Value	%	Previous year's expenses Value	%	All means of production Value	%
I	61.08	37.1	3.38	2.1	—	—	27.39	16.7	16.45	10.0	24.93	15.2	7.80	4.7	23.43	14.2	164.46	100
II (a)	124.26	45.4	2.25	0.8	—	—	58.81	21.5	27.22	10.0	20.37	7.4	15.16	5.5	25.81	9.4	273.88	100
II (b)	342.70	45.8	6.06	0.8	—	—	109.37	14.6	110.77	14.8	88.14	11.8	23.25	3.1	67.98	9.1	748.27	100
II (c)	544.28	51.7	6.17	0.6	—	—	111.98	10.7	172.08	16.4	119.92	11.4	14.99	1.4	81.91	7.8	1051.33	100
III	937.45	36.6	11.99	0.5	40.00	1.6	351.15	13.7	712.72	27.8	331.99	13.0	80.40	3.1	95.69	3.7	2561.39	100

Source: Sulkovskii (1930, 65–6)

Table 6.14.
Class Groups and Sown Area: Saratov

Average sown area in each class
group (ha per household)

Class groups	Vol'skii *raion*	Bazarno-Karbulakskii *podraion*	Petrovskii *raion*	Serdobskii *raion*
I	3.49	3.16	3.31	3.32
II (a)	2.54 ⎫		— ⎫	
II (b)	9.66 ⎬	5.80	6.79 ⎬	8.63
II (c)	14.11 ⎭		8.94 ⎭	
III	10.61	13.16	12.12	12.21

Source: Sulkovskii (1930, 117, 123, 126, 132)

Table 6.15.
Class Groups and Family Size: Saratov

Class groups	Volskii *raion* (including Bazarno-Karbulakskii *podraion*)	Petrovskii *raion*	Serdobskii *raion*	All
I	4.15	5.66	4.66	4.83
II (a)	4.00	—	6.00	5.00
II (b)	6.44	6.00	7.57	6.63
II (c)	7.75	7.25	7.33	7.45
III	9.66	7.00	8.00	8.09

Source: Sulkovskii (1930, 61)

Table 6.16.
The Ratio of Consumer and Labour Units per Household: Saratov

Class groups	Volskii *raion*	Petrovskii *raion*	Serdobskii *raion*	All
I	1.27	1.13	1.28	1.21
II (a)	1.06	—	1.42	1.23
II (b)	1.13	1.20	1.29	1.20
II (c)	1.50	1.37	1.23	1.35
III	1.28	1.23	1.20	1.24

Source: Sulkovskii (1930, 62)

sowed larger areas, they also cultivated more land per worker than the smaller, lower-class households. For the sample as a whole, group I had an average of 2.33 ha per worker, II(a) had 2.73 ha, II(b) 3.57 ha, II(c) 4.74 ha, and III 4.64 ha (Sulkovskii 1930, 63). As part of the general process of transition from petty-bourgeois to capitalist farming, Sulkovskii argued, not only would there be a greater concentration of land in the hands of wealthy households, but such land would also be cultivated more efficiently and intensively. To test this he employed two different ways of measuring intensiveness: on the one hand, in terms of the total value of capital invested in a farm, and on the other hand, in terms of the total costs of agricultural production per unit area of a farm. These he called respectively variants 1 and 2. The results, according to each method of measurement, are shown in Table 6.17.

As can be seen from the table, in every case there was a clear distinction between groups I and III, although the situation within group II was less clear, and in a few cases sections of group II scored higher than group III. Nevertheless, it seemed to Sulkovskii that the results in general, according to both types of measurement, confirmed his expectation of an increased intensiveness of production as one moved from more proletarian to more capitalist types of farming (Sulkovskii 1930, 79, 91–2).

In addition to evidence of the kind discussed in Table 6.17, which in itself was more detailed and more thoroughly analysed, at least than any other published work of the Agrarian Marxists, Sulkovskii produced information on various other aspects of peasant economic activity. His book included chapters or sections on differences in the sources and uses of income in different class groups, differences in relations with the market, and differences in cropping patterns and land use. In general, on the basis of his findings, he felt able to conclude that a gradual separation of an agrarian bourgeoisie and a proletariat was indeed taking place, although leaving behind a large group of small commodity producers whose own interrelations were still complex and contradictory. However, despite the general trends, the nature of class differentiation was far from simple even in relation to the emergent capitalist or proletarian groups. This could be seen particularly from Sulkovskii's analyses of accumulation in peasant farming, and of the relation between specialization in sunflower production and class differentiation.

As far as accumulation was concerned, the surprising finding of

Table 6.17.

Average Intensiveness of Production per Farm in Each Class Group (roubles)

Class group	Vol'skii *raion*		Petrovskii *raion*		Serdobskii *raion*		All	
	Variant 1	Variant 2	Variant 1	Variant 2	Variant 1	Variant 2	Variant 1	Variant 2
I	21.87	36.73	24.71	42.99	36.00	66.42	27.50	41.34
II (a)	45.91	87.35	—	—	37.03	57.94	41.47	72.64
II (b)	51.39	65.39	58.99	66.23	75.95	62.10	61.50	64.72
II (c)	47.09	59.72	61.40	61.12	87.16	67.95	63.15	64.30
III	98.43	71.02	90.17	60.62	173.99	91.14	129.91	74.92

Source: Sulkovskii (1930, 80)

the research was that farms with proletarian tendencies had the best figures, while the level of accumulation in farms with capitalist tendencies was significantly weaker. If cash was taken into account, group III farms were in deficit. Middle-peasant farms (group II(b)) showed the weakest performance, with an overall deficit both before and after taking cash into account. The figures are shown in Table 6.18.

Table 6.18.
Accumulation per Farm in each Class Group (roubles)

Class group	Means of production	Domestic buildings	Debt liabilities	Total	Cash	Total including cash
I	+21.84	+9.5	−4.65	+26.69	−4.82	+21.87
II (a)	+53.00	−9.37	+24.27	+67.90	−2.61	+65.29
II (b)	−12.77	+6.65	−3.93	−10.05	−17.36	−27.41
II (c)	+52.81	−14.78	+6.20	+44.23	−9.68	+34.55
III	+28.19	−2.51	−4.86	+20.82	−63.59	−42.77

Source: Sulkovskii (1930, 179)

However, although the findings here did not conform to Sulkovskii's expectations in terms of a straightforward process of class differentiation, he nevertheless argued, on the basis of a detailed analysis, that the figures could be explained only in terms of class groups. The basis for the different performance of each group consisted of a different combination of factors in each case, and therefore a different explanation was required for each group separately. Analyses that ignored class differentiation would not offer adequate explanation, therefore. Moreover, judging from the research findings, neither the extent of sown area nor a household's consumer–worker ratio seemed to have any significant relation with patterns of accumulation, thus further strengthening the case for a class analysis.

For households whose chief characteristic was proletarian, the main factors supporting accumulation were income received, either from wage work or from rental payments for land leased out to others. For the most part income from their own farming was not a significant source, except in so far as the household grew sunflowers as a cash crop. In contrast, *serednyak* households, if they succeeded in accumulating, did so on the basis of income from their own farming. Significantly, there was generally little off-farm income in households in this group to be used for accumulation.

The situation within the small capitalist group was more contradictory. There, the extent of a household's accumulation was found to be in inverse proportion to its income. Households not accumulating also tended to have a higher value of means of production, and tended to sow lower areas of land than households in the same group which were accumulating. According to Sulkovskii's analysis, there were two main reasons for this. First, he found that all the group III households with no accumulation or with annual accumulation of less than R10 had been founded before the revolution, whereas two-thirds of those with annual accumulation of more than R10 had been founded since the revolution. For capitalist farming, the revolution with its ensuing redistribution of land, and changed conditions of farming, required a reorganization of farming away from extensive cultivation to more intensive farming and non-agricultural interests. While some older farms were able to make this transition, those formed since the revolution seemed to have adapted better to the new conditions. Second, accumulation among the wealthier households had been affected by state policies, both in the early years of Soviet power, through direct confiscations, and more recently through taxation, in the direction of limiting the size of their farms (Sulkovskii 1930, 180–7).

Sulkovskii's analysis of the relation between class group membership and the production organization of sunflower cultivation also produced some surprising results. As a cash crop, and a factor encouraging the development of a commodity economy among the peasantry, it might have been expected that areas with a high concentration of sunflower production would also be areas of marked peasant class differentiation. However, in Saratov, Sulkovskii in fact found that, where specialization in sunflower production was greatest, differentiation and capitalist development was least. He concluded that 'the development of commodity relations together with the specialization of peasant farms in the production of sunflowers is connected with a lower tempo of differentiation of the countryside than if this development of commodity relations had taken a different course' (Sulkovskii 1930, 204).

For Sulkovskii, the situation found in Saratov was explained by the fact that sunflower production required a lower necessary input of means of production than most other crops, and that therefore it was possible for weak and poorly equipped farms to engage in it and produce for the market more easily than would be the case in other types of farming. Furthermore, given the lack of advanced mechanized stock on the better-off farms, the organization of production was not greatly different in these either. This was not, of course, as Sulkovskii pointed out, an argument about sunflower production in general, but about its specific circumstances and effects in Saratov at the time.

These last two aspects of Sulkovskii's findings, and what they show about the nature of the research that produced them, are of particular interest for a discussion of the work of the Agrarian Marxists. Sulkovskii's approach demonstrated how Agrarian Marxist methods and concepts might have been developed if Soviet agriculture had remained a predominantly petty-commodity-producing economy into the 1930s. There would then have been a place for sciences of applied agronomy and agricultural economics, which needed detailed knowledge not only of the class tendencies of peasant farms, but also of how class affected their production organization, and how a different organization of production could foster or inhibit class development. In itself, of course, Sulkovskii's book was not an example of such work, but it demonstrated the potential of the Agrarian Marxist approach. It showed that such an approach not only had a contribution in the realm of statistics on class differentiation, but also could provide a theoretical and methodological basis for a class-based agricultural science. Although the Samara research and Gaister's work had pointed the way in which the methodology of class analysis could be used for detailed empirical study, Sulkovskii's work went beyond this and showed the germs of an applied development to the work as well.

Furthermore, Sulkovskii's conclusions demonstrate the open-endedness of the research approach which could produce unexpected findings from the point of view of its initial hypotheses. This can be seen in three different conclusions drawn by Sulkovskii. First, he showed that proletarianization need not automatically follow from weaker peasant households selling labour for wages. Evidence from Saratov showed how wages could be a source of investment into the household farm. Second, the emergence of a group of households with capitalist tendencies did not represent an irreversible process of differentiation, either. The evidence showed that households with capitalist tendencies could fail to accumulate. If such a process were repeated over a few years, then presumably such households would have fallen back into the *serednyak* group. Third, the development of commodity production with the adoption of a particular cash crop such as sunflowers need not necessarily promote class differentiation, but could instead help maintain a relatively undifferentiated middle peasantry.[3]

3 Interpretation of the Findings

As noted above, the Agrarian Marxist research provided neither fully representative samples of the localities it studied, nor time series data to show changes overtime. It could not, therefore, provide clear evidence on the extent of the formation of separate classes in agriculture, or on the extent of changes in the class structure of the countryside in the 1920s. What it *was* able to show was that, over and above inequalities in the distribution of various factors of production, there were also clear signs of differentiation based on exploitation between households. Furthermore, such differentiation produced groups that not only were more or less wealthy, but differed from each other in various aspects of the organization of production and in the predominant types of social relations they entered into.

Despite the tentative and unfinished nature of the research, therefore, Kritsman and his colleagues tended to see their findings as supporting the idea that a gradual class differentiation of the peasantry was taking place. The originality of their research, in this view, was that it uncovered more clearly, and in more detail, the causes of differentiation and the nature of the social relations through which it developed. As a result, it was able to delineate the new emerging social classes more accurately than previous research approaches. As far as its basic empirical conclusions were concerned, all the researchers saw their work as confirming the classical Marxist assumption that differentiation resulted in the emergence of a class of agrarian capitalists, and a rural proletariat, leaving behind a transitional group who, while still undergoing differentiation, for the time being retained certain characteristics of a small-commodity-producing peasantry. Where some Agrarian Marxists differed from classical Marxism was on the question of whether this latter group constituted an independent 'middle peasantry'.

As a conclusion to this chapter, however, the question should be raised of whether alternative interpretations of the Agrarian Marxists' findings are possible. Raising this question also uncovers certain gaps or blind-spots in the analysis of the Agrarian Marxists which make conclusive judgements difficult. The possibility of a different interpretation arises in relation to two issues: first, on the nature of the upper, predominantly exploiting, group, and whether it was becoming truly capitalist; and second, on the nature of those peasants who were neither clearly capitalist nor clearly proletarian.

The question of an agrarian capitalist class

Although the researchers on each project felt able to identify an emerging capitalist class, it is noticeable that they usually qualified their judgement by referring to it as 'small capitalist' or 'semi-capitalist' and, moreover, that it was usually identified as a separate class on the basis of rather small measures of the various indicators of capitalist characteristics. For example, in the Volokolamsk study a household had to be only 20 per cent capitalist to be included in the 'small capitalist' group, while in Samara a household had to hire only one labourer for ninety days to be counted as capitalist. Given this limited extent of capitalist characteristics, even in the class identified as capitalist, and in view both of Kritsman's statements that state policies would be likely to limit the growth of agrarian capitalism, and of Sulkovskii's evidence of the tenuous and reversible nature of capital accumulation on some farms, the necessarily capitalist nature of the upper exploiting group identified by the research seems at least to be open to question.

Part of the problem of interpreting the nature of this group concerns the question of what should count as evidence of agrarian capitalism. The Agrarian Marxists tended to assume either that a given level of indicators of exploitation was sufficient to signify capitalist characteristics, or that such indicators, combined with others, of the extent of income or ownership of means of production should be used. However, in themselves, such indicators were not sufficient to distinguish a truly capitalist farm from a relatively wealthy peasant household engaged in petty-commodity production. If, as suggested in Chapter 1, Marx had identified expanded

reproduction as a key characteristic of capitalism which distinguished it from petty-commodity production, then a full capitalist
enterprise, including a capitalist farm, should be one where its
production is geared to creating and continually reinvesting a
surplus. The question not only of the appropriation of a surplus, but
also of the accumulation of capital, therefore becomes crucial in the
definition of capitalism.

However, a problem with the Agrarian Marxist approach was
that, although it developed a classification based on direct measures
of expropriation of a surplus, it did not also entail direct measures of
accumulation. While ownership of means of production could be
seen as an indirect indicator, since it reflected previous accumulation, it could not count as direct evidence. For the most part, the
accumulation of capital was a rather neglected issue in the work of
the Agrarian Marxists. Even Sulkovskii, although he studied the
issue in some detail, did not incorporate a measure of accumulation
into his scheme of classification, and so his evidence was not actually
used in the process of identifying capitalist farms.

Also involved in a Marxist concept of class is the question of
consciousness and political organization. A further sign, therefore, of
the emergence of a capitalist class in the countryside would have
been evidence that households in the upper groups identified by the
research actually recognized common class interests and began to
act politically in pursuit or defence of such interests as opposed to
more generally shared peasant interests. Such a development was
assumed to be taking place by members of the Left Opposition in the
1920s, and in a cruder version the same assumption was behind
official government fears of a '*kulak* grain strike' in the late 1920s. In
the light of these assumptions, it would have been useful if the
Agrarian Marxist projects had included research into whether
political attitudes and activities varied according to class group
membership. Unfortunately, this topic remained unresearched.

Finally, on the problem of an agrarian capitalist class, there is the
question of whether capitalist development in the countryside would
necessarily occur mainly in agricultural production. The various
projects all produced information on non-agricultural activities,
both where these were subsidiary to farming and where they were
the main source of income, and the general impression was that, not
only were there relatively few households whose main source of
income came from outside agriculture, but the number whose non-

agricultural activity was a capitalist enterprise was even smaller. However, what was not clear was the extent to which, hidden within the subsidiary trades and small-scale industrial production, there was any tendency for these to attract more of the investment of a household's surplus than their agricultural production. From studies of peasants in other parts of the world, it is clear that a surplus derived from farming is often invested in trading or transport enterprises. Furthermore, in view of Trotsky's remarks concerning the importance of small-scale trading in the Russian countryside (see Chapter 1 above), it may have been the case that Russian peasants were expanding trading enterprises by investing the surplus they had acquired from agriculture. Further impetus to such a trend could well have come from the concerns of well-off peasants to avoid being labelled as *kulaks*. Given the focus in the 1920s on the *kulaks* as a source of surplus grain, a suitable defensive tactic for such households would have been to invest in trade or small-scale industrial production. Unfortunately, the research of the Agrarian Marxists did not go into sufficient detail on these issues to draw any conclusion from their work.

The question of the 'middle peasants'

The concept of the 'middle peasant' or *serednyak* was one of the most entrenched in the conventional wisdom of Soviet Marxism of the 1920s. Not only had Lenin used the term frequently, but the whole justification of the NEP hinged on an understanding of the majority of the peasantry as being made up of a neutral group of peasants who, on the one hand, were not part of the proletariat and not necessarily likely to share economic or political interests with it, but on the other hand were not part of a nascent capitalist class whose long-term interests would be opposed to those of the Soviet state. Only in terms of an alliance between the proletariat and a neutral group of middle peasants who might in the long run be won over to socialism could the NEP be seen as still holding out the hope of a transition to socialism.

Alongside this view of the neutrality of the middle peasantry in the context of the long-term strategy of socialist construction, there was a prevalent view of the middle peasantry which saw it as made up of households that were each socially neutral in terms of class relations, remaining for the most part independent producers, neither exploiting nor being exploited. The official attitude to this group has been summarized by Carr as follows:

The characteristic of this group was that, while it owned or controlled the means of production with which it worked, and was to this extent capitalist, it did not generally exploit or employ the labour of others. . . . Hence the party was not unconditionally hostile to members of this group and was continually concerned to prevent them from falling under the predominant influence of the *kulaks*.

(Carr 1970, 112)

It was in the context of such thinking that Russian and Soviet classifications of the peasantry had always opted for the delineation of a large middle group made up of the majority of households who did not fall at the extreme ends of whichever scale of stratification was being used. Such a view had been shared by different researchers with otherwise different viewpoints. It began to be questioned however, by some of the Agrarian Marxists.

The various studies carried out by the Agrarian Marxists differed in the way they grouped their samples into class categories. The Samara and Saratov studies, as well as Gaister's use of budget survey data, all had a middle category of households which seemed to be tending neither towards proletarianization nor towards capitalist development, but the Volokolamsk study and the work of Naumov and Shardin did not make provision for such a group. It may be possible to some extent to attribute such differences to the varying degrees of differentiation of the areas under study in each of the surveys, but the different attitudes to grouping almost certainly were the result mainly of different opinions among the researchers.

Kritsman's views predisposed him to regard with suspicion the argument that there was a large, truly independent, middle peasantry with all the connotations of self-sufficiency and 'natural economy' which this term conveyed. He was therefore critical, for example, of the Samara study for its middle group of just over 40 per cent, which he thought was the result of the criteria chosen for the grouping. Probably closer to his own preferences was the scheme adopted in the Volokolamsk research, which contained only groups with varying degrees of either dependence (proletarianization) or entrepreneurship (capitalist development). In this scheme, there-fore, even households with only slight tendencies towards dependence or entrepreneurship were placed in a group according to their dominant tendency, however slight. In support of this, the researchers pointed to the fact that nearly all members of any potential middle-peasant group displayed at least elements of dependence in their operations and could not therefore be regarded as truly independent farmers.

For Kritsman and his colleagues, the results of their research clearly showed that, as a significant group of peasants farming independently by means of their own resources only, a 'middle peasantry' scarcely existed in Russia in the 1920s. What existed instead was what Kritsman described as 'a petty-bourgeois mass', all inextricably bound up in commodity relations, not only in so far as they sold their produce or bought consumer goods, but also in that they were engaged in market transactions over various factors of production required for farming. As a result of these various transactions, almost all households experienced relations in which they were either exploited or exploiting and many experienced both together. Taking the balance of their various relations, it was possible to put some households clearly into entrepreneurial or dependent categories, while others would have a balance of more or less equal mixtures of entrepreneurial and dependent tendencies. Only a few were truly independent in the sense of not being significantly involved in transactions with other households at all.

The critique of the whole idea of the 'middle peasants' as an independent peasantry was one of the most important results of the Agrarian Marxists' empirical research. By offering an understanding of them in terms of complex permutations of different kinds of social relations with other households, for the first time they could be studied seriously in their own right, and not treated merely as a residual category which was neither capitalist nor proletarian. The Agrarian Marxist approach at least lay the basis for further research on the relations of production and forms of organization of those peasants who were neither capitalist nor proletarian, although detailed research of this kind had not begun by the end of the 1920s. Within the new approach to the question developed by Kritsman and his colleagues, there lay the germs of a new understanding. However, in practice this was confused by their tendency, especially for example in the Volokolamsk research, to reject the whole idea of a middle group which was neither capitalist not proletarian along with the idea of an independent middle peasantry. Since in most cases, in all the surveys, households identified as capitalist or proletarian displayed only relatively slight signs of class characteristics, it was surely unwise to assume the current direction of a household's class tendencies would remain stable. The following year, with different weather or market conditions, a slightly proletarian household could easily have become a slightly capitalist one, or vice versa. It might therefore have been preferable to retain the idea of a middle group with no clear class characteristics, and perhaps to call it 'indeterminate' in terms of class character as a way of avoiding all the connotations of the term 'middle peasant'.

In various ways, the empirical research of the Agrarian Marxist has left an interesting heritage for modern researchers on peasant societies. Their results, however tentative, are of interest for historical research on Russia of the 1920s, while some of their methodological and conceptual innovations may well prove a useful source of ideas for modern studies of peasant issues in countries where peasant farming remains of importance. Such issues will be pursued further in Chapter 8.

Notes

1. For further evidence of a similar kind, see Studenskii (1929, 21).
2. The second row of this table totals 105 instead of 100. A possible explanation is that a 2 was mistaken for a 7, so that the 37.61 per cent in the fourth column should have been 32.61 per cent.
3. This point would seem to refute the criticism of Kritsman and his colleagues by Solomon, who argues that their work 'was addressed to a single problem ... and that problem was approached with certain assumptions to which the methodology was tailored' (Solomon 1977, 110).

7

The End of the Research

In the previous chapters an attempt has been made to chart the development of the research of the Agrarian Marxists on the class differentiation of the peasantry and to assess its methods, concepts, and results. It has been stressed that the research was exploratory in its methodology and tentative in its conclusions. By the end of the 1920s, however, there was a distinct possibility that many methodological issues could be resolved so that the group could establish a body of data on the basis of which clearer conclusions could be drawn. It was also hoped by Kritsman and his colleagues that their results could provide a basis for a more class-sensitive approach to both agrarian policy and extension work for peasant farming. Furthermore, by the end of the decade the group had begun to develop research on new issues other than the question of class differentiation. However, the high hopes enjoyed by Kritsman and his colleagues were soon to be cruelly shattered. In the last few years of the 1920s, just as the Agrarian Marxists were beginning to assert their predominance over rival approaches to agrarian questions, they began to attract criticisms of a more narrowly political nature. Then, at the end of 1929, the whole research enterprise was abruptly brought to an end following the government's decisions to collectivize the peasantry forcibly.

Some of the new areas of research developed by the Agrarian Marxists are outlined in Section 1 below, followed by a discussion of the main contemporary Soviet criticisms of their work in Section 2. An account of the ending of the research is given in Section 3.

1 Further Developments in the Work of the Agrarian Marxists

In extending their critical approach more widely, Kritsman and his colleagues developed two main new areas of concern: the study of the internal structure of the peasant household, and the elaboration of the policy implications of their research. As an undercurrent to all this work, there was also a continued development of theoretical critiques of the main alternative approach to the study of the peasantry by the Organization and Production School.

Research on the peasant household

Agrarian Marxist research in this field was carried out exclusively by M. Kubanin. In a series of articles (1928a, 1928b), and then in a book (1929) based on the same research,[1] Kubanin tried to develop an explanation of the tendency, made clear by the dynamic surveys both before and since the revolution, for a certain number of households, and especially economically strong ones, to split up. Hitherto discussion of this phenomenon had been largely the preserve of Chayanov and his colleagues, who saw it as part of the natural life cycle of the family unit responding to the changing balance of its consumer and producer components over the generations. As such, it was seen as evidence supporting the concept of demographic differentiation.

Implicit in this interpretation of the evidence was the idea that the peasant household was based on a consensual harmony of interests. Kubanin, however, drawing on evidence from a sample survey carried out by workers at the State and Law section of the Communist Academy in 1926, put forward the view that, in the conditions of change brought about by the growth of a commodity economy, the peasant household was increasingly prone to conflicts of interest between its members, leading to the household splitting up. Evidence for this was to be found, he thought, in that the survey interviews found more cases of internal conflicts reported from *serednyak* and *kulak* households than from *bednyak* households. Although all types of household would be undergoing changes brought about by commodity production, the heads of households of the *serednyak* and *kulak* households were taking on a new role as potential capitalist entrepreneurs. This led them to attempt to redefine their relations with other household members, taking on the role of employer in relation to the workers of the rest of the household. Where no other outlet seemed possible to younger household members who had thus become disadvantaged, the conflict simmered uneasily within the household, but where alternatives were recognized by the younger members, especially in wage labour, splits developed with the younger members leaving home.

For Kubanin, the relations between the resulting separate

households now became class relations. The 'mother' household, from which the younger members had split, kept the greater share of the formerly jointly owned means of production, leaving the 'daughter' household poorly equipped to take up independent farming. Those departing became either wage workers or dependent peasants undergoing a process of proletarianization. In this way the process of households splitting up, according to Kubanin, was both the result of a growing commodity economy and a contributory cause of the class differentiation of the peasantry.

Kubanin's work was greeted with enthusiasm by colleagues (e.g. Kritsman 1929b) and was clearly seen as a significant extension in the scope of Agrarian Marxist work and an important resource in the critique of neo-Populist approaches to the study of the peasantry. However, it must be said that, in the form it had taken by 1929, the work was rather speculative and was based only on a small amount of evidence. To have warranted the conclusions drawn from it, further research encompassing a wider range of questions would have been required. The bold claims made by Kubanin on a rather narrow base of evidence have led to his work receiving strong criticisms from Shanin (1972, 110–11) and Solomon (1977, 130–3).

For both of these modern critics of Kubanin, the main substantive objection seems to be that he assumed that commodity production had brought about the differentiation of the household into clear-cut classes of capitalists and proletarians. This, as both critics point out, is absurd because, as Solomon puts it, the conclusion follows that 'a capitalist would grant a portion of his resources to proletarians leaving his employ' (1977, 131). However, that was not what Kubanin was saying. His point was, rather, that the *process* of class differentiation was at work within the household, and especially within more entrepreneurially inclined households, and that differentiation was furthered by the splitting up of households in the condition of a growing commodity economy.[2]

Taken as the tentative beginning of a new line of enquiry, rather than in the form of more definite conclusions, Kubanin's work can be seen as interesting and imaginative. First, as Solomon has pointed out, 'Kubanin's study showed the family farm enmeshed in the process of rural stratification. In doing so it cast doubt on the assertion by the Timiryazev professors that, because its growth and decay were internally determined, the family farm would withstand capitalism' (Solomon 1977, 132).

Second, Kubanin's study took a first step for Marxist work on the peasantry in moving discussion down, from an exclusive concern with the household as its focus, to examine the relations of the different people making up the household. Given its overriding concern with class differentiation, Marxist work from Marx and Lenin through to Kritsman had dealt with the abstraction of the household as its basic unit of analysis, and in a sense had shared this with the Populists and with practically all writers on the peasantry. Thus, although they did not share the Populist view, perpetuated by Chayanov and his colleagues, of the consensual nature of the household, Marxist writers had not actually analysed the relations making up the household as a social institution. Although Kubanin did not take his analysis very far, his work was unique at the time in investigating the household as the product of power relations and inequality. While Kubanin would still hold that, for the purposes of class analysis, it was legitimate to use the abstraction of the household as a social unit in itself, he had now introduced the possibility of investigating the exercise of power and the relations of conflict management that created and sustained the household as a meaningful social unit.

However, the above claims for the novelty and value of Kubanin's work also serve to reveal its limitations. On the first point, although Kubanin had helped to locate the question of the splitting up of households in the context of class differentiation, he made the rather crude assumption that commodity relations necessarily strengthened the position of the patriarchal head of household and turned him into a budding capitalist, and his children into potential proletarians. A more subtle and open-ended analysis might have examined the question of the variability of responses to the growth of commodity relations, depending on a range of factors such as the existing structure and composition of different households, the kinds of agriculture they were engaged in, and the kinds of agriculture that new market opportunities might promote, alongside the question of what kinds of household might best be able to exploit different kinds of market opportunity.

An example of an alternative possible outcome is suggested here by Harrison (1977b) in his reworking of data from two dynamic surveys of the pre-revolutionary period. Harrison's explicit purpose was to challenge the Populist assumption that partition of households necessarily led to the relative impoverishment of all the resulting smaller households. Situating peasant households in the context of an expanding commodity economy, Harrison also raised the possibility of an alternative hypothesis to that of the Populists, suggesting, in a similar fashion to Kubanin, that partition could be 'economically rational [for the family as a whole or for a part of the family] and was a response of family structures to change in the external economy' (Harrison 1977b, 142). In putting forward his alternative hypothesis, however, Harrison had in mind not the Kubanin version but the possibility that in some cases, where new crops required intensive rather than extensive cultivation, a young small household might be better equipped to exploit new opportunities than an old household. Thus the potential capitalists in some cases might have been those breaking away from the parental household.

Second, although Kubanin had raised the question of the internal relations of the household and examined one effect they might have had on class relations, his focus remained very narrow. It would also have been interesting to examine the complex of relations through which social control was maintained within the household in order to understand better exactly how the shift to commodity production was related to the continuance or the partition of the household. Hypotheses could be generated concerning the ways in which different patterns of internal relations might either prevent or facilitate partition.

In relation to this question, Kubanin, along with his Agrarian Marxist colleagues, tended to think chiefly in terms of a unified household, in which, to use Harris's term, distribution within the household is conceived in terms of 'pooling': 'pooling involves first centralization and then reallocation. This process supposes a centre from which redistribution is effected. . . [the] unquestioned assumption that households are organized by and around a household head' (Harris 1981, 56). Although Kubanin had begun to see the household in terms of its component relations, he could only conceive of such relations producing a unified household under a patriarchal head. If this unit broke up, it split into two or more households still organized under new patriarchal heads.

Furthermore, the range of relations discussed by Kubanin was very narrow. In confining his discussion to the relation between the patriarchal head and the male younger generation, he ignored the whole question of the role of women within the household and their relations with the various men in the household division of labour, the internal power structure of the household, and its mechanisms of social control. From studies of peasants in other parts of the world, it is clear that a wide range of patterns of internal household relations and structures is possible, from a unified, patriarchally dominated type to a largely disaggregated type where men and women lead mostly separate lives both socially and in terms of the production relations. In the case of the Russian peasantry, this question was not researched by the Agrarian Marxists, or by anyone else, and therefore no definitive judgement can be made concerning the extent to which a unified partriarchal household predominated. While the growth of migrant labour, especially in the northern provinces before the revolution, and the more general absence of men during the war must have produced numerous farms run by women, little is known of what tensions and conflicts arose when men returned to the villages at the end of the war. It was certainly assumed by all schools of thought researching the peasantry that a unified household was maintained after the revolution.

Furthermore, the evidence available would suggest that in the 1920s, after the return of many people to the countryside and the redistribution of the land, the household was in fact the pre-dominant form of peasant social organization. However, although this would suggest that the concentration on the household as a unit in Agrarian Marxist research was not too much of a distortion of the reality of the Russian peasantry of the time, it was nevertheless a one-sided abstraction. The Agrarian Marxists showed no awareness in their writings of the significance of internal household relations which would either maintain or undermine the integrity of the household as a unit. In common with other approaches of the time, their work showed a general blindness to questions of sex roles and the position of women in peasant society. As a result, a whole dimension of social differentiation, and a whole range of possible social effects of capitalist development, were ignored, with unknown consequences for their overall understanding of the process of class differentiation.[3]

Policy issues

Like the question of internal household relations, the development of research more directly related to agricultural policy and the transition to socialist forms of agriculture was an area which the Agrarian Marxists had only tentatively begun to develop before their whole programme was brought to an end.

Of course, in a broad sense, they saw their whole work as policy-relevant. As noted in Chapter 3, Kritsman had argued that a well founded class analysis, and therefore the methodology to produce it, was vital for an understanding of the long-term social trends in relation to which policies for a socialist transition in agriculture would have to be devised. Moreover, in a paper on the agricultural five-year plan of 1924, devised mainly by Kondratiev, Kritsman showed strong interest in more detailed aspects of planning and in the relation between economic planning and the class differentiation of the peasantry.[4]

In his paper, first delivered to a meeting of Gosplan, Kritsman made a number of points. First, he argued that the plan put forward was too abstract, both in its discussion of agriculture and in its aims of industrialization. Implied in this was the idea that it was not enough to aim for improved productivity or organization in abstract without a clear statement of the social ends in view. Second, Kritsman argued that different branches of agriculture should be discussed separately in more detail and that distinctions should be made between commodity producing and subsistence sectors within them. Third, Kritsman held that planning for separate branches could not be carried out without taking into account the inter-relation between the differentiation of the peasantry and the levels of production of different crops (Kritsman 1925h, 68, 73–5).[5]

The issues raised by Kritsman in this early article were to be a continuing concern, if often only as a sub-theme, in various detailed studies carried out by the Agrarian Marxists. In particular, the impact of class differentiation on the organization of production and levels of productivity of different class groups was one of the questions discussed in the Samara study, in Gaister's book, and, most notably, in Sulkovskii's work on Saratov.

The organization of production and the question of different kinds of farm organization, their social relations, and their productivity then became more of a central focus of attention in the work of Ya. A. Anisimov, begun in 1928. Although the whole programme of work, and particularly what promised to be the more applied aspects of it, remained unfinished when Agrarian Marxist research was halted at the end of the decade, the start made by Anisimov in developing a systematic Marxist study of farm organization shows another potential path of development which the research might have taken in the 1930s. In a series of three articles, Anisimov began by providing a sociological history of farm organization studies, similar to that provided by Kritsman in agrarian statistics, linking the predominant ideas in studies of different periods to the main form of agriculture at the same time. In particular, for Anisimov, the work in this field of the Organization and Production School had arisen in relation to, and as an expression of, the problems of a petty-commodity-producing peasantry since the turn of the century; but, in the context of socialist state power and policies of socialist transition in agriculture, such work had become increasingly outmoded (Anisimov 1928a).

In this second article Anisimov went on to provide a more detailed critique of the Organization and Production School, focusing particularly on the works of Chelintsev and Makarov (Anisimov 1928b). Then, in a third article, and the last to be published, he began the task of trying to pull together the basis on which a systematic Marxist approach to farm organization could be developed. In doing this he echoed some of the points Kritsman had made three years earlier about national agricultural planning, applying the criticisms now to the existing ways in which plans for farm organization were discussed by Organization and Production School writers. For Anisimov, it was insufficient and inappropriate to tackle questions of farm organization in a framework of seeking the optimal relations of different factors of production to each other in a purely technical way, as he argued Chelintsev or Makarov had done. Instead, the social aims of farm organization and problems of encouraging collective forms of production had also to be considered and integrated into the analysis (Anisimov 1928c).[6]

The problem which Anisimov began to confront now was obviously the uncertainty about future government policy in the wake of the more punitive procurements policy introduced in the first months of 1928. Following the splits within the Party and the defeat of the Left Opposition, and now a seemingly left turn by the government, and in the context of an increasingly restrictive atmosphere for policy to be debated, it must have been a hazardous business developing ideas for a Marxist approach to farm organization. It is not surprising therefore that, at least in published form, Anisimov's work ended on a rather abstract note. The same problem can be seen with other authors who were beginning to tackle problems of farm organization. There were tendencies, for example, either towards a fairly superficial and inconclusive statement of issues of the kind produced by Lubyako and Naumov on organizational plans for *sovkhozy* (Lubyako and Naumov 1927), or towards more crudely polemical attacks on the Organization and Production School work on farm organization, such as that of Sivogrivov (1928).[7]

Thus, as with the research on internal household structure, although the developing interests of the Agrarian Marxists in more practical agrarian issues showed a commitment to developing new areas of research, the results of such work were not very well developed by the end of the 1920s.

2   Critics of Kritsman and his School

Given the controversial nature of the field of study in which Kritsman and his colleagues were working, there was remarkably little critical debate of their work. Their main rivals in the 1920s, the Organization and Production School, rarely confronted disagreements with the Kritsman group head-on, tending instead to pursue their own interests more tangentially. Moreover, on the key issue of class differentiation, the views of Chayanov and his colleagues were not completely unsympathetic. As noted above in Chapter 2, Chayanov accepted the reality of class differentiation, if only as one of a range of different types of differentiation occurring within the peasantry. He was not therefore opposed to research on this topic, seeing it as complementary to his own interests. He also was not very critical of the way Kritsman and his colleagues carried out their research on this question. While voicing technical criticisms, for example of the accounting procedures of the Volokolamsk study, Chayanov had positive things to say about Kritsman's general formulation of the question of class differentiation, and about the group's attempts to adapt the method of budget survey research to their ends. In the late 1920s, when some members of the Kritsman group introduced a harsher, more polemical, tone to their critique of Chayanov and his colleagues, the usual response was either a defensive one, or a deflection of criticisms[8] through a modification of their own research interests.

Ironically, stronger criticisms came from contemporary Russian

Marxist writers. Again, some of these were technical, especially in the case of Khryashcheva, who was unconvinced of the feasibility of synthesizing qualitative and quantitative indicators, and therefore critical of the attempts of Kritsman and his group to develop research based on the assumption that this was possible. For a Marxist, Khryashcheva had a very Positivist view of methodology which insisted on a strict dichotomy between 'facts' and 'values'. She insisted on maintaining a distinction between typologies of peasant farms, where the researcher's informed opinions were a legitimate basis, and attempts to measure the extent of differentiation within the peasantry, which had to be strictly 'factual' and therefore had to use measurable indicators which were not 'normative'. As a result, she maintained the necessity of using measures of the economic strength of households rather than measures of tendencies towards the predominance of certain kinds of relations favoured by the Kritsman school. She did not seem to see that this choice was in itself normative and based on certain unproven assumptions about the necessary coincidence between size, economic strength, and capitalist or proletarian tendencies in peasant households.[9]

More general criticisms came from a small number of other writers. The first appearance of these was at a conference in 1928, held at the Communist Academy, to discuss the work of Kritsman and his colleagues. Papers were delivered by Kritsman and most of his colleagues as well as a few critics. Of these, the leading speaker was Dubrovskii, who presented his criticisms in seven points. First, he raised the question of the groups into which the peasantry should be divided. The complexity of groups used in the Kritsman school's research, Dubrovskii claimed, served to confuse what should be a simple political point that, in conditions of capitalism, the peasantry was dividing into capitalist and proletarian groups, with the *serednyaks* in the middle (Dubrovskii 1928, 123).

Second, concerning the *serednyaks*, Dubrovskii argued that Kritsman was mistaken in seeing them as small commodity producers who combined elements of capitalism and proletarianization in their relations. Instead, they should be seen as non-capitalist farms, 'which only in the process of further development can turn into capitalist farms, but in our conditions cannot do so at all' (Dubrovskii 1928, 125).

Once such a view had been accepted, it followed, third, that the

Kritsman group's interpretation of the hire and lease of stock was wrong. For Dubrovskii, surplus value was not necessarily extracted by the owner of scarce stock from the labour of the hirer of them. This might be the case where the owner was a *kulak* and the hirer a *bednyak*, but there were many other cases of the hire or lease of means of production, involving *serednyaks*, or between peasants of the same class group, where the class characteristics could not be assumed in the way Kritsman had done. Kritsman, by assuming that all transactions involving means of production were relations of exploitation with clear class significance, was able to see elements of both capitalism and proletarianization in the vast majority of farms, and this led to a misunderstanding of the social character of the *serednyak* and to an overestimation of the extent of capitalist relations in the Soviet countryside (Dubrovksii 1928, 125–9).

Fourth, Dubrovksii took issue with Kritsman's view of the *bednyaks* as having become more dependent on stronger farms since the revolution because of their receipt of land without adequate stock to farm it as a result of the redistribution of the revolutionary period. For Dubrovskii, this seemed to contradict the party line that the situation of the *bednyaks* had improved under the Soviet state. That Kritsman was wrong he tried to prove by, on the one hand, pointing to a decline in the concentration of ownership of cattle among stronger farms compared with before the revolution, while *bednyaks* had received some stock from the better-off, and, on the other hand, arguing that, although many *batraks* had received land without sufficient stock, even so their position was relatively less dependent than it had been when they had had no land at all (Dubrovskii 1928, 129–30).

Fifth, Dubrovskii questioned Kritsman's interpretation of the revolution in the countryside. While Kritsman was right to see the first stage of the revolution as an anti-landowner revolution which was progressive in character, he was wrong in seeing the second stage, of expropriation of *kulak* farms, as predominantly petty-bourgeois in character, involving a petty-bourgeois expropriation of the *kulaks* with the Utopian aim of establishing independent peasant farming. Quoting from Lenin's polemic against Kautsky on the nature of the Bolshevik revolution (Lenin 1918d), Dubrovskii asserted that the *bednyaks*, whose struggle with the *kulaks* was the central feature of the second stage of the agrarian revolution, should be seen as part of the proletariat, therefore lending a proletarian character to the second stage (Dubrovskii 1928, 131–2). For Dubrovksii, this point was clearly linked to his fourth point concerning the improved position of the poor peasants as a result of the revolution.

Sixth, and in connection with his second and third points, Dubrovksii argued that, since Kritsman's views of the nature of the *serednyaks* and the significance of the hire and lease of stock had been so erroneous, it followed that evidence of transactions other than the hire and sale of labour power should not be used as indicators in the grouping of households. For Dubrovskii, on the basis that capitalism involved both the ownership of means of production which are transformed into capital and the hire of labour power, the chosen indicators for research should have reflected these characteristics. He therefore proposed using two indicators: a measure of a farm's means of production, and a measure of the extent of its hire or sale of labour power (Dubrovskii 1928, 133–4).

Finally, and very briefly, Dubrovksii drew attention to the role of socialized agriculture and called for much more attention to be paid to it in place of the exclusive concern with class differentiation which he claimed was evident in the work of the Kritsman school (Dubrovksii 1928, 135).

At the same conference in 1928, criticisms of the work of the Kritsman group were also heard from Sukhanov. However, whereas Dubrovskii's criticisms had been presented in a systematic way, Sukhanov's were rather rambling and confused. Basically, he seemed to be in agreement with Dubrovskii that Kritsman had overemphasized the significance of capitalist relations in peasant agriculture, mistaking generally antagonistic relations between households for specifically capitalist relations. For Sukhanov, part of the problem lay in Kritsman's use of hire and lease of means of production as indicators since, he argued, such relations were signs of trading capital but not capitalist agricultural production (Sukhanov 1928, 181–2). Kritsman's approach was also wrong in its attempt to do without indirect indicators, he thought, since these showed the size of the enterprise which was important for capital accumulation. For Sukhanov, a combination of direct and indirect indicators was necessary, presumably, given his criticisms of the use of hire and lease of stock mentioned above, involving sale or hire of labour power as the direct indicator along with some indicator of stratification (1928, 178–80).

Discontent with the use of data on the hire and lease of stock was also expressed by a third critic at the same conference, Vinogradov. He argued, in a similar fashion to Dubrovskii, that it was necessary to know whether a household hired or sold labour before the significance of insufficient means of production could be known. If a farm without necessary stock also sold labour power, then it would be a proletarian farm, but if it did not, then it would be 'a *bednyak* patriarchal farm' outside the system of capitalist relations of production. For Vinogradov, as for Dubrovskii, the peasantry was essentially a class of pre-capitalist society, which with the development of capitalism was gradually decomposing into a bourgeoisie and a proletariat. For Vinogradov, however, unlike Dubrovskii, this seemed to mean that it was illegitimate to talk of a stratification of the peasantry. He argued, claiming Lenin as his authority, that one should only talk of the decomposition, and not the differentiation, of the peasantry in relation to capitalism (Vinogradov 1928, 187–8).

Finally, and perhaps more surprisingly, at the 1928 conference there were criticisms from Raevich, who had been one of the main researchers in the Samara study. Raevich picked out for comment what he saw as Kritsman's stress on capitalist relations as the basic relations of the Soviet countryside and on the use of hire and lease of stock as indicators of such relations. However, the basic problem for Raevich lay in an assumption in Kritsman's approach that capitalist relations which could be indicated by the hire and lease of stock necessarily existed in the Soviet countryside. What was needed, thought Raevich, was a method of establishing the nature of the wider social context and the predominant relations in it, so that a more informed decision could be taken, for each piece of research separately, on the most appropriate method and indicators of grouping to be used (Raevich 1928, 105–6).

Since, with the exception of Raevich, the critics had not carried out research of their own on the class differentiation of the peasantry, their remarks were mainly of a theoretical and conceptual nature, with little firm grounding in information on the Soviet peasantry. For the most part, the tone of the debate at this 1928 conference was still cordial, although in the context of the criticisms a growing tendency was already present for the Kritsman school to be judged crudely in terms of their supposed deviations from the party line rather than in terms of the analytical value of their ideas. This was particularly clear in the accusations that Kritsman had overstressed the significance of capitalist relations in the Soviet countryside and underestimated the independence of the *serednyak*, and in Dubrovskii's criticism of Kritsman's description of the second stage of the agrarian revolution as petty-bourgeois.

The narrowly political, rather than scientific, nature of the polemic was to become more obvious in 1929 and 1930. The next major occasion for attacks on the work of Kritsman and his colleagues came at the Conference of Marxist–Leninist Scientific Research Institutes held in the spring of 1929. Here Kritsman chose to present the achievements of his colleagues' work to a wider audience through a discussion of Kubanin's work on the peasant household, which, as mentioned in Chapter 6 above, he saw as a valuable extension of the work of his school and as a strong basis for a critique of the work of Chayanov and his colleagues.

On this occasion the reception was more critical than it had been at the smaller 1928 conference. Some criticisms were pointed specifically at Kubanin's research and at its assumption that the antagonisms within the household could be seen in terms of the same kind of class relations as existed between households (Pavlov 1929, 84). Others however used the discussion to pursue further their more general criticisms of the approach of the Kritsman school. Both Dubrovskii (1929, 96) and Raevich (1929, 87) for example, returned to their theme of Kritsman's overemphasis of capitalist relations and consequent implied underemphasis on the potential for socialist transformation in the Soviet countryside, and they were supported on this occasion by Pavlov (1929, 85) and Ionov (1929, 93). Dubrovskii also repeated his criticism that the research of the Kritsman school had not paid sufficient attention to more co-operative forms of agriculture (1929, 97). Again, as at the 1928 conference, the main themes of the critics were to raise doubts about the orthodoxy of the Kritsman school's Marxism and to suggest they were deviating from the party line in their emphasis on capitalism.

Despite reasoned refutations, moreover, the critics persisted with their themes. Again in December 1929, at the First All-Union Conference of Agrarian Marxists, the critics launched their attacks— again, not based on alternative research of their own and supported only by assertions as to what the correct theoretical positions were and how the Kritsman school deviated from them.

Ironically, since the party line had now changed with the moves to collectivize the peasantry, Kritsman was no longer attacked for playing down the independence of the *serednyak* in his overemphasis of capitalist relations, but instead for underestimating the *kulak* threat. Dubrovskii was again the main critic, using as his text a footnote Kritsman had written (Kritsman 1926b, 117–18) to argue against any panic reaction to the growth of capitalist farming. In this note Kritsman had pointed out, purely as an illustration, that, even if in thirty years' time capitalist agriculture accounted for 60 per cent of all income in agriculture, given state policies supporting industrialization, and state control over the 'commanding heights' of the economy, agriculture in general might by then account for only 20 per cent of the national income, meaning that capitalist agriculture would account for only 12 per cent of the national income. At the time it was written it was quite an orthodox point to make (and indeed, even a year earlier, could have been used to refute Dubrovskii's charge that Kritsman was over-accentuating capitalist relations in agriculture), and in any case, it was never intended as part of an analysis of the nature or extent of the threat of agricultural capitalism if it were allowed to grow to such levels in the future. Dubrovskii, however, decided to interpret Kritsman's footnote as a 'thirty-year plan' for 'the capitalist development of the countryside' and to see Kritsman's arguments against a panic reaction as a serious mistake in underestimating capitalist development (Dubrovskii 1930, 321–2).

Apart from this new line of criticism, Dubrovskii also renewed his attacks on Kritsman's view of the agrarian revolution, Kubanin's views on the splitting up of peasant households, the Kritsman school's approach to the study of class differentiation, and their lack of concern with the problems of building a socialist agriculture, adding a new twist to the last point by arguing that their theoretical mistakes implied 'a right deviation in practice' (Dubrovskii 1930, 322–37). He was joined by Ignat'eva in general criticisms of a lack of Leninist orthodoxy in the work of the Kritsman school (Ignat'eva 1930, 347–52).

Although in terms of the decisions of the conference Dubrovskii's arguments were defeated and the Kritsman group was confirmed in its leadership of agrarian research, events in the wider political situation were soon to make the approach of the Kritsman school seem less and less relevant to the demands of the time. Criticisms continued in 1930 with, for example, a further attack on Kritsman's

view of the agrarian revolution (Livyant 1930). Whatever the degree
of logic or truth value of the criticisms, they provided a convenient
basis for accusations of the 'anti-Leninism' of the Kritsman school,
and therefore a justification of their removal from their positions.

3　The End of the Research

Ironically, the end came for the Agrarian Marxists on 27 December
1929, at the end of their first All-Union Conference, just as they had
successfully beaten off the attacks of Dubrovskii and their other
critics. The conference had established the Kritsman group as the
leading, and officially approved, school of thought in agrarian
questions in the Soviet Union, had given its backing to their
research approaches, and had taken various organizational decisions
which would entrust the formulation of guidelines for future
agrarian research to the group (*Trudy* . . . 1930). Then, on the last
day of the conference, Stalin chose to make his first public
announcement of the 'liquidation of the *kulaks* as a class' (*Trudy* . . .
1930, 448). Effectively, this was to mark the end of peasant family
farming in the Soviet Union, and therefore the liquidation of the
whole object of Agrarian Marxist research.

The political situation had of course been uneasy for the work of
the Agrarian Marxists since early 1928, when Stalin had revived
policies of forcible requisition of grain from the peasants. Officially,
to begin with, such moves had been presented as being aimed only
against the *kulaks*, who were said to be hoarding grain and beginning
the organization of a 'grain strike' against the government; but
during 1928 and 1929 it had become increasingly clear that the
moves were carried out against any peasants who had seizable
reserves. These policies had been followed by Stalin's announcement in his *Pravda* article, 'The Great Turn', that 'the *serednyak* has
moved towards the *kolkhozy*' and that a 'spontaneous' collectivization
of agriculture was therefore under way.[10]

Ironically, these government pronouncements, and the many
commentaries on them in the Soviet press of that period, were based
on class categorizations of peasant households for which they had no
evidence or theoretical justification at all. The years of hard thinking
and hard work, not only by Kritsman and his colleagues but by all
the researchers on rural issues in the 1920s, were suddenly
consigned to the rubbish dump of history. The rural research of the

1920s could no longer be of any use, because its object no longer existed. It was replaced by a forcibly collectivized peasantry.

The period of the collectivization of the peasantry saw the whole issue of class differentiation decided arbitrarily in a series of local actions based on little more than prejudice and hearsay. There could be no further role for the research of Kritsman and his colleagues. Their research had never envisaged the requirement of identifying the class character of individual households in order to enable punitive action against them, and nor could it. The whole approach of the Kritsman school had been developed in the context of the NEP, with its changing policy stresses over the years, but with a common theme that the Soviet state and proletariat had to live with the peasantry. This was seen either as a holding measure until the ripening of an international collapse of capitalism created new conditions for a socialist transition within the Soviet Union, or, in the context of a slow encouragement of the development of a socialized agriculture through fiscal policies, management of the terms of trade, and educational policies, alongside a containment of capitalist tendencies, again through peaceful measures. In any policies developed within such guidelines, a detailed understanding of the relations and organizational structure of the peasant farm and household, and in particular an analysis of the tendencies for various class relations to develop, were both necessary and useful. In such a situation, however, the object of research would always be the interests and motives of peasants, the pattern of their relations of production, and the nature of the forces acting on them in general.

Kritsman and his group had seen the tasks of their research to be the identification of class tendencies and the complex patterns of their coexistence within the peasantry (and often within one and the same household) in order to provide the information and understanding necessary to devise policies to constrain and structure these tendencies. The new crude policies of repression and 'administrative measures' were ignorant of all the complexities of peasant production, and their proponents would have found the detailed knowledge provided by Agrarian Marxist research to offer a threatening critique of the ignorance and crudeness of their policies. It was therefore clear that there could be no future for genuine Agrarian Marxist research. Kritsman and his colleagues held their posts until the end of 1930, and their lives until 1937, but in the course of that time they became increasingly marginalized; and, as collective paranoia spread through the ruling circles of Soviet society in the 1930s, they, following their opponents of the 1920s and most other sources of independent thought besides, were eventually completely suppressed. Following the almost general pattern of groups consigned to the role of 'oppositions' to Stalinist policy, they tried at first to accommodate and then to recant and attempt to serve by producing mindless works of propaganda. In most cases, however, this debasement was not sufficient to save their lives.[11]

Thereafter, for many years the work of the Agrarian Marxists seemed to have been forgotten. Neither in studies of the history of the Soviet Union in the 1920s, nor in research on the class differentiation of the peasantry in other societies, was their work discussed. However, in recent years their ideas have again begun to attract attention, although much of it has been negative. Their findings have also occasionally been used by historians, mostly in a partial way. In Chapter 8 below, an attempt is made to discuss more recent critics of the Agrarian Marxists, and to offer an alternative assessment of their work.

Notes

1. Unfortunately I have not been able to trace a copy of Kubanin's book. What follows is based on his articles and on Kritsman's introduction to Kubanin's book (Kritsman 1929b), which was republished in Kritsman (1929c).
2. Both critics also level more general criticisms in line with their general evaluation of the Agrarian Marxist approach as a whole. Solomon interprets Kubanin's work as largely motivated by the tactics of scoring points off Chayanov and his colleagues, while Shanin sees Kubanin's work as a good example of 'the essentially deductive and monistic thought typical of the period' (Shanin 1972, 110).
3. For further discussion of some of the general issues concerning peasant household structure and the position of women in peasant society see, e.g., Deere (1978), Deere and de Jainvry (1979); and Roberts (1986).
4. For discussion of Kondratiev's work on the plan (from a more sympathetic viewpoint), see Jasny (1972: 167–72).
5. For a detailed summary in English of Kritsman's critique of the plan, see the appendix to Littlejohn (1984: 81–4).
6. See also on this question the reviews of Chayanov's work on optimal sizes of agricultural enterprises by Kritsman (1923a) and Sulkovskii (1928a), and Sulkovskii's general review of agricultural economics (1928c).

7. Gaister was responsible for the publication of some useful empirical work on collectivized agriculture, but it too did not really develop any coherent theoretical basis on questions of new forms of farm organization for collective agriculture (Gaister 1929a, 1929b).

8. The latter approach was particularly adopted by Chelinstev, who began studies of socialized agriculture in the late 1920s (Chelinstev 1928, 1930).

9. Khryashchcva was also highly critical of Kubanin's research, although here again a large part of her objections were on technical grounds, concerning the way he had conducted his research (Khryashcheva 1928).

10. Stalin's article was published in *Pravda*, 7 November 1929. For detailed discussion of political developments concerning the peasantry in 1928 and 1929, see Lewin (1968, Chs. 9, 17); Carr (1974, Chs. 1–11).

11. For details of the political manœuvres to end the research, see Solomon (1977, 169–70). As with the leading members of the Organization and Production School, most of the Agrarian Marxist researchers died in the 1930s, probably in prison camps. Gaister, Kubanin, Vermenichev, and Sulkovskii all died in 1937, probably as part of the purges of that year. Different sources put Kritsman's death in 1937 of a kidney disease (Solomon 1977, 189) or in 1938 in prison (*Who . . .*, 1972, 317). The only major contributor to the research to survive the purges was Nemchinov, who avoided arrest and turned his attention to other areas of economics and statistics in the 1930s. He became one of the leading economists of the post-Stalin period, and died in 1964.

8

The Agrarian Marxists Today: An Assessment of their Research and its Modern Relevance

Since the ending of their research in 1930, the work of Kritsman and his colleagues has received little attention, either in the Soviet Union or in the West. While a few historians have drawn on their works for specific pieces of information, there has been little inclination to use Agrarian Marxist sources more comprehensively, and despite a growing interest among modern researchers of peasant societies in the works of Lenin and Chayanov, little attempt has been made seriously to appraise the research of the Agrarian Marxists. In the last few years, however, some attention, most of it critical, has been paid to the ideas and approaches of Kritsman and his colleagues, and to some extent their works are receiving more attention in historical discussion of Russia in the 1920s. In this final chapter an assessment of the work of the Agrarian Marxists will be offered, which, while critical, will argue that on many points their works deserve greater attention than has been realized hitherto, and in particular that their research has much which is positive to offer to modern peasant studies, and modern social research in general.

Section 1 offers an examination of the views of modern critics of Kritsman and his group. Sections 2, 3, and 4 then attempt an alternative assessment of their work, suggesting ways in which it has a contribution to make to modern scholarly work, in relation to the methodology of research on peasants and capitalism, the history of the Russian countryside during the NEP, and the relation of Marxist concepts to empirical social research.

1 Modern Critics of the Agrarian Marxists

In the Soviet Union since the 1930s, relatively few writers have made reference to Kritsman and his colleagues, either in historical research or in sociological discussions. Notable exceptions include Danilov, Chagin, and Bokarev. Danilov has made significant use of at least some aspects of Agrarian Marxist research in his historical writings on the NEP (see Section 3 below), while Chagin and Bokarev have made assessments of their theory and methods. For Chagin, Kritsman's work was one of the leading examples of concrete social research in the Soviet Union in the 1920s. However, he devotes relatively little space to a discussion of Kritsman's ideas, his main criticism being that Kritsman ignored the specific circumstances of the 'dictatorship of the proletariat' which gave the process of class differentiation a different significance than it had under capitalism (Chagin 1971, 92, 104). This is of course essentially a reflection of the standard Soviet criticism developed towards the end of the 1920s by, for example, Dubrovskii. It is also put forward by Danilov (1979: 25). Bokarev devotes more space to Agrarian Marxist work than Chagin, concentrating on their contribution to peasant budget research in his book on that subject. However, he too offers only a partial account of their work, concentrating more on the problem of establishing the lines of division between classes than on the Agrarian Marxists' original work on conceptual issues and indicators of differentiation (Bokarev 1981, 17–21, 118–28).

Among writers in English, while historians such as Carr, Davies, and Lewin have made use of their work, criticisms and comments have come mainly from three authors: Shanin, Solomon and Harrison. For Shanin, the Marxism of Kritsman and his colleagues was essentially a theory which predetermined the answers which empirical research should find. 'The main group of party scholars, led by Kritsman, developed research whose direction was governed by ideological commitment to detect a rising tide of polarisation' (Shanin 1972, 60).

Shanin sees Kritsman and his school, therefore, as working with the deductive approach based on 'Grand Theory', which offered a monistic explanation, thus failing to consider some major determinants of peasant society, and resulting in a partial and misleading set of conclusions. They shared such problems with the other main approach of the period, that of Chayanov and his colleagues, which also offered a monistic approach based on a 'Grand Theory'. While Chayanov offered a form of 'biological determinism', however, Kritsman and his school offered an 'economic determinism' (Shanin 1972, 101–12).

For Shanin, the answer lies in rejecting both approaches and, making use of Khryashcheva's work, offering an explanation based on a 'theory of the middle range', involving a 'multi-factorial analysis' (1972, 62, 109–12). Against this view, however, while it is true that neither Kritsman's nor Chayanov's theories are multi-factorial, in the sense of isolating a number of different, separate variables as causes, it does not follow that their explanations are therefore 'monistic'. As shown above, both Kritsman and Chayanov, in their different ways, recognized complex interrelations of variables, and each chose to abstract particular aspects of that complexity to which they gave priority in their explanations. Indeed, by retaining a sense of the interrelation of variables, it can be argued that they offered a more adequate approach than Shanin's multi-factorial analysis.[1]

Somewhat similar criticisms of the Marxist theory used by Kritsman and his school are offered by Solomon. Like Shanin, she sees the Agrarian Marxists as being bound by a general Marxist theory with which they had to fit their facts. 'Before 1927 the Agrarian Marxists concentrated almost entirely on designing and executing studies that would support their hypothesis that the Soviet peasantry was pursuing the capitalist path to socialism' (Solomon 1977, 128).

However, according to Solomon, the Agrarian Marxists had also adopted ideas from Lenin, based on his concepts of 'state capitalism' and 'cooperation', which led them to refine 'a theory of rural development according to which the Russian peasantry in its transition to socialism could skip the stage of capitalism'. A problem then arose when their findings, which were the results of an approach based on the general Marxist theory of class differentiation, conflicted with the expectations embodied in the Leninist theory of the nature of Soviet rural development.

In response to the dissension between their novel theory arrived at by assertion and their empirical findings, the Agrarian Marxists set aside discussion of theory and concentrated on data collection. They structured their research projects around the hypothesis that capitalism was on the rise in the countryside and. . . never used their findings to modify their original theory.

(Solomon 1977, 32–3)

As a result, for Solomon, the Agrarian Marxists became 'almost entirely atheoretical' in their approach. Rather than being concerned with honest enquiry, she implies that they were merely a group of dogmatic Marxists attempting to fit the facts to one theory while ignoring any awkward discrepancies that arose thereby in relation to a second theory which they also espoused. In trying to prove that class differentiation was necessarily occurring, Solomon argues that the Agrarian Marxists lost sight of that central figure of the NEP countryside, the middle peasant. This was most obvious in the Volokolamsk research, where, she argues, they set up a self-fulfilling prophecy by excluding the category of middle peasantry to begin with, and therefore masking its existence in their results (Solomon 1977, 63). Furthermore, for Solomon, by focusing exclusively on differentiation, they conveniently omitted to mention their original concerns with co-operatives and socialist construction. Thus, Kritsman and his colleagues failed to develop a broad view of Soviet peasant society in general, or to engage in issues of more practical concern. As such, their approach was severely limited in comparison with the work of Chayanov and his school (Solomon 1977, 33 *et passim*).

This view of the Agrarian Marxists is related to a more general approach which structures the whole presentation of Solomon's argument. She is concerned mainly with the sociology of academic research, and as a result, in her treatment of the ideas of the Kritsman group, she explores their work as half of a debate with the Chayanov school in order to draw conclusions about the nature of the academic politics of the period. Unfortunately, this tends to detract from an assessment of the ideas and findings of either school in terms of their methodologies or their analyses of Russian peasant society, and presents instead a rather misleading view where all statements, papers, and publications of the researchers are seen as tactical ploys in the continuing competition for ascendancy in their own little academic environment. The effect is to ignore the actual theory, in all its complexity, with which the Agrarian Marxists were attempting to work.

As an alternative to the interpretations of Shanin and Solomon, it is more accurate to see the Agrarian Marxists as offering a more open-ended approach, which did not seek simply to prove the propositions of a dogmatic general theory. Moreover, contrary to Solomon's view, their approach should not be seen as comprising two contradictory theories from which incompatible hypotheses were drawn. The Agrarian Marxists supported Lenin's general characterization of the transitional nature of the Soviet Union in the NEP period and the general strategy he derived from it involving tolerance for 'state capitalism' and support for co-operatives as a way of expanding and socializing production. At the same time, they wished to investigate the extent to which other features of the same transitional society, and especially petty-commodity production in agriculture, might provide a basis for class differentiation and capitalist development. Seen in this light, there are not two separate static theories from which different hypotheses can be drawn in the manner of positivist methodology, but one dialectical theory, which offers a view of a complex and contradictory society in which different tendencies, such as socialized and individual forms of agricultural production, are likely to conflict.

Given such an approach, along with a commitment to the encouragement of socialized forms of agriculture, it followed that the Agrarian Marxists should attempt to discover the strength of the counter-tendency towards private commercialized farming in order to understand the strength of the barriers to their own preferred solution. They could best do this by empirical research into the nature and extent of exploitation and capitalist development among the peasants.

In choosing to investigate class differentiation, the Agrarian Marxists were well aware that they were abstracting from a more complex reality. However, their method of abstraction, as shown in preceding chapters, did not preclude a discussion of other 'structures' with which the petty-bourgeois economy was seen to coexist; nor were collective and co-operative forms of agriculture entirely ignored, especially in the last few years of the 1920s. Moreover, as has been shown above, the Agrarian Marxists' methods did not predetermine their results. Despite their assumptions that they would find class differentiation resulting from the growth of a commodity economy, their results revealed a more complex situation involving some differentiation, but also ways in which the prevailing relations of exploitation were helping to maintain the existence of a petty-commodity-producing peasantry.

In brief, then, there would seem to be no grounds either for the claims of Solomon and Shanin that the Kritsman group was merely finding evidence to fit a dogmatic theory or, for that matter, for Soviet critics' claims that there was too much stress on capitalist relations in the Agrarian Marxists' view of the Soviet peasantry. This, of course, is not to argue that their treatment of peasants who were neither capitalist nor proletarian was fully adequate, nor that their discussion of the relation between petty-commodity production and other forms of production was sufficiently developed. On these issues, as well as on remaining problems in their research methods and approaches to calculating income and exploitation, there was still much work to do by the end of the 1920s.

There were also unresolved problems on another point raised by Solomon, and by some contemporary critics: that of the relation of the research of the Agrarian Marxist to political practice. This issue in explored further by Harrison, who is equally critical of a lack of practical orientation in the work of Kritsman and his colleagues, but who, unlike Solomon, recognizes the value of their attempt to develop a Marxist approach to the peasantry. For Harrison, the lack of a practical application in Agrarian Marxist work is a result of problems in the history of the way Marxism developed rather than something inherent in it as a theory. In relation to agrarian issues, Harrison argues, Marxism has largely been a 'subordinate Marxism'.

By 'subordinate' I do not primarily mean 'theoretically wrong'; I mean primarily a particular relationship to bourgeois intellectual life. Subordinate Marxism criticizes bourgeois theory at the level of assumptions, conceptions, and forms of knowledge. . . . It criticizes bourgeois practice by rejecting the ideas which shape it. . . . it does not possess an alternative, socialist practice relevant to the world as it actually exists.

(Harrison 1979, 92)

In many ways, for Harrison the work of the Agrarian Marxists fitted this picture.

As they began to organize their own independent work, they directed it against both the theoretical conceptions and the forms of knowledge produced by the Chayanov tradition. However, they were unable to match the Chayanov tradition's breadth of scientific endeavour. Consequently in their own work they sought to reduce the area of scientific controversy to one subject. . . . At the same time, they failed to develop their own practical theory, and could not construct an alternative socialist mode of rural intervention. . . . The Agrarian Marxists had no relationship to practice at all.

(Harrison 1979, 95)

Although there is some basis to this criticism, in that most of the energies of the Kritsman group were spent in empirical research and they did not intervene to any significant extent in the political debates of the time, it is nevertheless an exaggeration to say that the group 'had no relationship to practice at all'. In general, as shown in the chapters above, Kritsman and his colleagues saw their work as part of a wider analysis of the political situation of the USSR in the 1920s which involved them in a commitment to the political line developed by Lenin early in the decade. This involved achieving a better understanding of tendencies towards class differentiation in order to combat them through support for the poor peasants and the encouragement of socialized forms of agriculture.

Basically, for Kritsman a socialist development of agriculture had to be the result of the active participation of the majority of the peasants in its construction, and while some peasants were probably lost to the attractions of the capitalist path, the majority were still there to be won over for socialism. He advocated replacing the well-known slogan of the party, 'the union of the proletariat and peasantry under the leadership of the proletariat', with a rephrased version, 'the union of the proletariat with the majority of the peasants. . . ' (Kritsman 1925i, 27). If the well-being of this majority could be shown to improve as a result of more collective forms of production, then they could be won over. In this the role of the co-operatives, as Lenin had envisaged, was vitally important.

For Kritsman, however, the co-operatives were not simply a vehicle for the socialization of agriculture, or, as some of their critics claimed, a vehicle for the enrichment of the *kulaks*. They were

a field of struggle between capitalist and socialist tendencies of development. Where they are not dominated by capitalist elements they are the product of the interlocking of the petty-bourgeois and state economies. This opens the way for petty-bourgeois farms towards their own transcendence which, like the conversion of petty-bourgeois into capitalist farms, is based on independent small farms; but, in contrast to capitalism, independence is not individual but collective, not under the leadership of capitalism but of the proletariat.

(Kritsman 1927, 10)

Thus, given that a major problem for peasants was either the risk or the actuality of falling into dependence on their richer neighbours because of their lack of necessary means of production, there were two ways they could become securely independent. One was through success in a commodity economy, becoming increasingly entrepreneurial in character, but the other was by combining forces with similarly weak or insecure neighbours, and moreover receiving material support from the state for their preparedness to do so. For Kritsman this had been Lenin's vision, and it was still the policy the government should adopt.

In all this, research which could accurately and sensitively reveal the nature and extent of class differentiation was vital, since it was necessary to know which households should be encouraged into co-operatives and were worthy of state support for doing so. Furthermore, information on the details of the production organization of farms in different class groups would help in the task of giving them both fiscal encouragement and agronomic support in their voluntary transition into more collective patterns of farming. As shown in Chapter 6 above, the still experimental research of Kritsman and his colleagues, and especially the work of Sulkovskii, was already beginning to make a contribution in this direction.

In fact, contrary to Harrison,[2] although the Agrarian Marxists were concerned with practical issues, the main way in which they could be criticized for a lack of involvement in political practice was in their unwillingness to engage directly in the politial debates of the period. Until 1927 it is possible to know some of Kritsman's views. For example, he was prepared to criticize some of the legislation which made capitalist farming easier after 1925; he called for more support for co-operative and collective agriculture and for opposition to the growing bureaucratic and hierarchical attitudes in administration; and he continued to refer to the wider context of the need for an international proletarian revolution before socialism could be fully achieved in the Soviet Union, all in a period when such ideas were increasingly unpopular in government circles (Kritsman 1925c, 1925i, 1927a).

On the other hand, given the interest of the Opposition in the question of the differentiation of the peasantry, it is perhaps surprising that the Agrarian Marxists did not intervene more in their debates with those in ruling positions. The Kritsman group were drawn into comment directly only when the Opposition took some of Gaister's figures from his analysis of TsSU budgets and argued from them that a large *kulak* element was now clear in the Soviet countryside. However, since they had arrived at their figures by adding the totals of group V, capitalist households, to those of group IV, entrepreneurial households, Gaister was able to publish a further article denying the validity of the Opposition's interpretation of his work and stressing the *serednyak* nature of his group IV (Gaister 1927c, 18; 'Counter Theses. . . . ' 1927).

Given Kritsman's view that there was no need to fear an imminent re-emergence of a strong class of rural capitalists, he probably agreed with Gaister's dissociation of his work from the view of the Opposition, although in other ways he must have quietly sympathized with their criticisms of growing bureaucracy and their opposition to the idea of socialism in one country. However, after his more central role in economic debates in the early 1920s, Kritsman was never a very active or prominent participant in the later debates on these matters.

Given the seriousness with which he treated Lenin's ideas on the contradictory nature of the peasantry, and the need for both co-operatives and cultural revolution to encourage them along ways leading to socialism, Kritsman must have been disappointed in the lack of state support during the 1920s for encouraging poor peasants into co-operatives, and the lack of serious attention to class differentiation among government circles. However, for some reason, perhaps because he feared official interference with his research if he intervened too openly in political debates, Kritsman did not launch any very public attacks on government policy. In this context, his various remarks that state control of the 'commanding heights' of the economy would be sufficient to contain capitalist development did not really confront the main issues of what the state should have been doing in relation to the peasantry. Gradually after 1927 the more political remarks of the Agrarian Marxists tended uncritically to reflect official policy as a harsher approach was adopted to so-called *kulaks* and less voluntary moves towards collective agriculture were introduced. Like many more prominent figures, including members of the Opposition such as Preobraz- henskii, the Agrarian Marxists seem to have opted for loyalty to the Soviet state rather than outright criticisms of it.

In summary, while aspects of the views of the critics such as Shanin, Solomon, and Harrison can be accepted, their general presentation of the approach of the Agrarian Marxists is misleading. In the remaining sections of this chapter an alternative assessment of the research of Kritsman and his colleagues is offered.

2 Research on the Relation between Capitalism and Peasant Production

Since the end of the 1920s, research on the relation between peasants and capitalism has become of importance in South America, Africa, and Asia. In the development of this research, the two main general perspectives which dominated the Russian research have remained very influential, the one arguing for the existence of a separate peasant economy operating according to its own logic, and the other seeing peasant production as basically determined by capitalist relations. Moreover, some Russian writers, particularly Chayanov and Lenin, have had a strong influence on modern thinking. On the other hand, the work of the Agrarian Marxists has until recently been largely unknown to modern researchers. It will be argued below, however, that, both in its concepts and in its research methods, Agrarian Marxist work has much to offer modern research.

As far as the conceptualization of peasant society is concerned, perhaps the most important modern debate has concerned the question of whether peasant production should be understood as occurring within a general capitalist mode of production, and therefore basically determined by it, or as determined by the logic of some other mode, seen by different writers as a 'peasant mode', a 'household mode', or the survival of the feudal mode. While at a general level such non-capitalist modes are seen as subordinated to, or articulated with, the capitalist mode, at the specific level of peasant production their own internal logic is seen as determining the way peasant society operates.[3]

At the same time, there has been a growing recognition that both in the Third World and in Europe the class differentiation of the peasantry has not occurred as clearly or as extensively as classical Marxist theorists would have expected.[4] For some writers this has been seen as evidence against the idea of locating peasant production within the capitalist mode; but on the other hand, various Marxist writers have also attempted analyses of peasant societies where capitalist development is seen to have produced outcomes other than the classic pattern of differentiation. It is the work of these writers that it is interesting to compare with the research of the Agrarian Marxists.

Modern Marxist writers offer a range of different interpretations.

Some still approach the problem in a basically Leninist framework, taking evidence of inequalities between peasant households as signs of potential class differentiation, which has however been arrested by various 'blocking' mechanisms (e.g. Shivji 1976; Mamdani 1976). Others however have examined more closely the patterns of relations within peasant society to try and discover how they are linked to capitalism. Banaji, for example, has argued that, instead of a full class differentiation, capitalist development has helped create a 'concealed' proletarian class still engaged in forms of labour process and of relations of exploitation of peasant production. Although the peasant farm still has the outward appearance of an independent unit of production, in fact it is

a quasi-enterprise with the specific social function of wage labour (in the strict sense, value-producing labour). . . . In the first place, the 'price' which the producer receives is no longer a pure category of exchange, but a category, that is, a relation, of production, a concealed wage. . . . Secondly, the monopsonistic determination of 'prices' under this system, or the fact that the contracts which fix this price may often also stipulate the volume of output required and its specific quality, are necessary expressions of the capitalists' command over labour power. . . . Finally, subsistence production now figures, under this system, as the specific form of reproduction of labour power within a capitalist process of production.

(Banaji 1977b, 34)

Capitalist control over peasant production has come about, argues Banaji, as a result of increasing indebtedness. This can be seen in his analysis of detailed empirical material on the Deccan in the late nineteenth century.

Over time, a household. . . would find itself subsisting 'at the mercy of' its creditor, who would in this way come to establish *control over the reproduction process* from one cycle to the next. Elements of the production process would be 'advanced' to the peasant either in money form, or directly in material form, and the peasant would then surrender the whole crop by way of 'interest' payments.

(Banaji 1977a, 380–1)

The effect of such a relationship with capitalism was for Banaji that, while a limited amount of differentiation in the more conventional sense took place, with 'big peasants' employing the labour of semi-proletarian households, many more poor, and also middle, peasants were increasingly trapped by debt into dependence on money-lenders or 'big peasants' who supplied credit to them. The effect of such dependence was that value was extracted by capitalists from the labour of the peasants on their own farms (Banaji 1977a, 397–403).

A slightly different approach, although also based on detailed study of peasant production, is offered by Roseberry using data from the Andean region of Venezuela. Like Banaji, Roseberry notes that direct peasant producers were losing control over their means of production to 'merchant/usurers' to whom they were increasingly in debt. However, for Roseberry, Banaji's term 'concealed labour' is misleading, because it implies that the producers in question were already proletarian, beneath a peasant disguise. From the evidence of his own study, Roseberry suggests that this was not the case. The coffee-producing households he studied were not proletarian because they still retained a degree of control over their means of production, but on the other hand they were not really peasants, either. 'They were family farmers investing in commercial production. In the process of investing they were forced to enter into a relation with capital which meant they could no longer be considered peasants. While some, as entrepreneurs, might propser and accumulate resources, most had embarked on a process of proletarianization' (Roseberry 1978, 13).

An alternative interpretation is offered by Bernstein. In his view, as a result of the growth of a commodity economy, peasant production is penetrated by different forms of capital, with the result that commodity relations become built into the reproduction cycle of the peasant household. 'While the immediate organization of the production process remained in the hands of the peasants, their production and reproduction was determined by the development of commodity relations. . . which tied the producers more closely to particular kinds of production.' (Bernstein 1977, 64).

However, despite the influence of the commodity economy on peasant production, it does not transform it to the logic of accumulation as would be the case in capitalist production. The peasant economy remains based on simple reproduction. This means that, although capitalism does appropriate a surplus from peasant production, it does not do so in the same way as it would in the fully capitalist sector. Appropriation is achieved instead by 'the simple reproduction squeeze'. This involves households responding to pressures such as rising indebtedness or falls in the prices of their products by cutting their own consumption or lengthening their working day. 'The objective of the simple reproduction "squeeze" is to act as one of the mechanisms of intensifying the labour of the household to maintain or increase the supply of commodities without capital incurring any costs of management and supervision of the production process' (Bernstein 1977, 65).

For Bernstein, the outcomes of such a relation to capital are various but can be reduced to two main types: either peasant production is maintained as a cheaper way of producing certain commodities for capital than if capitalists intervened more directly in the production process, or a process of class differentiation and 'de-peasantization' takes place. However, differentiation should by no means be seen as a necessary, or even usual, outcome of capitalist penetration of peasant production (Bernstein 1977, 67–9).

Modern work such as Bernstein's[5] opens up new possible approaches not anticipated by Kritsman and his colleagues, in comparison with which their assumptions are shown to be somewhat historicist and dogmatic. However, what the modern approaches have achieved is not necessarily to supplant those of earlier writers such as Kritsman, but to increase the range of ideas which should inform and help structure further research on the relation between capitalism and peasant farming. As Williams has commented in a recent paper,

The debate on the impact of capitalism on the peasantry originally focused on the question: is peasant farming giving way to capitalist agriculture?. . . . An alternative theory suggests that capitalism incorporates peasants by subordinating them to credit and marketing arrangements in such a way that they lose control over the disposal of their produce and even over the production process itself. Opposed to both is the view that peasants continue to reproduce themselves as peasant households and maintain some degree of control. . . .

The answers to these questions cannot be deduced from a theory of history, nor from the logic of capital, or of the peasant economy. Different circumstances produce different results.
(Williams 1984, 60)

What is required, therefore, is the development of further research which is sensitive to a range of different circumstances and outcomes, and here, the Agrarian Marxists provided some useful ideas which offer an alternative to more recent approaches and potentially provide a general understanding of the nature of peasant society within which different outcomes are possible.

At the level of the peasantry as a whole, as far as the 1920s in Russia were concerned, the outcome for Kritsman was the limited differentiation, but at the same time the preservation, of a class of petty-commodity producers, within which processes of both the dissolution and the reconstitution of petty-commodity production were continually taking place. As such, Kritsman's view was perhaps closest to Roseberry's among the modern researchers, seeing the peasants as petty-bourgeois or, in Roseberry's case, family farmers, in transition to capitalism and therefore undergoing class differentiation in the long run.

However, while Kritsman, reflecting the predominant Marxist ideas of his time, abstracted the processes of differentiation and de-peasantization as the main long-term trends to be focused on in his analysis of the Russian peasantry, his general conceptualization of peasants does not necessarily preclude other outcomes. In this, his work marks an important break from Second International Marxism, and even from Lenin. As far as comparison with modern writers is concerned, while the range of outcomes he foresaw was narrower than is allowed for in some recent studies, such as those of Bernstein or Williams, Kritsman's general conceptualization allows a similar openness, although on the basis of a different understanding of the social character of the peasantry.

Kritsman's starting point was neither the idea that peasants are really hidden proletarians, nor the idea that they are involved in a non-capitalist form of production which has been subordinated to capital. Instead, he located the Soviet peasantry in a capitalist context (in that, in the absence of effective socialist construction, he thought capitalist development would inevitably follow) and also identified the peasantry as a class within capitalism with a different character from either the bourgeoisie or the proletariat. Capitalist tendencies were established by the prevalence of commodity production in the Soviet countryside, and this helped produce the contradictory character of the peasant household which could, at the same time, be both exploiting and exploited in its social relations.

Specifically, Kritsman offered an understanding of the class character of peasants as petty-bourgeois, that is, as petty-commodity producers, defined by a fundamental tension in their relations of production. Proposing a similar view to that of Marx (discussed in Chapter 1, Section 1), where peasant producers were seen as embodying the roles of both capitalist and proletarian in the same person, Kritsman conceptualized peasant households as similarly contradictory. As part of their conditions of existence, all peasant households would experience tensions between forces encouraging differentiation (towards either capitalist or proletarian class positions), and forces encouraging their preservation or reconstitution as petty-bourgeois farms. These tensions were reflected on the one hand in the pervasiveness of exploitation between households which the Agrarian Marxist research uncovered, and on the other hand in the precariousness of any clear-out differentiation into capitalists or proletarians.

Implicit in Kritsman's conceptualization of the peasantry is the idea that, while generalized commodity production implies the predominance of the capitalist mode of production in agriculture, and therefore peasant production is not to be understood as separate from capitalism, this does not require class differentiation or the eventual eradication of petty-commodity production. Both differentiation and the continued contradictory existence of the petty-bourgeoisie are, in principle, equally possible outcomes, and the particular situation can be discovered only by empirical research for each different society, taking into account its own peculiarities. In other words, Kritsman's approach laid the basis for an open-ended research strategy on the basis of Marxist theory. As such, it presented, and still presents, a powerful argument against Populist approaches, which reject both Marxism in general and the significance of the capitalist mode in particular for the study of the social character of the peasantry. While such an open-ended approach is not explicit in Kritsman's writings, it nevertheless underlies his whole work and helps establish his theoretical significance for modern research on the relation between peasants and capitalism.

In addition to their theoretical legacy, Kritsman and his group also offered some important innovations in their methodology and research methods which could have interesting applications in modern research. When the work of the modern writers is compared with that of Kritsman and his colleagues, some interesting similarities emerge. Like Banaji and Roseberry, Kritsman also was attempting to explore beyond the superficial reality of the forms through which labour was organized and exploitation took place, to the relations of production behind them. While both Kritsman and the modern researchers have extended their analysis of relations through which value is appropriated beyond the hire and sale of labour, the work of Kritsman and his colleagues would suggest a more extensive range than even Banaji and Roseberry. The latter writers bring transactions in money, credit, and means of production into consideration, but only in the context of increasing indebtedness to money-lenders or 'big peasants'. While Kritsman and his colleagues also studied such relations, the implication of their work is that further exploitation may also occur between 'middle' and 'poor' peasants where some happen to have some factors of production which are in scarce supply and which others need. Although the significance of such relations may have been particularly clear following the redistribution of land and general devastation of the countryside which had occurred in Russia, they may well be important in modern situations following land reforms or devastation by, for example, drought or civil war or both. Furthermore, it may be the case that, even where appropriation through the employment of the wage labour is predominant, other forms of appropriation are significant, although largely unstudied (see, e.g., Leys 1975, 192). In fact, perhaps one of the most important insights of the Agrarian Marxists was the pervasive nature of relations of exploitation within and between all categories of peasants.

This detailed focus on relations of exploitation is of particular importance in the search for alternatives to approaches which define the question of peasant relations of production in terms of a 'stratification problematic'. There are many modern examples, both of works seeking to show a differentiation process and of works arguing for the continued existence of an independent and more homogeneous peasantry, where the evidence cited is in terms of either the existence or lack of inequalities between households.[6] However, only in a few cases in recent years, and especially in India, have research approaches been developed using more direct indicators of class character, comparable with those of the Agrarian Marxists.

One of the most sophisticated modern attempts at empirical research on peasant class differentiation is to be found in the work of Utsa Patnaik, and, as a means of judging the modern relevance of Agrarian Marxist ideas, comparison will be made between their work and that of Patnaik.[7] For the specific question of class differentiation, Patnaik has proposed a method of analysis of peasant households using a single index, known as a 'labour exploitation ratio' (E), which measures 'the use of outside labour relative to the use of family labour'. The use of labour is measured in two ways; both directly, in terms of the hire and sale of labour, and indirectly, in terms of the rent and lease of land. The latter can be used as a measure of use of labour because the rent paid by a weak household owning insufficient land constitutes surplus labour which is appropriated by the owner of the land. By converting rental payments into an equivalent value of labour time, Patnaik proposes to calculate the balance of alienated labour and appropriated labour of a household in relation to the amount of its own labour used on its own farm. Depending on the resulting ratio, each household can then be classified into a particular class group.

Large landowners and capitalist farmers will be distinguished by a large positive value of its exploitation ratio (E) because they will have a large component of appropriated labour and a negligible amount of family labour on their own land. Rich peasants will also have a positive value of E, although perhaps not as large as for the landowner/capitalist group. Their ratio will have a large component of appropriated labour, but this will be balanced by their own household labour to a larger extent than in the previous group. In a middle-peasant household there will be more of a balance between the labour it appropriates from others and the alienation of its own labour. Its own labour on its own farm will be more significant than in the higher groups. The value of E for this group could be either slightly positive or slightly negative. For poor peasants the value of E will be more clearly negative, reflecting a larger extent of alienated labour. The household will depend more on selling labour and less on working on its own farm than households in the middle group. Finally, the full-time wage workers will have no labour on a plot of their own and a strongly negative value of E, reflecting their total dependence on selling their labour to others (Patnaik 1976, A84–5).

Unfortunately, although Patnaik's approach contains much which is interesting methodologically, hardly any existing survey data on Indian peasant farming lend themselves to analysis using such methods, and as yet, only preliminary results are available from newly developed research using Patnaik's methods. However as an approach to the question of class differentiation, it marks a clear advance on most others currently used in research on modern peasant socities. It is also interesting in that it forms only one part of

Patnaik's research, which also comprises a different set of methods designed specifically to identify capitalist farms, as distinct from large landowners or big peasants. Patnaik first put forward this approach in two articles in 1971 in response to research with similar aims developed by A. Rudra. For Patnaik specifically, the degree of capitalist orientation of farms could be recognized from the following seven criteria:

1. higher-than-average value of cash wages (and cash outlays generally) per acre;

2. higher-than-average ratio of sales to value of output;

3. higher-than-average value of modern capital equipment per acre;

4. higher-than-average value of profit per acre;

5. higher-than-average value of output per acre;

6. higher-than-average value of modern capital equipment per unit wage outlay;

7. higher-than-average value of output per unit wage outlay.

According to Patnaik, such a set of criteria is necessary for the identification of capitalist farms, rather than simply the employment of wage labour and the involvement in commodity production, because these latter characteristics can be found also in pre-capitalist forms of production. For Patnaik, the key characteristic of a capitalist enterprise is that it accumulates capital, reinvesting part of the surplus it has appropriated from the labour of others. Therefore, she argues, a whole range of variables is needed to identify capitalist farms, reflecting higher-than-average levels of reinvestment of a surplus, as well as higher-than-average involvement in markets and employment of wage labour (Patnaik 1971a, 124–7; 1971b, 193).

Taken together, the two aspects of Patnaik's approach represent one of the most comprehensive attempts so far to devise empirical survey research on the relation between capitalism and peasant farming. In some ways there are similarities with the Agrarian Marxist approach; in other ways there are clear advantages over it; while in other aspects again the Agrarian Marxist approach may still prove more satisfactory. The main similarities are seen first in the use by Patnaik, like the Agrarian Marxists, of direct indicators of exploitation as measures of class differentiation, in preference to indicators of inequality, and second in the recognition of the importance of calculating the tendencies of a household to exploit or be exploited *in relation to* its tendencies towards independent production, using its own resources on its own land.

Patnaik's work, in comparison with that of Kritsman, also offers some possible advances. First, it at least attempts to use units of labour time as a common unit of measurement for different relations of exploitation, a feature that is perhaps especially important in research aiming to operationalize Marxist concepts based on the labour theory of value. Second, and more important, Patnaik's approach combines a measure of the accumulation of capital with a measure of the expropriation of a surplus. As noted in Chapter 6, the lack of such a measure was a serious problem for Agrarian Marxist researchers. Without it, they either fell back on attempting to decide on class membership on the basis of tendencies to exploit or be exploited only (as in the case of the Volkolamsk research), or they used indirect indicators of accumulation based on a notion of the 'economic strength' of a household (for example, the Urals research of Nemchinov).

However, in other important respects Patnaik's approach may be criticized as incomplete in the range of factors it takes into account, and the approach of Kritsman and his colleagues might offer something useful in return. First, as noted above, Patnaik's approach is based on a single indicator of exploitation. This has been criticized by various writers (e.g. Shanin 1980, 87; Athreya *et al.* 1983, 36) because it would seem to leave out important relations through which a surplus can be appropriated, including credit relations and off-farm trades. By comparison, in their slightly different ways, from one project to the next, the Agrarian Marxists attempted to use multiple indicators of exploitation, including transactions not only in labour and land, but also in livestock, farming implements, and machinery, credit, and off-farm trades and crafts.

Moreover, although the Agrarian Marxists' position was not clearly worked out on this, it may be that their use of systems of measurement of exploitation based on money or points was more practical than Patnaik's use of units of labour time is likely to be. At first sight it might seem that, if research is based on the assumptions that capitalist relations lie at the basis of peasant production, and that the labour of the direct producer is the source of the value appropriated from peasant production by capital, then it would be theoretically correct to measure exploitation in terms of units of labour time. However, to the extent that the peasant households under study are, for the most part, not yet proletarianized, then their own labour used on their own land, even when it is used in relation to other households' means of production, has not yet taken the form of a commodity. This would also be the case for a household's own labour used on rented land. In these conditions peasants still have some significant control over the disposition of their labour, unlike the wage workers. If this is the case, then it follows that there is in fact a better theoretical justification for the use of money prices or points as general equivalents to measure different relations of exploitation.

Furthermore, at a more practical level, it is not clear how Patnaik would actually calculate the rent of land in units of labour time, as she has proposed. While she has given a sophisticated theoretical justification (1980, 484–5), there are as yet no results of empirical studies to show how successful this may be in practice. Certainly, other writers have expressed doubts about using units of labour time as a measure. Shanin, for example, has described it as unworkable, and has stated a preference for the approach adopted by Nemchinov (Shanin 1980, 87, 92–5); but in view of the fact that Nemchinov used money values as his general equivalent, and in view of Shanin's earlier expressed doubts about the suitability of this form of measurement for peasant farming (Shanin 1972, 131–2), it is not clear what method of measurement he would actually propose.

There are also doubts about Patnaik's assumption that an average labour time of the kind assumed by Marx for capitalist production could in fact prevail in peasant household production. If the doubts are correct, this would pose great problems for research aiming to generalize about class relations on the assumption that the appropriation of a given number of units of labour time represents the same degree of exploitation in different parts of the same society. More specifically, as Athreya and colleagues have argued (1983, 36–9), doubts about the existence of an average labour time pose particular problems for Patnaik's approach because she wishes to distinguish three types of labour—labour hired in, labour hired out, and family labour—each of which, it is assumed, share the same proportion within them of necessary and surplus labour. On the basis of the authors' empirical work on India, this seems dubious, because they argue, first, that family labour is more often used in 'labour-extensive' tasks such as tending livestock or maintaining irrigation, whereas hired labour is more likely to be used in crop production, and, second, that hired labour employed on farms with different class characters, and therefore different patterns of organization requiring different levels of intensity of labour, will not be homogeneous either.

In view of such problems, it may well be that, despite their lack of explicit discussion of the reasons for their choice of measures of exploitation, the Agrarian Marxists' solutions will prove more practicable. If there is still significant household control over the actual disposition of its labour, albeit constrained by the demands of capitalism more widely, and if the productivity of labour is not sufficiently homogeneous to make generalization possible, then perhaps it is more realistic to take the actual measures for various factors that are used by peasants themselves in the transactions, and treat them as prices rather than as values in a Marxist sense. Furthermore, in view of the complexity of expressing different prices in terms of money, or of finding out the precise monetary expression for transactions carried out using other measures, then perhaps the use of a points system such as that used in the Samara research more realistically represents the level of accuracy actually achievable by research.

Clearly, many of these issues concerning concepts and methods of research are not yet resolved and further debate will continue. Modern research on these issues is still in its relative infancy, and the work of the Agrarian Marxists was not allowed to develop from its first attempts to resolve the problems. Any conclusions from the above discussion must therefore remain tentative. The main point made here is simply to illustrate the continuing relevance of Agrarian Marxist work for the continuing task of refining research approaches on questions of the relations between capitalist and peasant production.

3 Agrarian Marxist Research and the History of the NEP Period

As far as historical research is concerned, the information provided by Agrarian Marxist studies has so far been of limited use, given that historians have been concerned mainly with broad questions such as the overall proportions of different social classes in the Soviet countryside, their political roles and interests, and their relative share of the marketable grain surplus. Although the Agrarian Marxists had hoped eventually to produce figures which would have been useful for the study of such questions, as noted in Chapter 5, they were only beginning to produce analyses of data at a nationwide level by the end of the 1920s, and such figures were highly problematic in comparison with the requirements they had set for their own local surveys. As a result, recent historians of the period have tended to be attracted by the seeming completeness and comprehensibility of stratification data such as those used by Khryashcheva or Strumilin.

There has been a wide range of interpretations of the extent and significance of the differentiation of the peasants among historians. It ranges from Soviet writers such as Trapeznikov, (1981, Vol. 1, 486–91, Vol. 2, 66–9), who writes of growing differentiation, sharpening class struggle, and attempts by the *kulaks* to foment civil war, through Bettelheim (1978, 85–126), who recognizes some differentiation but thinks it need not have led to the abandonment of the NEP compromise if different policies had been followed, to Shanin (1972, 45–137), who argues for the basis class homogeneity of the whole of the peasantry in relation to the state and sees differentiation as largely cyclical in character. However, in all these arguments the data relied on to support the different interpretations have been stratification figures reflecting inequalities of distribution of different factors of production. For both Trapeznikov and Shanin, the main original sources have been TsSU surveys and the analysis of Khryashcheva, while Bettelheim's main source is the work of Strumilin, which, while more sophisticated than the TsSU figures, was nevertheless based on a stratification rather than a class approach.

While, admittedly, there are no completely satisfactory figures based on a class analysis with which to replace the stratification data, nevertheless it is disappointing that historians have not been more aware of the critique produced by Kritsman and his colleagues of the data they seem content to use. Few have seen fit to report in any detail on the debates of the 1920s concerning how to collect figures on stratification, and ironically, in the case of the main writer who has reported these debates at any length (Lewin 1968, 43–9), his conclusion seems to be that the whole debate was so confused that no clear conclusions could be drawn. However, recently the work of the Agrarian Marxists has begun to receive more attention as a source for historical research. In the Soviet Union, Danilov has made use of Gaister's analysis of TsSU budget data, as well as the work of the commission on the 1926 census, in his account of the class structure of the countryside in the 1920s (1979, 313–20), and he has also referred to Agrarian Marxist writers, especially Kubanin, in his discussion of peasant household structure (1977, 235–64).

Meanwhile, in the West, Littlejohn has helped make the problems behind the figures on peasant differentiation in the Soviet Union better known through his translation of Kritsman's critique of existing studies on the subject in the mid-1920s (Kritsman 1926b 1984). In addition, he has also shown how Kritsman's understanding of the nature of the peasantry during the 1920s can help in historical interpretation of the problems and prospects of the NEP. Connecting various aspects of Kritsman's ideas, including his opinion that class differentiation was proceeding only slowly in the 1920s, his faith in the power of the Soviet state to adopt measures to counteract the formation of a developed capitalist class in the countryside, and his belief that more favourable policies towards poor peasant farms and the encouragement of co-operation could have helped both in socialist construction and in the preservation of the NEP, Littlejohn interprets Kritsman in support of the view of various recent historians (e.g. Bettelheim 1978, Grosskopf 1976) that the end of the NEP was the 'result of its faulty implementation' rather than the result of the growing threat of a *kulak* class. Furthermore, this can be linked with the argument that industrialization was carried out on the basis of a surplus appropriated from the workers rather than from the peasants, implying that forced collectivization and the suppression of a small but growing *kulak* class were not necessary for industrialization (Littlejohn 1984, 60–76).

While Littlejohn is surely correct in his interpretation of Kritsman's stress that a *kulak* class posed no immediate threat in terms of its economic strength, and that socialist state policies could effectively undercut the existing trends of class differentiation, he may nevertheless have underestimated Kritsman's concern at the growth of agrarian capitalism.[8] After all, he was worried enough to go against the conventional party wisdom of the mid-1920s in setting up the research programme of the Agrarian Marxists to study class differentiation, and in presenting his critiques of the class blindness of the existing agricultural plan and official agrarian statistics. He and his colleagues were often also suspicious of *kulak* involvement in peasant co-operative arrangements and party organizations, seeing possible ulterior class motives at work beneath the surface.

Since Kritsman openly expressed fewer political opinions towards the end of the 1920s than he had formerly, it is difficult to be sure of his views, but it would seem equally plausible to use his work in support of a view which, admittedly in the longer term than the end of the 1920s, saw a gradual growing threat in the increasing power of the *kulaks*. It can be pointed out, for example, that Kritsman and his colleagues were not entirely unhappy at the increasingly anti-*kulak* turn of official policy towards the end of the decade, and this may not have been entirely the result of opportunism. Like some members of the Left Opposition, they may initially have seen Stalin's policy shift as representing a cruder version of some of their own views and, as such, preferable to the previous 'Bukharinist' policies. Furthermore, Kritsman's optimism in the mid-1920s concerning the capacity of state policies to undercut the growth of a *kulak* class was presumably based on the assumption that changes in favour of support for poor peasants and for the encouragement of co-operation and socialized production would be introduced during the 1920s or early 1930s. Without such policy changes, the increasing political influence of the *kulaks*, their increasing economic power over their neighbours as sources of credit and scarce means of production, and their influence in local trade in the absence of effective state organization would all have served to increase their power relative to the rest of the peasantry. In these respects, therefore, Kritsman's views should not be equated too closely with those of Bettelheim or Grosskopf, although Littlejohn's basic points that Kritsman's views were incompatible with the idea of a *kulak* 'grain strike', and compatible with moves towards industrialization and socialist construction within NEP, are well founded.

Despite such differences of interpretation over the implications of Kritsman's work for an analysis of the NEP, the basic point stands that Littlejohn's discussion illustrates the value of Agrarian Marxist work for attempts at such historical analysis. Further uses may also be possible. For example, if the trend reflected in recent studies of the revolutionary period is also to apply to the 1920s, with more attention being paid to local-level studies and to the way history is the complex result of the activities of ordinary people in their localities,[9] then the specifically detailed local nature of much of the Agrarian Marxists' research may prove to be a very useful resource.

4   Agrarian Marxist Research as a Model for a Marxist Rural Sociology

Finally, in addition to the more specific considerations discussed in Sections 2 and 3 above, the work of Kritsman and his school can also be seen as a contribution to the development of a Marxist rural sociology. As such, its origins have been traced above both in developments in classical Marxist theory and in the Russian tradition of empirical social research on the peasantry. Although a number of problems have been noted with the work of the Agrarian Marxists, it can be suggested that, in synthesizing Marxist theory with the Russian rural research methods, some important and valuable innovations were made, both in a theory of the peasantry in conditions of petty commodity production and in the methods of study of the relations of production and social structure of such a peasant society. In particular, Kritsman and his colleagues, through their conceptualization of the Russian peasantry in terms of class relations rather than more rigidly defined concrete classes or groups, have made a contribution to the study of peasant societies which is still relevant today, offering a means of understanding the essential transitional nature of such societies which is lost if too rigid a concept of class structure is employed.

Similarly, through their detailed work on specifying the particular relations of exploitation through which they considered class differentiation to be taking place in the Russian conditions of the 1920s, and the way in which data on the occurrence of such relations could be used as indicators of class differentiation, Kritsman and his colleagues have also made a lasting methodological contribution to modern rural sociology. For while the particular relations of exploitation, and therefore the particular most suitable indicators of class differentiation, may vary from society to society, the approach that they adopted of identifying the relations most appropriate for their own conditions, and of utilizing data on them in empirical research, offer an important example to be followed.

In a previous work (Cox, 1979a), I suggested that appropriate criteria for judging the adequacy and success of an attempt at a Marxist sociology should include the way such research develops and employs a concept of class, the extent to which it develops a realist methodology, and the extent and nature of its role in providing a critique of the society in which it exists. On each of these counts, it is interesting to compare the work of the Kritsman school with more recent attempts at a Marxist rural sociology in the Soviet Union.

In terms of its conceptualization of class, the Agrarian Marxist approach offered a means of defining the changes of the society being studied in terms of the social relations of production and exploitation which avoided resort to the abstract notions of property pervasive in modern Soviet sociology. Moreover, the major tendencies of social change were explained in terms of the dynamics of class relations with respect to changes in the forces of production, instead of by resort to the influence of changes in technology in abstraction from the relations between classes that determine its development and application. This is brought out especially clearly if, for example, the comparison is made between the way in which modern Soviet sociologists explain how scientific and technological change brings about changes in patterns of stratification through its effect on productivity, the labour process, and standards of living, in a basically evolutionary, systemic fashion,[10] and the way in which Kritsman explained how the class struggles of the agrarian revolution created a countryside characterized by a struggle between capitalist interests and the socialist state to influence the mass of petty-bourgeois farmers, each offering a means of achieving economic independence and security by different routes, and thus attempting to establish the conditions for capitalism or socialism in the Russian countryside.

Use of this example can also illustrate the basic methodological differences between the work of the Kritsman school and modern Soviet sociology. In modern Soviet sociology, the working class and the *kolkhoz* peasantry are pre-defined by the theory. The role of the sociologist is most often an ascientific one of illustrating the theory or resolving narrowly defined problems which do not challenge the theory. Alternatively, in the more sophisticated work of, for example, Arutyunyan (1971), the task is to attempt a positivist approach in deducing hypotheses from the pre-defined theory for empirical testing.[11] In Kritsman's work, by contrast, to quote the phrase used by Lukacs in a different context, 'orthodoxy refers exclusively to method' (Lukacs 1922, 1). The classes existing in the society under study had to be discovered through research, and conventional wisdom concerning their definition or political interests was to be treated with suspicion. Thus Kritsman developed a critique of the conventional classifications of the peasantry based on sown area statistics, and of conventional views about the political progressiveness or otherwise of the petty-bourgeoisie and the class alliances it was likely to form, which, as he said, were based on Western European experience, and not necessarily applicable to the Soviet Union (Kritsman 1925e, 14).

Thus Kritsman's approach illustrated the use of a realist method, seeking to discover the processes of social relations which were hidden from phenomenal reality, but which were the real causes of that reality.[12] This involved for him, following Marx, the use of the dialectical method where things were to be conceived in their interrelations, which were constantly in a process of change. 'Among the majority of those who consider themselves followers of Marx, there exist definite clichés apparently stemming from Marx's teachings. . . . But reality is constantly changing and needs each time the special use of Marxist method' (Kritsman 1925e, 14).

For Kritsman, it was only through an open-minded enquiry which sought its own evidence and drew conclusions which were faithful to it, that the reality of class relations in a given situation could be discovered. The importance of this was that it was through the relations and struggles of these classes that the social structure at any given time was constituted, and therefore that it was only through an analysis of class relations that the nature of society and its tendencies could be known. The *a priori* assumption of the nature of society and its constituent classes, which is typical of modern Soviet sociology, would be quite foreign to the approach employed in Kritsman's work.

Finally, the differences can be seen also on the question of the relation between research and practice. The aim of the work of Kritsman and his colleagues was to help decide on practice by informing the debates through which policy issues would be decided. Far from simply taking their cue from policy-makers, when the research began in the mid-1920s Kritsman was swimming against the tide of policy dominated by the ideas of Bukharin. This contrasts sharply with the work of modern Soviet sociologists, who have to restrict their concerns to problems in the implementation of general policy rather than raising basic issues. However, it is perhaps in questions of the relation to practice that the Agrarian Marxist research has most in common with modern Soviet sociology. By the time the research of the Kritsman school was established, open debate within the party had already become increasingly circumscribed, and, as noted above, as the decade went on Kritsman's political comments on policy became rarer. Although it was still possible in the 1920s to do research which implied criticism of ruling views, it was dangerous to use it to launch an overt attack on governing circles. In this sense the work of Kritsman and his colleagues was becoming increasingly restricted in the extent of the social critique it could offer, and was already beginning to experience some of the constraints which are the norm for social research in the Soviet Union now.

Taken as a whole, however, the research of Kritsman and his school represents the peak of a remarkable flowering of Marxist empirical social research in Russia in the 1920s. It remains to this day a rare example of a Marxist method being used in detailed empirical and policy-oriented research. It marks a peak in the history of sociological research in the Soviet Union which is unlikely to be attained again in the foreseeable future. The contribution offered by the Agrarian Marxists to the conceptualization of peasant society could offer valuable insights for the development of the study of peasants in the modern world. Moreover, the example of the Agrarian Marxist researchers in terms of method is still relevant more generally to sociological research today.

Notes

1. For more detailed criticisms of Shanin's argument see Cox (1979b).
2. For further argument against Harrison's interpretation, see Littlejohn (1984, 68–9), where he suggests that, at least implied in Kritsman's analysis, there were ideas for policy in relation to credit, pricing, and trading organization.
3. For examples of the argument concerning the articulation of modes, see Rey (1973) and Wolpe (1980).
4. See, for example, Djurfeldt (1981), Mann and Dickinson (1978), and Williams (1976).
5. For further discussion and examples of modern works on these issues, see e.g. Harriss (1982b), Goodman and Redclift (1981).

6. For further details, see Cox (1983b, 211–15) and Williams (1976, 143–4, 147).
7. The literature on class differentiation within the Indian peasantry is both extensive and of high quality. Unfortunately, it cannot be discussed in detail here. The work of Patnaik is taken only as a representative example, albeit one of the most distinguished examples of this body of modern research, as a means of assessing the work of the Agrarian Marxists.
8. Littlejohn writes for example: 'Yet it is clear from Kritsman's analysis that the *kulaks* were often not a direct political danger; they were often in the Party and beneficiaries of its policies in many unintended ways. Neither were they a serious economic danger, given the strength of the state sector, even if they were economically powerful in their own localities' (Littlejohn 1984, 69).
9. See e.g. Smith (1983).
10. Cox (1979a, 23–4); *Sovremennaya* . . . (1970); Amvrosov and Staroverov (1974).
11. For my discussion of Arutyunyan's methodology see Cox (1979a, 71–84, 89).
12. For discussion of the realist approaches to social science and contrasts with positivist approaches, see Keat and Urry (1975).

Appendix

The Economic Regions of European Russia and the Locations of the Agrarian Marxists' Research Projects

Reference has been made at various points in the text to the different economic regions of European Russia. While the precise details of how the regions were distinguished and where their boundaries were drawn has varied between different writers, in general there was a broad agreement on this question. A commonly used scheme before the revolution was that of P. P. Semenov, who divided European Russia into twelve regions as follows (see also the accompanying map):

Region	Constituent guberniyas
1. Far North	Arkhangel'sk, Vologda
2. Lakes	Olonets, parts of Tver, Pskov, Novgorod, St Petersburg
3. Baltic	Estland, Livland, Kurland
4. Moscow Industrial (or Central Industrial)	Moscow, parts of Tver, Yaroslavl, Kostroma, Nizhegorod, Vladimir
5. Central Agricultural	Kaluga, Tula, Ryazan, Penza, Tambov, Voronezh, Kursk, Orel
6. Urals	Vyatka, Perm, Ufa, Orenburg
7. Volga	Kazan, Simbirsk, Samara, Saratov, Astrakhan
8. Little Russia	Chernigov, Poltava, Kharkov
9. New Russia	Bessarabia, Kherson, Ekaterinoslav, Taurida
10. South West	Kiev, Volhynia, Podolia
11. Belorussia	Minsk, Mogilev, Smolensk, Vitebsk
12. Lithuania	Kovno, Vilna, Grodno

After the revolution, in 1921, a commission of Gosplan drew up a slightly different scheme made up of eleven regions with some variations on the above scheme. However, informally, reference was still made by various writers to the pre-revolutionary regions. It is these that have been used in the text above. (For a detailed discussion of the various schemes of regions and the criteria for them, see Baranskii 1926, 5–41.)

In general, the land in the northern regions and in the Central Industrial Region was less fertile, and these regions were mainly deficient in grain. The sown area of farms tended to be small. These areas, or parts of them, were sometimes known as the 'consumer zone', in contrast to those regions to the south which had more fertile soil, slightly larger farms, and a greater productivity: those areas were able to produce a grain surplus and were sometimes referred to as the 'producer zone'. There were, however, important differences between the provinces of the Central Agricultural Region and the 'border' regions to the south in New Russia, and to the west in the Volga region. Compared with the border areas, the concentration of population in the Central Agricultural Region was such that farms tended to be smaller and less productive.

The implications of regional variations for the differentiation of the peasantry is unclear. In so far as pressure for land made more extensive farming and the expanding of commodity production of grain difficult in the Central Agricultural Region, it was generally thought that little differentiation could be expected there. More likely areas were the border lands to the south and west, where more extensive farming was possible, and the Moscow Industrial Region, where, despite the poor fertility of the soil, industrial and urban markets provided incentives for the production of dairy produce, vegetables, and flax, as well as stock breeding (Antsiferov 1930, 39–40). However, to a significant extent this may have been an impression created by the predominant use of sown area as the main indicator of differentiation. Both Lenin and Kritsman considered that class differentiation was taking place in the Central Agricultural Region as well as in the rest of Russia, but not necessarily through expansion of grain cultivation directly (Lenin 1899, 114–20, Kritsman 1925d, Part 4, 42).

Furthermore, even if clear class groups were not emerging in the Central Agricultural Region to the same extent as elsewhere, this would not exclude the possibility of the development in the Central Region of relations of exploitation of the kind that Kritsman identified elsewhere in Russia. If this region had suffered the same shortages of stock that were common elsewhere, then such relations were very likely. Unfortunately, however, the Kritsman group did not carry out any research of their own in this area.

Bibliography

Alavi, H. (1975), 'India and the Colonial Mode of Production', *Socialist Register*, London.

'Alin' (1928), Review of Vermenichev *et al.* (1928), *Planovoe khozyaistvo*, No. 4.

Amvrosov, A. A., and Staroverov, V. I. (1974), 'Nauchno-tekhnicheskaya revolyutsiya i razvitie sotsial'noi struktury sel'skogo naseleniya SSSR', *Nauchny kommunizm*, No. 4.

Anisimov, Ya. A. (1927), 'Differentsiatsiya Krest'yanskogo Khozyaistva', *Puti sel'skogo khozyaistva*, No. 6.

—— (1928a), 'Postanovka nekotorykh voprosov ob organizatsii sel'skogo khozyaistva v proshlom', *Puti sel'skogo khozyaistva*, No. 1.

—— (1928b), 'Osnovnye polozheniya organizatsionno-proizvodstvennoi shkoly v uchenie ob organizatsii krest'yanskogo khozyaistva', *Puti sel'skogo khozyaistva*, No. 2.

—— (1928c), 'K postanovke nekotorykh voprosov ob organisatsii sel'skogo khozyaistva, primenitel'no k usloviyam SSSR', *Puti sel'skogo khozyaistva*, No. 4/5.

—— (1928d), 'Diskussiya o klassovykh gruppirovkakh krest'yanskikh khozyaistv', *Na agrarnom fronte*, No. 8.

—— Vermenichev, I., and Naumov, K. (1926a), 'K voprosu o sotsial'nom sostave moskovskoi derevni', *Na agrarnom fronte*, No. 5/6.

——, —— and —— (1926b). 'O progreshnosti podvornogo metoda obsledovaniya krest'yanskogo khozyaistva', *Na agrarnom fronte*, No. 11/12.

——, ——, and —— (1927), *Proizvodstvennaya kharakteristika krest' yanskikh khozyaistv razlichnykh sotsial'nykh grupp*, Moscow.

Antselovich, N. (1925a), 'Voprosy zashchity i organizatsii batrashestva', *Na agrarnom fronte*, No. 4.

—— (1925b), 'Raboche-krest'yanskii soyuz i batrachestvo', *Na agrarnom fronte*, No. 5/6.

Antsiferov, A. N. (1930), *Russian Agriculture during the War*, New Hartford, Conn.

Arutyunyan, Yu. V. (1966), 'Iz opyta sotsiologicheskikh issledovanii sela v 20 gg.', *Voprosy istorii KPSS*, No. 3.

—— (1971), *Sotsial'naya struktura sel'skogo naseleniya SSSR*, Moscow.

Athreya, V., Boklin, G., and Djurfeldt, G. (1983), 'Identification of Agrarian Classes: A Methodological Essay with Empirical Material from South India', *Arbejdspapir*, No. 21, Sociologisk Institut, Copenhagen.

Atkinson, D. (1983), *The End of the Russian Land Commune*, Stanford, California.

Banaji, J. (1972), 'For a Theory of Colonial Modes of Production', *Economic and Political Weekly* (Bombay), Vol. 7, No. 52.

—— (1977a), 'Capitalist Domination and the Small Peasantry: Deccan Districts in the Late Nineteenth Century', *Economic and Political Weekly*, special issue, August; reprinted in Rudra *et al.* (n.d.): page references are to this edition.

—— (1977b), 'Modes of Production in a Materialist Conception of History', *Capital and Class*, No. 3.

Baranskii, N. (1926), *Ekonomicheskaya Geografiya Sovetskogo Soyuza*, Moscow and Leningrad.

Baron, S. H. (1963), *Plekhanov: The Father of Russian Marxism*, Stanford, California.

—— (1974), 'Plekhanov, Trotsky, and the Development of Soviet Historiography', *Soviet Studies*, Vol. 26, No. 3.

Baskin, G. I. (1927a), 'Vliyanie urozhaev na differentsiatiyu krest'yanskogo khozyaistva', *Puti sel'skogo khozyaistva*, No. 4.

—— (1927b), 'Batrachestvo v Samarskoi gubernii', *Na agrarnom Fronte*, No. 3.

Baturinskii, D. (1926), 'Problema naemnogo truda v sel'skom khozyaistve', *Na agrarnom fronte*, No. 5/6.

Bernstein, H. (1977), 'Capital and Peasantry', *Review of African Political Economy*, No. 10.

Bettelheim, C. (1976, 1978), *Class Struggles in the USSR*, Vols 1 and 2, London.

Blum, J. (1971), *Lord and Peasant in Russia*, Princeton, NJ.

Bokarev, Yu. P. (1981), *Byudzhetnye obsledovaniya krest'yanskikh khozyaistv 20-kh godov kak istoricheskii istochnik*, Moscow.

Bolshakov, A. M. (1924), *Sovetskaya derevnya 1917–24*, Leningrad.

—— (1925), *Sovetskaya derevnya za 1917–25 gg.*, Leningrad.

—— (1927), *Derevnya 1919–1927*, Moscow–Leningrad.

Brykin, N. (1925), *V novoi derevne: ocherki derevenskogo byta*, Leningrad.

Bukharin, N. I. (1920), *Ekonomika perekhodnogo perioda*, Moscow; translated and published as part of N. I. Bukharin, *The Politics and Economics of the Transition Period*, ed. K. Tarbuck, London, 1979.

—— (1925a), *Pravda*, 24 April.

—— (1925b), *Put k sotsializmu i raboche–krest'yanskii soyuz*, Moscow– Leningrad.

Byres, T. J. (1980), 'Peasants as Unfinished History', *Economic and Political Weekly*, No. 31.

Carr, E. H. (1966), *The Bolshevik Revolution*, 3 Vols, Harmondsworth.

—— (1969), *The Interregnum*, Harmondsworth.

—— (1970), *Socialism in One Country*, Harmondsworth.

—— (1974, 1976), *Foundations of a Planned Economy*, Vols 1 and 2, Harmondsworth.

Chagin, B. A. (1967), 'Razvitie sotsiologicheskoi mysli v SSSR v 20e gody', *Filosofskie Nauki*, No. 5.

—— (1971), *Ocherk istorii sotsiologicheskoi mysli v SSSR*, Leningrad.

Chayanov, A. V. (1912a), *Ocherki po teorii trudovogo khozyaistva*, Moscow.

—— (1912b), *Len i drugie kul'tury v organizatsionnom plane krest'yanskogo khozyaistva nechernozemnoi Rossii*, Moscow.

—— (1915), *Byudzhety krest'yan Starobel'skogo uezda*, Khar'kov.

—— (1922), 'Optimal'nye razmery zemledel'cheskikh khozyaistv', in *Problemy zemleustroistva*, Moscow.

—— (1924a), 'Zur Frage einer Theorie der nichtkapitalistischen Wirtschaftssysteme', *Archiv für Sozialwissenschaft und Sozialpolitik*, Band 51; translated as 'On the theory of non-capitalist economic systems' in Thorner *et al.* (1966).

—— (1924b), *Ocherki po ekonomike trudovogo sel'skogo khozyaistva*, Moscow.

—— (1924c), 'Znachenie mashiny v trudovom i kapitalisticheskom khozyaistve', in Chayanov (1924b).

—— (1925), *Organizatsiya krest'yanskogo khozyaistva*, Moscow; page references are to the English translation, published as 'Peasant Farm Organisation' in Thorner *et al.* (1966).

—— (1927), 'O differentsiatsii krest'yanskogo khozyaistva', *Puti sel'skogo khozyaistva*, No. 5.

—— (1929a), *Byudzhetnye issledovaniya*, Moscow; page references to Paris, 1967 edn, ed. B. Kerblay.

—— (1929b), *Krest'yanskoe svekloseyanie tsentral'no-chernozemnoi oblasti*, Moscow.

Chelintsev, A. N. (1927a), 'K voprosu o differentsiatsii krest'yanskogo khozyaistva', *Puti sel'skogo khozyaistva*, No. 4.

—— (1927b), 'Sel'skokhozyaistvennye raiony, poraionnye perspektivy sel' skogo khozyaistva i napravlenie meropriatii sel'skokhozyaistvennoi politiki', *Puti sel'skogo khozyaistva*, No. 9.

—— (1928), 'O printsipakh stroitel'stva i proizvodstvennykh tipov kolkhozov', *Puti sel'skogo khozyaistva*, No. 11.

—— (1930), 'Spetsializatsiya sel'skogo khozyaistva po raionam SSSR', *Sotsialisticheskaya rekonstruktsiya i sel'skoe khozyaistvo*, No. 2.

—— Matyukhin, V. V., and Nikishin, I. I. (1928), *Dinamika krest'yanskogo khozyaistva*, Moscow.

Chelovek . . . (1973), *Chelovek—nauka—tekhnika*, Moscow.

Chesnokov, M. (1927), 'Sotsial'no-ekonomicheskie gruppirovki v rybatskoi derevne nizov'ev r. Dona', *Na agrarnom fronte*, No. 1.

Cohen, S. (1974), *Bukharin and the Bolshevik Revolution*, London.

'Counter-theses . . .' (1927), 'Counter-theses of the Opposition on the Five Year Plan', *Pravda*, 19 November.

Cox, T. (1979a), *Rural Sociology in the Soviet Union: Its History and Basic Concepts*, London.

—— (1979b), 'Awkward Class or Awkward Classes? Class Relations in the Russian Peasantry before Collectivisation', *Journal of Peasant Studies*, Vol. 7, No. 1.

—— (1983a) *The Development of Empirical Sociology in the Soviet Union: The Rural Research of Kritsman and His School*, PhD thesis, University of Glasgow.

—— (1983b), 'Inequality and Class in Research on Peasant Societies', *Sociologia Ruralis*, Vol. 23. No. 3/4.

—— (1984), 'Class Analysis of the Russian Peasantry: The Research of Kritsman and His School', in Cox and Littlejohn (1984).

—— and Littlejohn, G. (eds,) (1984), *Kritsman and the Agrarian Marxists*, London.

de Crisenoy, C. (1978), *Lénine face aux moujiks*, Paris.

—— (1979), 'Capitalism and Agriculture', *Economy and Society*, Vol. 8, No. 1.

Danilov, V. P. (1977), *Sovetskaya dokolkhoznaya derevnya: naselenie, zemlepol 'zovanie, khozyaistvo*, Moscow.

—— (1979), *Sovetskaya dokolkhoznaya derevnya: sotsial'naya struktura, sotsial'nye otnosheniya*, Moscow.

—— and Slavko T. I. (1972), 'O putyakh issledovaniya dannykh nagolovykh svodok po sel'skomu khozyaistvu SSSR za 1924/5–1927/8 gg', *Istoriya SSSR*, No. 5.

Davies, R. W. (1980a), *The Industrialisation of Soviet Russia*, Vol. 1. London.

—— (1980b), *The Industrialisation of Soviet Russia*, Vol. 2. London.

—— (1984), 'E. H. Carr and the Kulaks', *New Left Review*, No. 145.

Day, R. B. (1973), *Leon Trotsky and the Politics of Economic Isolation*, London.

—— (1981), 'Leon Trotsky on the Problems of the Smychka and Forced Collectivisation', *Critique*, No. 13.

Deere, C. D. (1978), 'The Differentiation of the Peasantry and Family Structure: A Peruvian Case Study', *Journal of Family History*, Vol. 3, No. 4.

——, and de Jainvry, A. (1979), 'A Conceptual Framework for the Empirical Analysis of Peasants', *American Journal of Agricultural Economics*, Vol. 61, No. 4.

Deichman, I. (1924), *Kooperatsiya v derevne, kak ona est*, Rostov on Don–Moscow.

Den, V. (1929), *Istochniki vazhneishikh otraslei khozyaistvennoi statistiki SSSR*, Leningrad.

Deutscher, I. (1965a), *The Prophet Armed*, London.

—— (1965b), *The Prophet Unarmed*, London.

Djurfeldt, G. (1981), 'What Happened to the Agrarian Bourgeoisie and the Rural Proletariat Under Monopoly Capitalism?', *Acta Sociologica*, Vol. 24, No. 3.

—— (1982), 'What Happened to the Agrarian Bourgeoisie and the Rural Proletariat Under Monopoly Capitalism? A Reply', *Acta Sociologica*, Vol. 25, No. 3.

Bibliography   255

Draper, H. (1977), *Karl Marx's Theory of Revolution*, Vol. 1, London.

Drozdov, I. (1928), 'Dinamika gruppovogo sostava Chernigovskoi derevni', *Na agrarnom fronte*, No. 9.

Dubrovskii, S. (1926), 'Vopros o krest'yanstve i o postroenii sotsializma u sovremennoi oppozitsii', *Na agrarnom fronte*, No. 11/12.

—— (1927), 'Rassloenie krest'yanstva i rabota partii v derevne', *Na agrarnom fronte*, No. 11/12.

—— (1928), 'Contribution to "Diskussiya o klassovykh gruppirovkakh krest'yanskhikh khozyaistv v Komakademii"', *Na agrarnom fronte*, No. 5.

—— (1929), 'Analiz krest'yanskogo dvora', *Na agrarnom fronte*, No. 8.

—— (1930), Speech to the Conference of Agrarian Marxists; in *Trudy*. . . (1930), Moscow.

Dunn, S. and Dunn, E. (eds), (1974), *Introduction to Soviet Ethnography*, Berkeley, California.

Emmons, T. (1968), *The Russian Landed Gentry and the Peasant Emancipation of 1861*, Cambridge.

——, and Vucinich, W. S. (eds) (1982), *The Zemstvo in Russia: An Experiment in Local Self-Government*, Cambridge.

Ennew, J., Hirst, P., and Tribe, K. (1977), ' "Peasantry" as an Economic Category', *Journal of Peasant Studies*, Vol. 4, No. 4.

Entelis, G. S. (1974), *Preobrazovanie sotsial'no-klassovoi struktury sel'skogo naseleniya*, Kishinev.

Fedorov, E. F. (1925), *Religiya i byt v kommunisticheskom obschchestve*, Moscow.

Fenomenov, M. Ya. (1925), *Sovremennaya derevnya*, 2 Vols, Leningrad.

—— (1926), *Izuchenie byta derevni v shkole*, Moscow.

Fernbach, D. (ed.) (1973a), *Marx: The Revolutions of 1848*, Harmondsworth. ·

—— (ed.) (1973b), *Marx: Surveys From Exile*, Harmondsworth.

Filtzer, D. (1978), 'Preobrazhenskii and the Problem of Soviet Transition', *Critique*, No. 9.

—— (1979), 'Introduction', in E. A. Preobrazhensky, *The Crisis of Soviet Industrialisation*, New York.

Foster-Carter, A.(1978), 'The Modes of Production Controversy', *New Left Review*, No. 107.

Gaister, A. I. (1927a), 'Arenda i sdacha zemli', *Na agrarnom fronte*, No. 6.

—— (1927b), 'Sootnoshenie klassov i grupp v derevne', *Na agrarnom fronte*, No. 10.

—— (1927c), 'Rassloenie derevni i oppozitsiya', *Na agrarnom fronte*, No. 11/12.

—— (1928a), *Rassloenie sovetskoi derevni*, Moscow.

—— (1928b), 'Diskussiya o klassovykh gruppirovkakh krest'yanskikh khozyaistv', *Na agrarnom fronte*, No. 6/7.

—— (1929a), *Dostizheniya i trudnosti kolkhoznogo stroitel'stva*, Moscow.

—— (ed.) (1929b), *Kollektivizatsiya sovetskoi derevni: predvaritel'nye itogi sploshnykh obsledovanii, 1928 i 1929 gg*, Moscow.

—— (1929c), 'Analiz krest'yanskogo dvora', *Na agrarnom fronte*, No. 8.

Gontareva, I. I. (1928), *Schetovodny analiz krest'yanskogo khozyaistva*, Moscow.

Goodman, D. and Redclift, M. (1981), *From Peasant to Proletarian*, Oxford.

Gordeev, G. S. (1928), 'Uchenie ob Intensivnom i Ekstensivnom Sel'skom Khozyaistve', *Na agrarnom fronte*, No. 3.

Govorov, A. S. (1925), *Pereustroistvo sovremennoi derevni*, Samara.

Grigorov, L. (1925), *Ocherki sovremennoi derevni*, Moscow—Leningrad.

Grosskopf, S. (1976), *L'alliance ouvrière et paysanne en URSS (1921—8): le problème du blé*, Paris.

Gurevich, M. (1925), *K voprosu o differentsiatsii krest'yanskogo khozyaistva Ukrainy*, 2 Vols, Kharkov.

—— (1927), *Voprosy sovremennogo krest'yanskogo khozyaistva Ukrainy*, Kharkov.

Gurvich, I. A. (1896), *Ekonomicheskoe polozhenie russkoi derevni*, Moscow; page references to the edn of Moscow 1941.

Gutkind, P., and Wallerstein, I. (eds) (1976), *The Political Economy of Contemporary Africa*, London.

Harding, N. (1977), *Lenin's Political Thought*, Vol. 1, London.

—— (1981), *Lenin's Political Thought*, Vol. 2, London.

Harris, O. (1981), 'Households As Natural Units', in Young *et al.* (1981).

Harrison, R. M. (1974), *Theories of Peasant Economy: Critique of the Works of the Organisation of Production School of Agricultural Economy, with Particular Reference to A. V. Chayanov*, DPhil, Thesis, University of Oxford.

Harrison, M. (1975), 'Chayanov and the Economics of the Russian Peasantry', *Journal of Peasant Studies*, Vol. 2, No. 4.

—— (1977a), 'The Peasant Mode of Production in the Work of A. V. Chayanov', *Journal of Peasant Studies*, Vol. 4, No. 4.

—— (1977b), 'Resource Allocation and Agrarian Class Formation', *Journal of Peasant Studies*, Vol. 4, No. 2.

—— (1978a), 'The Soviet Economy in the 1920s and 1930s', *Capital and Class*, No. 5.

—— (1978b), Review of Solomon (1977), *Journal of Peasant Studies*, Vol. 6, No. 1.

—— (1979), 'Chayanov and the Marxists', *Journal of Peasant Studies*, Vol. 7, No. 1.

Harriss, J. (1982a), *Capitalism and Peasant Farming*, Oxford.

—— (ed.) (1982b), *Rural Development: Theories of Peasant Economy and Agrarian Change*, London.

Hindess, B. (ed.) (1977), *Sociological Theories of the Economy*, London.

History . . . (1939), *History of the Communist Party of the Soviet Union, Short Course*, Moscow.

Hobsbawm, E. J. (ed.) (1980), *Peasants in History: Essays in Honour of Daniel Thorner*, Oxford.

Hunt, A. (1976), 'Lenin and Sociology', *The Sociological Review*, Vol. 24, No. 1.

Hussian, A., and Tribe, K. (1981), *Marxism and the Agrarian Question*, 2 Vols, London.

Ignat'eva (1930), in *Trudy*. . . (1930).

Ikonnikov, S. N. (1971), *Sozdanie i deyatel'nost' obedinennykh organov TsKK– RKI v 1923–34 gg.*, Moscow.

'Ionov', (1929), 'Analiz krest'yanskogo dvora', *Na agrarnom fronte*, No. 8.

Jasny, N. (1972), *Soviet Economists of the Twenties*, Cambridge.

Johnson, R. E. (1982), 'Liberal Professionals and Professional Liberals: The Zemstvo Statisticians and Their Work', in Emmons and Vucinich (1982).

Kak Zhivyot. . . (1925), *Kak zhivyot derevnya*, Archangel.

Kavraiskii, V., and Nusinov, I. (1927), *Klassovoe rassloenie sibirskoi derevni*, Novosibirsk.

—— and —— (1929), *Klassy i klassovye otnosheniya v sovremennoi sovetskoi derevne*, Novosibirsk.

Kazanskii, F. (1926), 'Sotsial'nye gruppy i ekonomicheskie gruppirovki v sovremennoi ural'skoi derevne', *Na agrarnom fronte*, No. 5/6.

Keat, R., and Urry, J. (1975), *Social Theory As Science*, London.

Kerblay, B. (1968), *Les Marches paysans en URSS*, Paris.

—— (1971), 'Chayanov and the Theory of Peasantry as a Specific Type of Economy', in Shanin (1971).

Khatayevich, M. (1925), *Partiinye yacheiki v derevne*, Leningrad.

Khleboslov, A. V. (1926), *Volost' kak ona est'*.

Khryashcheva, A. I. (1923), *K voprosu o nepravil'nykh priemakh issledovaniya dinamiki krest'yanskogo khozyaistva*, Moscow.

—— (1924a), 'O rabotakh otdela osnovnoi sel'sko-khozyaistvennoi statistiki Ts.SU' *Voprosy statistiki*, Nos. 1–3.

—— (1924b), 'Rassloenie krest'yanstva v usloviyakh NEP'a' *Sotsialisticheskoe khozyaistvo*, No. 2.

—— (1925a), 'K voprosu ob isuchenii rassloeniya krest'yanstva', *Na agrarnom fronte*, No. 1.

—— (1925b), 'K voprosu o printsipakh gruppirovki massovykh statisticheskikh materialov v tselyakh izucheniya klassov v krest'yanstve', *Voprosy statistiki*, Nos. 1–3.

—— (1925c), 'Differentsiatsiya promyslov krest'yanskogo naseleniya', in Kritsman *et al.* (1925).

—— (1925d), 'Usloviya evolyutsii krest'yanskogo khozyaistva', *Sotsialisticheskoe khozyaistvo*, No. 5.

—— (1926), *Gruppy i klassy v krest'yanstve*, Moscow.

—— (1928), 'Usloviya drobimosti krest'yanskikh khozyaistv', *Ekonomicheskoe obozrenie*, No. 9.

Kingston-Mann, E. (1972), 'Lenin and the Beginnings of the Marxist Peasant Revolution', *Slavonic and East European Review*, Vol. 50, No. 121.

—— (1980), 'A Strategy For Marxist Bourgeois Revolution: Lenin and the Peasantry, 1907–1916', *Journal of Peasant Studies*, Vol. 7, No. 2.

Korenevskaya, N. N. (1954), *Byudzhetnye obsledovaniya krest'yanskikh khozyaistv v dorevolyutsionnoi Rossii*, Moscow.

Krest'yanskoe ... (1923), *Krest'yanskoe khozyaistvo za vremya revolyutsii*, Moscow.

Kritsman, L. N. (1921a), *Kapitalisticheskoe rabstvo — velikaya rabochaya revolyutsiya — osvobozhdenie rabochego klassa*, Moscow.

—— (1921b), *Obshchestvennyi trud rabochego i edinolichnyi semeinyi trud krest' yanina*, Moscow.

—— (1921c), *O edinom khozyaistvennom plane*, Moscow.

—— (1922), 'O russkoi revolyutsii', *Vestnik Sotsialisticheskoi akademii*, No. 1.

—— (1923a), 'Krupnoe i melkoe khozyaistvo v zemledelii', *Vestnik Sotsialisticheskoi akademii*, No. 3; republished in Kritsman (1929c).

—— (1923b), 'O nakoplenii kapitala i "tretikh" litsakh', *Vestnik Sotsialisticheskoi akademii*, No. 5.

—— (1923c), 'Ot tyagi k zemle k tyage k rynku', *Sotsialisticheskoe khozyaistvo*, No. 4/5; republished in Kritsman (1929c).

—— (1924a), 'Sel'skoe khozyaistvo v sisteme narodnogo khozyaistva v pervye tri goda novoi ekonomicheskoi politiki', in a pamphlet, *Tri goda novoi ekonomicheskoi politiki*, Moscow; republished in Kritsman (1929c).

—— (1924b), 'Sovremennaya Melko-burzhuaznaya politicheskaya ekonomiya', *Vestnik Kommunisticheskoi akademii*, No. 7; also published as the foreword to Chayanov (1924b), and in Kritsman (1929c); page references to Chayanov (1924b).

—— (1925a), 'Arifmetika i znanie dela (o trudakh zemplana i o professorakh Kondratieve i Oganovskom)', *Na agrarnom fronte*, No. 1.

—— (1925b), *Geroicheskii period russkoi revolyutsii*, Moscow; also published in *Vestnik Kommunisticheskoi akademii*, No. 9, 1924.

—— (1925c), 'Kolkhoznoe dvizhenie (o ego literaturnom otrazhenii)'; republished in Kritsman (1929c).

—— (1925d), 'K voprosu o klassovom rassloenii sovremennoi derevni', in four parts, respectively, in *Na agrarnom fronte*, Nos. 2, 7/8, 9, 10.

—— (1925e), 'Lenin i put' k sotsializmu', *Na agrarnom fronte*, No. 3, paper delivered to the Communist Academy, 24 January, 1925; republished in Kritsman (1929c).

—— (1925f), 'Ob osnovakh perspektivnogo plana razvitiya sel'skogo i lesnogo khozyaistva' *Na agrarnom fronte*, 7/8.

—— (1925g), 'Perezhitiki ideologii krepostnichestva v nashei statistike', *N agrarnom fronte*, No. 1; republished in Kritsman (1929c).

—— (1925h), 'Plan sel'skogo khozyaistva i industrializatsiya', paper presented to the presidium of Gosplan in 1925; republished in Kritsman (1929c).

—— (1925i), 'Soyuz proletariata i bol'shinstva krest'yanstva v SSSR posle pobedy revolyutsii', *Bolshevik*, No. 2; republished in Kritsman (1929c).

—— (1925j), 'Stikhiya oproverzheniya i ee zhertva (po povodu piśma prof. Oganovskogo)', *Na agrarnom fronte*, No. 2.

—— (1926a), 'Klassovaya differentsiatsiya krest'yanstva v sovremennoi sovetskoi derevne', *Vestnik Kommunistichestkoi akademii*, No. 14; republished in Kritsman (1929c), and page numbers refer to 1929c.

—— (1926b), *Klassovoe rassloenie sovetskoi derevni (po dannym volostnykh obsledovanii)*, Moscow; republished in Kritsman (1929c).

—— (1926c), 'Razvitie kapitalizma i progress tekhniki', *Vestnik Kommunisticheskoi akademii*, No. 16.

—— (1926–7), 'O statisticheskom izuchenii klassovoi struktury sovetskoi derevni', *Na agrarnom fronte*, Nos. 2, 1926; 7, 1927; 8/9, 1927; 10, 1927; republished in Kritsman (1929c).

—— (1927a), 'Desyat' let na agrarnom fronte proletarskoi revolyutsii', *Na agrarnom fronte*, No. 11/12; republished in Kritsman (1929c).

—— (1927b), *Novy etap. (K. proektam 'Obshchikh nachal zemlepol'zovaniya i zemleustroistva')*; republished in Kritsman (1929c).

—— (1928a), 'Klassovye gruppirovki krest'yanskikh khozyaistv', *Na agrarnom fronte*, No. 4; paper presented to the Communist Academy, January 1928; republished in Kritsman (1929c).

—— (ed.) (1928b), *Materialy po istorii agrarnoi revolyutsii*, Vol. 1., Moscow.

—— (1928c), 'Ob analize klassovoi struktury krest'yanstva', introduction to Gaister (1928a); republished in Kritsman (1929c).

—— (1928d), 'O samarskom obsledovanii', foreword to Vermenichev *et al.* (1928); republished in Kritsman (1929c).

—— (1929a), 'Ob osnovnykh metodakh razrabotki massovykh statisticheskh materialov nashei agrarnoi revolyutskii', in Kritsman (1929c).

—— (1929b), 'O vnutrennikh protivorechiyakh krest'yanskogo dvora', introduction to Kubanin (1929); republished in Kritsman 1929c).

—— (1929c), *Proletarskaya revolyutsiya i derevnya*, Moscow–Leningrad.

—— (1930a), Biography of Kritsman in *Malaya Sovetskaya Entsiklopediya*, Vol. 4.

—— (1930b), 'The Process of Socialisation of Agriculture in the USSR', *Proceedings of the Conference of Agricultural Economists*, New York.

—— (1930c), 'O kharaktere nashei revolyutsii', *Na agrarnom fronte*, No. 4.

—— (1984), 'Class Stratification of the Soviet Countryside', (ed. and trans. G. Littlejohn), in Cox and Littlejohn (1984).

——, and Larin, Ya. (1920a), *Ocherk khozyaistvennoi zhizni i organizatsiya narodnogo khozyaistva sovetskoi Rossii*, Moscow.

—— and —— (1920b), *Organizatsiya narodnogo khozyaistva v sovetskoi Rossii 1927–20*, Moscow.

——, Popov, P., and Yakovlev, Ya., (eds) (1925), *Selśkoe khozyaistvo na putyakh vosstanovleniya*, Moscow.

Kubanin, M. (1928a), 'Sotsial'no-ekonomicheskaya suchchnost' problemy drobimosti', *Na agrarnom fronte*, No. 1.

—— (1928b), 'Sotsial'no-ekonomicheskaya suchchnost' problemy drobleniya krest'yanskikh khozyaistv', *Na agrarnom fronte*, Part 1, No. 8; Part 2, No. 11.

—— (1929), *Klassovaya sushchnost' protsessa drobleniya krest'yanskikh khozyaistv*, Moscow.

Kuplenskii, A., Rudakova, E, and Sulkovskii, M. (1930), *Klassovye gruppy krest'yanskikh khozyaistv i ikh proizvodstvennaya kharakteristika,*, Moscow.

Larin, Ya. (1925a), 'Boevye voprosy batrachestva', *Na agrarnom fronte*, No. 1.

—— (1925b), 'Obschechestvennaya rol' batrachestva', *Na agrarnom fronte*, No. 3.

—— (1927a), 'Chastnyi kapital v sel'skom khozyaistve', *Na agrarnom fronte*, No. 4.

—— (1927b), *Chastnyi kapital v SSSR*, Moscow–Leningrad.

—— (1928), *Soltsial'naya struktura SSSR*, Moscow.

Lehmann, D. (ed.) (1974), *Agrarian Reform and Agrarian Reformism*, London.

Lenin, V. I. (1893a), *New Economic Developments in Peasant Life (On V. Y. Postnikov's 'Peasant Farming in South Russia')*; references to Lenin, *Collected Works*, Vol.1, Moscow, 1960.

—— (1893b), *On the So-called Market Question*; references to Lenin, *Collected Works*, Vol. 1, Moscow, 1960.

—— (1894a), *What the 'Friends of People' Are and How They Fight the Social Democrats*; page references to Lenin, *Collected Works*, Vol 1, Moscow, 1960.

—— (1894b), *The Economic Content of Narodism*; page references to Lenin, *Collected Works*, Vol. 1, Moscow, 1960.

—— (1897a), *A Characterisation of Economic Romanticism*; reprinted in Latin, *Collected Works*, Vol.2, Moscow, 1960.

—— (1897b), *The Heritage We Renounce*; reprinted in Lenin, *Collected Works*, Vol. 2, Moscow, 1960.

—— (1899), *The Development of Capitalism in Russia* (1st edn); reprinted according to text of 2nd edn (1908) in Lenin, *Collected Works*, Vol. 3, Moscow, 1964.

—— (1902), *The Agrarian Programme of Russian Social-Democracy*; page references to Lenin, *Collected Works*, Vol. 6, Moscow, 1961.

—— (1907), *Preface to The Development of Capitalism in Russia* (2nd edn); page references to Lenin, *Collected Works*, Vol. 13, Moscow, 1964.

—— (1908), *The Agrarian Programme of Social Democracy in the First Russian Revolution 1905–1907*, in Lenin, *Collected Works*, Vol. 13, Moscow, 1962.

—— (1910), *The Capitalist System of Modern Agriculture*, in Lenin, *Collected Works*, Vol. 16, Moscow, 1963.

—— (1913), *The Purpose of Zemstvo Statistics*, in Lenin, *Collected Works*, Vol. 20, Moscow, 1964.

—— (1914), *New Data On the Laws Governing the Development of Capitalism in Agriculture*, in Lenin, *Collected Works*, Vol. 22, Moscow, 1964.

—— (1916), *Imperialism, The Highest Stage of Capitalism*, in Lenin, *Collected Works*, Vol. 22, Moscow, 1964.

—— (1918a), *'Left-wing' Childishness and the Petty Bourgeois Mentality*, in Lenin, *Collected Works*, Vol. 27, Moscow, 1965.

—— (1918b), *On the Famine*, in Lenin, *Collected Works*, Vol. 27, Moscow, 1965.

—— (1918c), *Speech to the First All-Russian Congress of Land Departments, Poor Peasant Committees, and Communes*, in Lenin, *Collected Works*, Vol. 28, Moscow, 1965.

—— (1918d), *The Proletarian Revolution and the Renegade Kautsky*, in Lenin, *Collected Works*, Vol. 28, Moscow, 1965.

—— (1919), *Speech to the First All-Russian Conference on Party Work in the Countryside*, in Lenin, *Collected Works*, Vol. 30, Moscow 1965.

—— (1920a), *Left-wing Communism, An Infantile Disorder*, in Lenin, *Collected Works*, Vol. 31, Moscow, 1966.

—— (1920b), *Preliminary Draft Theses on the Agrarian Question*, in Lenin, *Collected Works*, Vol. 31, Moscow, 1966.

—— (1921a), *The Tax in Kind*, in Lenin, *Collected Works*, Vol 32, Moscow, 1965.

—— (1921b), *Theses for a Report on the Tactics of the RCP*, in Lenin, *Collected Works*, Vol. 32, Moscow, 1965.

—— (1922), *O tezisakh tov. Preobrazhenskogo*, in Lenin (1930).

—— (1923), *On Cooperation*, in Lenin, *Collected Works*, Vol.33, Moscow, 1966.

—— (1930), *Sochineniya*, Vol. 27, Moscow.

—— (1960), *Collected Works*, Vol.1, Moscow.

—— (1966), *Preliminary Draft Theses on the Agrarian Question*, in Lenin, *Collected Works*, Vol. 31, Moscow.

—— (1968), *Notebooks on the Agrarian Question*, in Lenin, *Collected Works*, Vol. 40, Moscow.

Lewin, M. (1966), 'Who Was the Soviet Kulak?', *Soviet Studies*, Vol. 18.

—— (1968), *Russian Peasants and Soviet Power*, London.

—— (1975), *Political Undercurrents in Soviet Economic Debates*, London.

Leys, C. (1975), *Underdevelopment in Kenya: The Political Economy of Neo-colonialism*, London.

Lezhnev-Finkovskii, T., and Savchenko, K. D. (1925), *Kak zhivyot derevnya*, Moscow.

Libkind, A. (1928), Review of Kavraiskii and Nusinov (1927), in *Na agrarnom fronte*, No. 1.

Litso . . . (1925), *Litso donskoi derevni*, Rostov-on-Don.

Littlejohn, G. (1977), 'Chayanov and the Theory of Peasant Economy', in Hindess (1977).

—— (1984), 'The Agrarian Marxist Research in its Political Context: State

Policy and the Development of the Soviet Rural Class Structure in the 1920s', in Cox and Littlejohn (1984).

Livyant, Z. (1930), 'V osnovnom voprose revolyutsii nuzhna yasnost', *Na agrarnom fronte*, No. 4.

Lositskii, A. E. (1924), *Sovremennoe sostoyanie skotovodstva v Rossi*, Moscow.

—— (1927), 'Raspredelenie krest'yanskikh khlebnykh zapasov', *Statisticheskoe obozrenie*, No. 4.

Lubyako, V., and Naumov, K. (1927), 'K voprosu o postroenii organisatsionnykh planov sovkhozov', *Puti sel'skogo khozyaistva*, No. 12.

Lukacs, G. (1922), *History and Class Consciousness* (English translation London, 1971).

McEachern, D. (1976), 'The Mode of Production in India', *Journal of Contemporary Asia*, Vol. 6, No. 4.

Makarov, N. P. (1927), 'Differentsiatsiya krest'yanskogo khozyaistva', *Puti sel'skogo khozyaistva*, No. 4.

Mamdani, M. (1976), *Politics and Class Formation in Uganda*, London.

Mann, S., and Dickinson, J. M. (1978), 'Obstacles to the Development of a Capitalist Agriculture', *Journal of Peasant Studies*, Vol. 5, No. 4.

Marx, K. (1850), *The Class Struggles in France*, in Fernbach (1973b).

—— (1852), *The Eighteenth Brumaire of Louis Bonaparte*, in Fernbach (1973b).

—— (1858), *Grundisse* (English translation, M. Nicolaus, ed., Harmondsworth, 1973).

—— (1863), *Theories of Surplus Value* (English translation, Moscow, 1963).

—— (1865), *Capital*, Vol. III (English edn, London, 1974).

—— (1867), *Capital*, Vol. I (English edn, London, 1970).

—— and Engels, F. (1848), *Manifesto of the Communist Party* (English edn, Harmondsworth, 1967).

—— and —— (1882), Preface to the first Russian edn of the *Communist Manifesto*; reprinted in the Harmondsworth, 1967, edn.

—— and —— (1955), *Selected Correspondence*, London.

Meerson, G. (1925), 'Semeino-trudovaya teoriya i differentsiatsiya krest' yanstva na zare tovarnogo khozyaistva', *Na agrarnom fronte*, Nos. 3 and 4.

Meyer, G. (1974), *Studien zur sozialökonomischen Entwicklung sowjetrusslands 1921–23*, Cologne.

Millar, J. R. (1970), 'A Reformulation of A. V. Chayanov's Theory of the Peasant Economy', *Economic Development and Cultural Change*, January.

Miller, M. (1967), *The Economic Development of Russia 1905–1914*, (2nd edn), London.

Morosanov, A., and Yermolenko E. (1925), 'Akmolinskaya derevnya', *Na agrarnom fronte*, Nos. 7/8, 9.

Murin, V. A. (1925), *Byt i nravy derevenskoi molodezhi*, Moscow.

Naumov, K. I. (1928a), 'Problem differentsiatsii krest'yanskikh khozyaistv', *Puti sel'skogo khozyaistva*, No. 4/5.

Bibliography 263

—— (1928b), 'Diskussiya o klassovykh gruppirovkakh krest'yanskikh khozyaistv', *Na agrarnom fronte,*, No. 6/7.

—— and Shardin D. (1928), 'Opyt postroeniya klassovoi gruppirovki krest'yanskikh khozyaistv', *Na agrarnom fronte*, No. 4.

Nelson, E. (1983), 'Capitalism in Western Agriculture: A Comment' *Acta Sociologica*, Vol. 26, No. 3/4.

Nemchinov, V. S. (1926a), 'Zadachi statistiki v svyazi s resheniem III sessii oblispolkoma', *Byulleten' Uralskogo oblastnogo statisticheskogo upraveleniya*, No. 1; reprinted in Nemchinov (1967).

—— (1926b), 'O statisticheskom izuchenii klassovogo rassleoniya derevni', *Byulleten' Uralskogo oblastnogo statisticheskogo upraveleniya*, No. 1; reprinted in Nemchinov (1967).

—— (1927a), 'O Sotsial'no-ekonomicheskikh gruppirovkakh krest'yanskikh khozyaistv', *Vsesoyuznoe statisticheskoe soveshchanie 1927 goda*, Moscow; reprinted in Nemchinov (1967).

—— (1927b), 'Programma i organizatsiya dinamicheskikh perepisei', *Vsesoyuznoe statisticheskoe soveshchanie 1927 goda*, Moscow; reprinted in Nemchinov (1967).

—— (1928a), 'Opyt klassifikatsii krest'yanskikh khozyaistv', *Vestnik Statistiki*, No. 1; reprinted in Nemchinov (1967).

—— (1928b), 'Diskussiya o klassovykh gruppirovkakh krest'yanskikh hozyaistv', *Na agrarnom fronte*, No. 8.

—— (1967), *Izbrannye proizvedeniya*, Vol. 1, Moscow.

Nove, A. (1972), *An Economic History of the Soviet Union*, Harmondsworth.

Obozhda, V. A. (1977), 'K voprosu o sotsial'no-ekonomicheskoi gruppirovke krest'yanskikh khozyaistv dokolkhoznyi derevni', in *Matematicheskie metody v istoriko-ekonomicheskikh i istoriko-kul'turny issledovaniyakh*, Moscow.

Orlov, M. (1929), Review of Kavraiskii and Nusinov (1929), *Planovoe khozyaistvo*, No. 7.

'Ot redaktsii' (1932), *Na agrarnom fronte*, No. 1.

Pallot, J. (1982), 'Social Change and Peasant Land-holding in Pre-revolutionary Russia', *Research Paper No. 30*, School of Geography, University of Oxford.

—— (1984a), '*Khutora* and *Otrub* in Stolypin's Program of Farm Individualisation', *Slavic Review*, Vol. 42, No. 2.

—— (1984b), 'Open Fields and Individual Farms: Land Reform in Pre-revolutionary Russia', *Tijdschrift voor Economische en Sociale Geografie*, Vol. 75, No. 1.

Patnaik, U. (1971a), 'Capitalist Development in Agriculture: A Note', *Economic and Political Weekly*, No. 39.

—— (1971b), 'Capitalist Development in Agriculture: Further Comment', *Economic and Political Weekly*, No. 52.

—— (1976), 'Class Differentiation Within the Peasantry', *Economic and Political Weekly*, No. 39.

—— (1980), 'Empirical Identification of Peasant Classes Revisited', *Economic and Political Weekly*, No. 9.

—— (1983), 'Classical Theory of Rent and Its Application to India', *Journal of Peasant Studies*, Vol. 10, No. 2/3.

Pavlov, A. (1929), 'Analiz krest'yanskogo dvora', *Na agrarnom fronte*, No. 8.

Pavlovsky, G. (1930), *Agricultural Russia on the Eve of the Revolution*; page references to the 1968 edn, New York.

Platform . . . (1927), *Platform of the Left Opposition*, Moscow (English edn, London, 1963).

Plekhanov, G. (1885), *Our Differences*; reprinted in Plekhanov (1961).

—— (1895), *The Development of the Monist View of History*, reprinted in Plekhanov (1961).

—— (1961), *Selected Philosophical Works*, Vol. 1, London.

Popov, A. (1928), Review of Gaister (1928a), *Planovoe khozyaistvo*, No. 4.

Postnikov, V. Y. (1891), *Yuzhno-russkoe krest'yanskoe khozyaistvo*, Moscow.

Preobrazhenskii, E. A. (1922a), *Osnovyne printsipy politiki RKP, v sovremennoi derevne*; references to Lenin (1930).

—— (1922b), *Ot NEPa k sotsializmu*; references to the English translation, *From NEP to Socialism*, London, 1973.

—— (1926), *Novaya ekonomika*, Moscow; references to the English translaion, *The New Economics*, Oxford, 1965.

—— (1979), *The Crisis of Soviet Industrialisation*, ed. D. Filtzer, New York.

Raevich, G. (1925), 'Teoriya krest'yanskogo khozyaistva i ponyatie "rabotnik" ', *Na agrarnom fronte*, No. 11/12.

—— (1926—8), 'K issledovaniyu krest'yanskogo dokhoda', *Na agrarnom fronte*, Nos. 3 (1926), 5/6 (1926), and 1(1928).

—— (1928), 'Diskussiya o klassovykh gruppirovkakh krest'yanskikh khozyaistv', *Na agrarnom fronte*, No. 8.

—— (1929), 'Analiz krest'yanskogo dvora', *Na agrarnom fronte*, No. 8.

Raikes, P. (1982), 'Djurfeldt's "What Happened to the Agrarian Bourgeoisie and Rural Proletariat Under Monopoly Capitalism?" A Comment', *Acta Sociologica*, Vol. 25, No. 2.

Report . . . (1928), *Report of the Fifteenth Congress of the C.P.S.U.*, London.

Rey, P. P. (1971), *Colonialisme, neo-colonialisme, et transition au capitalisme*, Paris.

—— (1973), *Les Alliances de classes*, Paris.

Roberts, P. (1986), 'The Sexual Politics of Labour' in Young (1986).

Robinson, G. T. (1932), *Rural Russia Under the Old Regime*, London.

Roseberry, W. (1978), 'Peasants As Proletarians', *Critique of Anthropology*, No. 11.

Rosnitskii, N. (1925), *Polgoda v derevne*, Penza.

—— (1926), *Litso derevni*, Moscow—Leningrad.

Rudra, A., *et al.* (n.d.), *Studies in the Development of Capitalism in India*, Bombay.

Sawer, M. (1978), 'The Politics of Historiography: Russian Socialism and the Question of the Asiatic Mode of Production', *Critique*, No. 10/11.

Sayer, D. (1979), *Marx's Method*, Hassocks, Sussex.

Sem'ya (1925), *Sem'ya i brak v proshlom i nastoyashchem*, Moscow.

Shafir, Ya. (1924), *Gazeta i derevnya*, Moscow—Leningrad.

Shanin, T. (ed.) (1971), *Peasants and Peasant Societies*, Harmondsworth.

—— (1972), *The Awkward Class*, Oxford.

—— (1973), 'The Nature and Logic of Peasant Economy', *Journal of Peasant Studies*, Vol. 1.

—— (1975), 'Promysly', *Journal of Peasant Studies*, Vol. 2, No. 2.

—— (1980), 'Measuring Peasant Capitalism', in Hobsbawm (1980).

Shcherbina, F. (1900), *Krest'yanskie byudzhety*, Voronezh.

Shestakov, A. (1925), 'Naemnyi trud v sel'skom khozyaistve', *Na agrarnom fronte*, Nos. 1 and 2.

Shingarev, A. I. (1907), *Vymirayushchaya derevnya*, St Petersburg.

Shivji, I. (1976), *Class Struggles in Tanzania*, London.

Shulimov, G. (1927), 'O differentsiatsii dekhkanskikh khozyaistv zemledel' cheskikh raionov Uzbekistana', *Na agrarnom fronte*, No. 2.

Sivogrivov, A. (1928), 'Predmet, metod i zadachi organizatsii sel'skogo khozyaistva', *Puti sel'skogo khozyaistva*, No. 3.

Smith, K. (1979), 'Introduction to Bukharin: Economic Theory and the Closure of the Soviet Industrialisation Debate', *Economy and Society*, Vol. 8, No. 4.

Smith, R. E. F. (1975), 'Crafts and Trades', *Journal of Peasant Studies*, Vol.2, No. 4.

Smith, S. A. (1983), *Red Petrograd: Revolution in the Factories 1917—1918*, Cambridge.

Solomon, S. G. (1975), 'Controversy in Social Science: Soviet Rural Studies in the 1920s', *Minerva*, No. 13.

—— (1977), *The Soviet Agrarian Debate: A Controversy in Social Science 1923— 1929*, Boulder, Colorada.

Sovremennaya . . . (1970), *Sovremennaya nauchno-tekhnicheskaya revolyutsiya*, Moscow.

Stalin, J. V. (1924), *The Foundations of Leninism*; reprinted in Stalin, *Collected Works*, Vol. 6, Moscow, 1952.

—— (1926), *On the Problems of Leninism*; reprinted in Stalin, *Collected Works*, Vol. 8, Moscow, 1952.

—— (1952), *Economic Problems of Socialism in the USSR*, Moscow.

Strumilin, S. G. (1925), 'Dinamika batratskoi armii v SSSR', *Na agrarnom fronte*, No. 7/8.

—— (1928), 'Rassloenie sovetskoi derevni', *Planovoe khozyaistvo*, No. 3.

—— (1929), 'Rassloenie sovetskoi derevni 1927—8 gg,' *Planovoe khozyaistvo*, No. 8.

Studenskii, G. A. (1926), *Opyt issledovaniya organizatsii krest'yanskogo khozyaistva tsentral'no-chernozemnoi oblasti*, Part 1, Moscow.

—— (1927), *Problemy organizatsii krest'yanskogo khozyaistva*, Moscow.

—— (1929), *Osnovnye voprosy metodiki byudzhetnykh i shchetovodnykh issledovanii*, Samara.

Sukhanov, N. (1927), 'O differentsiatsii krest'yanskogo khozyaistva', *Puti sel'skogo khozyaistva*, No. 6/7.

—— (1928), Contribution to 'Diskussiya o klassovykh gruppirovkakh krest'yanskikh khozyaistv', *Na agrarnom fronte*, No. 6/7.

Sulkovskii, M. (1928a), Review of Charanov, *Optimalńye razmery sel'skokhozyaistvennykh predpriyatii*, *Na agrarnom fronte*, No. 4.

—— (1928b), 'Opyt sotsial'no-klassovoi gruppirovki krest'yanskikh byudzhetov podsolnechnogo raiona', *Na agrarnom fronte*, No. 5.

—— (1928c), 'Predmet i metod sel'sko-khozyaistvennoi ekonomii', *Na agrarnom fronte*, No. 12.

—— (1929a), 'Dokhody, ikh obrazovaniya i ispol'zovaniya v razlichnykh klassovykh gruppakh krest'yanskikh khozyaistv', *Na agrarnom fronte*, No. 7.

—— (1929b), 'Nakoplenie v krest'yanskikh khozyaistv', *Na agrarnom fronte*, No. 8.

—— (1929c), 'Evolyutsiya i raspad neonarodnichestva', *Na agrarnom fronte*, No. 11/12.

—— (1929d), 'Analiz krest'yanskogo dvora', *Na agrarnom fronte*, No. 8.

—— (1930), *Klassovye gruppy i proizvodstvennye tipy krest'yanskikh khozyaistv*, Moscow.

Svavitskii, N. A. (1924), 'Kombinatsionnye tablitsy kak priem izucheniya tipov i faktorov krest'yanskogo khozyaistva v zemskikh podvornykh perepisyakh', *Vestnik Statistiki*, Nos. 7–9.

—— (1961), *Zemskie podvornye perepisi*, Moscow.

Terletskii, E. (1925), 'Differentsiatsiya ukrainskogo krest'yanstva i kolkhozy', *Na agrarnom fronte*, No. 2.

Thorner, D., Kerblay, B., and Smith, R. E. F. (eds) (1966), *Chayanov: The Theory of Peasant Economy*, Homewood, Ill.

Trapeznikov, S. P. (1981), *Leninism and the Agrarian and Peasant Question*, 2 Vols., Moscow.

Trotsky, L. (1922), *1905*, Moscow; page references to the English translation, New York, 1972.

—— (1923), Second Speech to the 12th Congress of the Russian Communist Party, *Dvenadtsatyi s'ezd Rossiiskoi kommunisticheskoi partii*, Moscow.

Trudy . . . (1930), *Trudy pervoi vsesoyuznoi konferentsii agrarnikov-marksistov 20/XII–27/XII 1929 g*, Moscow.

Ts. S. U. (1927), *Statisticheskii spravochnik SSSR 1927*, Moscow.

—— (1929), *Statisticheskii spravochnik za 1928*, Moscow.

Utechin, S. V. (1964), *Russian Political Thought*, London.

U. (Uzhanskii?), S. (1925), Review by 'S. U.' of Chayanov, *Kratkii kurs kooperatsii*, *Na agrarnom fronte*, No. 4.

Uzhanskii, S. G. (1928), *Differentsiatsiya derevni* Moscow–Leningrad.

Venturi, F. (1960), *Roots of Revolution*, London.

Vermenichev, I. (1928a), 'Ob odnoi vylazke novonarodnika', *Na agrarnom fronte*, No. 10.

—— (1928b), 'Diskussiya o klassovykh gruppirovkakh krest'yanskikh khozyaistv', *Na agrarnom fronte*, No. 5.

—— (1929), 'Analiz krest'yanskogo dvora', *Na agrarnom fronte*, No. 8.

——, Gaister, A., and Raevich, G. (1928), *710 khozyaistv samarskoi derevni*, Moscow.

Vil'do, Yu., Uzhanskii, S., and Tsil'ko, F. (1925), 'Svekloseyanie v svyazi s rassloeniem derevni', *Na agrarnom fronte*, No. 5/6.

Vinogradov, (1928), 'Diskussiya o klassovykh gruppirovkakh krest'yanskikh khozyaistv', *Na agrarnom fronte*, No. 6/7.

VKP(b) (1936), *VKP(b) v rezolyutsiyakh*, Part 1, Moscow.

Vol'f, M. (1927), Foreword to Gurevich (1927).

Volgin, V. P., Gordon, G. O., and Luppol, I. K. (1928), *Obshchestvennye nauki SSSR 1917–27*, Moscow.

Volin, L. (1970), *A Century of Russian Agriculture*, Cambridge, Mass.

Voronov, I. (1927), 'Obrabotka krest'yanskoi pashni v khozyaistvakh raznoi moshchnosti', *Na agrarnom fronte*, No. 3.

Vorontsov, V. P. (1882), *Sudby kapitalizma v Rossii*, St Petersburg.

Vucinic, A. (1976), *Social Thought in Tsarist Russia*, Chicago.

Walicki, A. (1969), *The Controversy Over Capitalism*, Oxford.

Weinberg, E. A. (1974), *The Development of Sociology in the Soviet Union*, London.

Wheatcroft, S. G. (1974), 'The Reliability of Russian Pre-war Grain Output Statistics', *Soviet Studies*, Vol. 26, No. 2.

Who . . . (1972), *Who Was Who in the Soviet Union*, NJ.

Williams, G. (1976), 'Taking the Part of Peasants', in Gutkind and Wallerstein (1976).

—— (1984), 'Why Is There No Agrarian Capitalism in Nigeria?' (unpublished paper), Oxford.

Winter, M. (1982), 'What Happened to the Agrarian Bougeoisie and Rural Proletariat Under Monopoly Capitalism? A Reply to Goran Djurfeldt', *Acta Sociologica*, Vol. 25, No. 2.

Wolpe, H. (ed.) (1980), *The Articulation of Modes of Production*, London.

Yakovlev, Ya. (1923), *Derevnya kak ona est: ocherki Nikolskoi volosti*, Moscow–Leningrad.

Yakovlev, Ya. A. (1924), *Nasha derevnya* (1st edn), Moscow-Leningrad.

—— (1925a), *Nasha derevnya* (2nd edn), Moscow–Leningrad.

—— (1925b), 'Ob oshibakh khlebo-furazhnogo balansa TsSU i ego istolkovatelei', *Planovoe khozyaistvo*, No. 12.

—— (1925c), *Pravada*, 9 December, 10, and 16.

—— (1926), *Ob oshibakh khlebo-furazhnogo balansa TsSU i ego istolkovatelei*, Moscow.

—— (ed.) (1928), *K voprosu o sotsialisticheskom pereustroistve sel'skogo khozyaistva*, Leningrad–Moscow.

Yancheskii, N. L. (ed.) (1924), *Zak zhivyot i chem boleet derevnya*, Rostov-on-Don.

Yermolenko, A. (1925), 'Kazakhstanskaya derevnya', *Na agrarnom fronte*, No. 9.

Young, K. *et al.* (eds) (1986), *Serving Two Masters*, London.

——, Wolkowitz, C., and McCullagh, R. (eds) (1981), *Of Marriage and The Market*, London.

Zauzolkov, F. (1925), *K kharakteristike sotsial'nogo sostava rabochego klassa*, Moscow.

Zheleznev, F. (1926), *Voronezhskaya derevnya*, Voronezh.

Index